The Author

J. EDWIN ORR earned a D. Ph. from Oxford University in England, an Ed.D. from UCLA, and a Th.D. from Northern Baptist Seminary. Internationally honored as a careful scholar and an authority on revival, Dr. Orr has been a guest lecturer to countless university campuses around the world. The author of over thirty books with total sales well over a million, his works include *A Hundred Questions About God*—which sold over 100,000 and *Full Surrender*—a volume that has been published in fifteen languages and has been selling strong for fifteen years, each year excelling its sales record of the previous year.

THE FLAMING TONGUE

The Impact of Twentieth Century Revivals

THE FLAMING TONGUE

The Impact of Twentieth Century Revivals

by

J. EDWIN ORR

MOODY PRESS

CHICAGO

ISBN: 0-8024-2801-0

The author acknowledges with gratitude a generous research grant from National Library Foundation of Valley Forge.

Printed in the United States of America

CONTENTS

48527

PREFACE

The writer of this treatise has been interested in the subject of Evangelical Awakenings for forty years, and has engaged in research in the subject for at least thirty years, publishing a couple of standard texts on the topic.

It was Dr. Kenneth Scott Latourette himself who pointed out to the writer the great need of further research into the revivals and awakenings of the past hundred years in many countries of the world, and he continued to encourage such projects, never failing to read the writer's typescripts, nor neglecting to answer correspondence.

Professor F. F. Bruce, of the University of Manchester, requested the present writer to supply the concluding volume of his Church History series, published in 1965, sub-titled 'Evangelical Renewal and Advance in the Nineteenth Century,' sketching the progress of Evangelical Awakenings therein— and providing perspective for detailed research.

In the narrative which follows, it has been necessary to accumulate facts, country after country, in order first to establish that an evangelical revival did occur in each of the countries studied, to satisfy readers all over the world, but at the risk of boring others unfamiliar with faraway locations and strange place-names.

In the second place, the language of the original reports has often been reproduced, partly to give the essence of the story, and partly because the use of evangelical language (as found in the world's best seller) seemed appropriate to describe the impact of evangelical truth on men. Some who accept military language in the history of war, or anthropological language in the study of man, or ecclesiastical language in the history of the church, nevertheless object to such terms as 'converted' or 'filled with the Spirit' because of the antipathy of the natural man to experiences of the sort.

The writer has designated this as an 'exploratory study.' It has been next to impossible to enlist the help of scholars in the usual way, when so often a specialist in a particular field would confess that the material was unfamiliar to him and express his wonderment that a movement of such magnitude had escaped everyone's attention. This was not true of either Wales or Korea, on which a number of books have been written about the early twentieth century Awakening, interest continuing lively till this day. But it is true of the other countries of Europe, Asia, Africa and the Americas where published works of any kind are lacking.

The writer in years gone by enjoyed personal friendship and acquaintance with leading figures of the Awakening— Evan Roberts in Wales, Frederick Wood, Harry Turner and Lindsay Glegg in Ireland, Scotland and England, Albert Lunde, Prince Oscar Bernadotte and Nils Sörensen in Scandinavia, William Fetler and the Princess Lieven after flight from Russia. The same was so of Andrew Stewart, Robert Laidlaw and William Douglas, who saw the power of God in Australia, New Zealand and South Africa. But none ever discussed the Awakening worldwide, nor did Oswald Smith in Canada or Rodney Smith in the United States. And the writer visited many mission fields without ever encountering anyone who was aware of the wider movement a generation previous.

Thanks must be expressed to scores of scholars who read typescripts in various stages of development, and to career missionary researchists at the School of World Mission in Pasadena, who discussed details in their graduate classes. All were keen in urging publication.

In the countries of the West, the encouraging years of the 1950s gave way to the turmoil and decline of the 1960s, but in Latin America and Black Africa the Churches have rapidly expanded. As in Indonesia, the growth has been accomplished in ways reminiscent of the Awakenings. Who knows that the tide is about to turn? When the Enemy comes in like a flood, the Spirit of the Lord will raise up a standard against him. Meanwhile, one must tell one's children and one's children's children, and generations yet to be born, the wonderful works of God in modern times.

There have been instances in the history of the Church when the telling and retelling of the wonderful works of God have been used to rekindle the expectations of the faithful intercessors and prepare the way for another Awakening.

J. EDWIN ORR, 1968.

NINETEENTH CENTURY RETROSPECT

The Awakening of Wesley's day was a worldwide movement, at least as widespread around the world as were the congregations of Evangelical Christianity. The Awakening of the decades before and after the year 1800 was even more widespread, as Evangelical Christianity expanded; and, like its predecessor, it has lacked little in the telling of it. The Awakening of 1858-59 was effective on five of the six great land masses and set in motion the evangelization of the neglected continent; but there is no standard work on the movement, though it continued effective for a lifetime.

By 1900, Evangelical Christianity had become worldwide, and within a decade another worldwide Awakening of phenomenal power had swept its churches and affected the nations. And—incredibly—not only is there lacking a standard work on the amazing impact of the movement, but an almost total ignorance about it among Christian scholars is manifest.

In this study of the Evangelical Awakening of the early twentieth century, the misunderstood misnomer 'revivalism' (though popular in modern secular and religious writings) will not be used. Dr. William G. McLoughlin, Jr. defines his term 'modern revivalism' as 'professional mass evangelism.' No sophist however smart could justify the use of such words to describe the spontaneous spiritual movement which swept Wales or Korea or other countries in the early 1900s.

The logic of words suggests 'revival' for the revitalizing of a body of Christian believers, and 'awakening' for the stirring of interest in the Christian faith in the related community of nominal Christians or unbelievers.

Christians, individually or collectively, may engage in evangelism or social action, the former the presentation of the Good News of Jesus Christ with the object of bringing men to vital faith in God, which is their great commission, and the latter the application of Christian truth to human situations, whether individual or social. Thus evangelism and social action may issue from a revival or awakening, or they may not, if hindered by circumstances.

There were four great outpourings of the Holy Spirit in the nineteenth century, resulting in revivals and awakenings and their extension by evangelism and social action.

The upheavals of the late eighteenth century, especially the American and French Revolutions, were followed by a decline in Christian witness so serious that, in the judgment of Kenneth Scott Latourette, it seemed as though Christianity became 'a waning influence, about to be ushered out of the affairs of men.' Even in the dynamic society of the United States, the plight of the churches was desperate, the Episcopal Bishop of New York (for example) considering the situation hopeless and simply ceasing to function. In despair, Christian leaders began to pray for Divine intervention; the answer came in a series of four great waves of evangelical advance which made the nineteenth century the 'Great Century' of evangelism and Christian action.

When John Wesley died, Evangelical Christendom was confined to Great Britain, Scandinavia, parts of Germany, Holland and Switzerland, minorities in France and Hungary, and territory east of the Alleghenies in North America, while Latin America was closed by the intransigent governments of Spain and Portugal, Africa was unexplored, Islam was hostile to the Gospel, the East India Company made missionaries unwelcome in India, and none resided in China, Japan or Korea. South Seas islanders lived in savagery.

The 'turn of the century' awakenings sent off pioneer missionaries to the South Seas, to Latin America, Black Africa, India and China. There rose denominational missionary societies such as the Baptist Missionary Society, the American Board and other national missions in Europe. At the same time, the British and Foreign Bible Society was founded, followed by the American Bible Society and other national Bible Societies, as well as societies for promotion of Christian literature.

The awakenings raised up evangelists on the American frontier, sent the Haldanes up and down to revive Scotland, produced Hans Nielsen Hauge to transform Norway and provoked revival and evangelism in England, Germany, Holland and other European countries, directly equipping churches with Sunday Schools, home missions, city missions and the auxiliaries taken for granted today.

Then a second wave of revival reinforced the foreign missionary invasion of all the continents, and continued its great social impact upon the sending countries. Captain Allen

Gardiner pioneered in the wilds of South America and died tragically. Missionaries reconnoitred the citadels of Islam. William Carey was followed by societies ready to evangelize India. Robert Morrison opened a way for missionaries to settle in the treaty ports of China. Evangelism in Oceania was followed by extensive awakenings in Hawaii and other Polynesian kingdoms. Missionaries pushed north from the Cape of Good Hope as David Livingstone explored the hinterlands of Africa.

Granted freedom under law, social reforms were bound to follow in the homelands. Revived Evangelicals mobilized opinion and tackled many social injustices, supported modern trade unions and legislated reform of working conditions. None of this was accomplished by force—all of it by verbal persuasion against which the reactionaries could not stand, even though they resisted strenuously.

Along with prevention of social injustice came a multitude of agencies created to care for the unfortunate, until at last the very State itself, the still unregenerate society, began adopting the standards of the New Testament as the norm of civilization, even anti-Christian revolutionists adopting Christian idealism, though trying to legislate righteousness by dictatorship and not by persuasion.

William Wilberforce mobilized Evangelicals and political opinion in Britain to secure an abolition of the slave trade and emanicipation of slaves throughout the British Empire, an event of the greatest importance, after which the naval might and diplomatic power of Britain crushed the traffic.

An Anglican, John Howard, pioneered prison reforms, which were carried on by Elizabeth Fry in London. Theodore Fliedner adopted the same ideas in Germany, building homes and hospitals, training deaconesses and nurses, a most famous pupil being Florence Nightingale who later influenced Henri Dunant, another evangelical, Red Cross founder.

The connection between Evangelical Revival and popular education is not hard to establish. In Lollardy and Reformation, scholars were ready to share the blessings of education; and Puritans established universities and colleges in places where none previously existed. The Revivalists of the eighteenth century founded academies and colleges as a matter of course. The nineteenth century awakenings led to the foundation of numerous schools, high schools and colleges both in the United States and Europe and elsewhere—extending education until the State took over a fully-fledged project.

Great Britain was the first of the countries of the world to be industrialized, and its workers were caught in a treadmill of competitive drudgery which kept them straining full sixteen hours a day. Evangelical leaders, including Shaftesbury and members of the Clapham Sect, brought about an end to much of the sorry exploitation and promoted all sorts of social improvements. No less an authority than Prime Minister Lloyd George credited to the Evangelical Revival the movement 'which improved the condition of the working classes in wages, hours of labour and otherwise.' This was paralleled in the United States by what have been called 'the Sentimental Years,' when organized good works and betterment flourished in the American States, and organizations such as the Seamen's Missions were founded.

Inevitably there came about a decline in the spirituality of the churches affected by the post-1800 Awakenings. Not only was the attack of unbelievers renewed, but anti-evangelical notions claimed a following in the Anglican, Lutheran, and Reformed constituencies, and even among Baptists, taking the form of non-cooperation with other Christian denominations, and developing into a hyper-Anglicanism, hyper-Lutheranism, and hyper-Calvinism—even a hyper-Baptist factionalism manifesting itself in areas of strength.

In the autumn of 1857, there were signs of an awakening—success in revival and evangelism in Canada, and an extraordinary movement of men to prayer in New York City which spread from city to city throughout the United States and over the world. Churches, halls and theatres were filled at noon for prayer, and the overflow filled churches of all denominations at night in a truly remarkable turning of a whole nation toward God.

The same movement also affected the United Kingdom, beginning in 1859 in Ulster, the most northerly province in Ireland; approximately ten percent of the population professed conversion in Wales and Scotland as well, and a great awakening continued in England for years. Repercussions were felt in many other European countries.

The phenomena of revival were reported in countries all around the world, including South Africa and India, during the decade that followed the awakening in the sending countries: wherever an Evangelical cause existed, revival resulted.

Out of the 1859 Awakening in Britain arose a phalanx of famous evangelists—aristocrats and working men. Spurgeon built his Tabernacle on the crest of the movement. The War between the States (in which there was extraordinary revival and evangelism) delayed the emergence of great American evangelists from the 1858 Awakening, though Moody himself served his apprenticeship in that movement in Chicago.

The 1858-59 Awakenings extended the working forces of of Evangelical Christendom. Not only were a million converted in both the United States and the United Kingdom, but existing evangelistic and philanthropic organizations were revived and new vehicles of enterprise created. The Bible Societies flourished as never before, Home Missions and the Salvation Army were founded to extend the evangelistic-social ministry of the Revival in a worldwide mission. The impact on the Y. M. C. A. organization was noteworthy, and a remarkable recruitment of university students followed.

The mid-Century Awakenings revived all the existing missionary societies and enabled them to enter other fields. The practical evangelical ecumenism of the Revival was embodied in the China Inland Mission founded by Hudson Taylor in the aftermath of the British Awakening, the first of the interdenominational 'faith missions.' As in the first half of the century, practically every missionary invasion was launched by men revived or converted in the Awakenings. The first permanent missionary enterprises of Protestants in Brazilian territory, for example, began in 1859.

In the 1870s, D. L. Moody rose to fame as a world evangelist. Beginning modestly in York in the year 1873, Moody moved Sunderland, Newcastle, Edinburgh, Dundee, Glasgow, Belfast, Dublin, Manchester, Sheffield, Birmingham, and Liverpool, using methods of the 1858 Revival in prayer and preaching. About 2,500,000 people in aggregate heard him in twenty weeks in London, a lasting imprint made on Britain. In 1875, Moody returned to his native land a national figure, campaigning equally successfully in Brooklyn, Philadelphia, New York, Chicago, Boston and other cities. From then on, he served cities on both sides of the Atlantic.

It is curious to notice that Charles Darwin's most significant publication (1859) occurred at the time of the Awakening in Great Britain and the United States, heralding a clash between the sceptics who interpreted many new scientific conclusions as anti-theistic and traditional theologians who far too readily agreed with their faulty interpretations. And yet, far from antagonizing the academic world, the Revival resulted in the most extraordinary invasion of the major universities and colleges by Christian forces and the most successful recruitment of university-trained personnel in the history of higher education or evangelism. No one could have imagined that in thirty years the number of student volunteers sailing for the mission fields from the 'home' countries would approximate thirty thousand.

In the social impact of Mid-Century Revivals, greater effects were seen in the industrialized United Kingdom. Lord Shaftesbury continued his extraordinary parliamentary projects for the betterment of humanity. Great orphanages were founded. A Society was formed for the Prevention of Cruelty to Children (1889), while Josephine Butler rallied evangelical opinion to abolish licensing of prostitution.

In Great Britain, the evangelical interest motivated so much of the agitation for the betterment of conditions for working people, many leaders in the Labour Party itself being avowed Evangelical Christians. In the United States, there also was a growing concern with purely social issues such as the rights of the working man, poverty, the liquor trade, slum housing and racial bitterness.

To achieve this reform, the crusaders of the Evangelical Awakenings did not stoop to engage in class warfare. Rather, under the guidance of the Spirit, they enlisted the privileged to serve the poor. The Seventh Earl of Shaftesbury single-handed accomplished as much in his lifetime as had been achieved by any dozen parliamentarians— yet he remained an aristocratic nobleman.

Out of this evangelical concern grew a liberal social gospel whose advocates became indifferent by degrees to the dynamic of the Christian gospel, the transforming of personal lives by the power of Jesus Christ, evangelism enlisting converts and workers and initiating reforms achieved by dedicated individuals and societies.

The nineteenth century closed in a glow of optimism. People looked forward to the twentieth century as to a coming utopia. Christians were likewise optimistic, and their hope had become one of ushering in the Kingdom of God before bringing back the King.

Little did anyone know that in the second decade of the twentieth century, war unparalleled in ferocity and scope would engulf the world. As Sir Edward Grey truly observed: 'The lights are going out all over Europe, and we shall not see them lighted again in our generation.' A period of war and revolution engulfed the world. It was preceded by an extraordinary worldwide Awakening.

1

THE PREPARATION IN WALES

Church membership in Wales was declining in the last decade of the nineteenth century,[1] all of the denominations (Nonconformist and Anglican)[2] suffering the effects of a loss of power in the pulpits and of a worldly spirit in the pews.

Writers in various denominational papers complained of low attendance at Sunday services, fellowship and prayer meetings, and of a decline in Bible reading and in family worship; a Divine visitation was the only remedy,[3] they said. Evan Phillips, a Moderator of the Presbyterian Assembly (the Welsh Calvinistic Methodist Church), declared in June of 1900 that Revival was the great need,[4] and until met, all efforts to supply every other need would be in vain. In 1902, a month before his death, Dean David Howell announced:[5]

> Take notice! If it were known that this is my last message to fellow countrymen before being summoned to judgment—the chief need of my country and my dear nation at present is a spiritual revival through the outpouring of the Holy Spirit.

In the 1900s, a number of Welsh leaders were hoping for the inauguration of a Keswick-style Convention in Wales. Many young Welsh ministers had been helped by the teaching of F. B. Meyer; they invited him to come and minister to them regarding deeper truths. Meyer replied that a Keswick Convention would be held at the beautiful Welsh spa, at Llandrindod Wells, a prime mover being Mrs. Jessie Penn-Lewis.[6] Here the young Welsh pastors were greatly blessed, continuing with liberty in prayer for an awakening in Wales. In August 1904, a second convention was held at Llandrindod Wells, Drs. F. B. Meyer and A. T. Pierson ministering.

A Baptist minister, R. B. Jones, was one of the younger ministers challenged by the message of the Llandrindod Wells Convention.[7] He and his friends journeyed widely, conducting missions for the deepening of the spiritual life of the Church. Joseph Jenkins, W. S. Jones, E. Keri Evans and Seth Joshua participated in such efforts, though not all were advocates of Keswick teaching.

These Keswick conferences served, in the psalmist's words, to gather the saints to God, 'those who had made a covenant with sacrifice,'[8] and in them began a reviving.

Many of the evangelists active in Wales in the late 1890s and early 1900s were experienced men. During the middle 1870s, the Rev. John Pugh had begun an evangelistic ministry in the Calvinistic Methodist Church of Wales. Later to be designated the Forward Movement, it stressed open-air evangelism. Pugh moved to Cardiff.

John Pugh found a kindred spirit in Seth Joshua, who (with his brother Frank) had been converted in a Salvation Army meeting, and Seth Joshua also tackled Cardiff. Pugh and the Joshuas extended work all over South Wales.

Also challenged by the virile evangelism of the Salvation Army was Rosina Davies, who held evangelistic missions in the valleys for a score of years, and exercised a fuitful ministry in the North Wales town os Rhos near Wrexham in that significant year, 1904.[9]

The Rev. Seth Joshua was born 10th April 1859, in the year of the mid-nineteenth century Revival in Wales.[10] He was converted twenty-three years later. In 1891, Seth Joshua joined forces with the Forward Movement of the Calvinistic Methodist (now the Welsh Presbyterian) Church in which he was ordained, operating in Cardiff, Newport and Swansea.[11] In 1904, he was denominational evangelist. His missions in Wales in the spring encountered much resistance —trying his spirit and forcing him to private prayer and study. He sought counsel and fellowship from friends in London and Llandrindod Wells.

Seth Joshua was not committed to 'Keswick.' He appreciated its contribution to holiness, but considered its approach as only one of many; and he had a healthy fear that holiness could be cultivated at the expense of service.[12]

Seth Joshua felt afraid of the prevailing emphasis on intellectual qualifications rather than spiritual attainments, hence he began to pray God to take a lad from the mines or fields of Wales, to revive His work in Wales. Little did he realise that the call of that chosen instrument would be confirmed in one of his own meetings.

The Welsh Revival of 1904 may be traced to the chapel of the Rev. Joseph Jenkins at New Quay, Cardiganshire, dated as early as February 1904.[13] Joseph Jenkins had been born during the Revival of 1859 in Wales. He too was moved by the work of the Salvation Army. He too was influenced by John Pugh of the Forward Movement. He was appointed to New Quay in 1892. Jenkins was helped at the Llandrindod Wells Convention also. A number of 'Keswick' conferences was arranged, keeping him busy in Cardiganshire in 1904.[14]

Deeply burdened about the lack of concern in both heart and voice in preaching, Jenkins sought a deeper knowledge of Christ, using Andrew Murray's meditations on the School of Prayer. Greatly burdened by the indifference among the Christians around him, and particularlym concerned about the apathy of his own young people, in the early part of 1904 he called the latter before him and talked most seriously about obeying the Holy Spirit.

One Sunday morning, in a prayer meeting for young people, the pastor asked for testimonies of spiritual experience. Then several attempted to speak on different topics, but the minister tried to redirect them to the subject. At last, a young girl, Florrie Evans, who had been converted a few days before, rose and spoke with a tremor in her voice, saying, 'I love Jesus Christ, with all my heart.' This word, given in sincerity, impressed the Young People's Society.[15]

As in nearby Carmarthenshire, some forty-five years before in the 1859 Awakening, when a young girl's testimony provoked an outbreak of extraordinary power, the blessing in New Quay became noised abroad. There was an open door for the revived young people who, led by their minister, conducted testimony meetings throughout the area.

After six months of sustained movement there in New Quay, Seth Joshua arrived in September 1904 and found a remarkable 'revival spirit' in the place. On Sunday 18th, he reported that he had 'never seen the power of the Holy Spirit so powerfully manifested among the people as at this place just now.' His meetings lasted far into the night. The New Quay movement was about to spread:[16]

> 19th. Revival is breaking out here in greater power . . . the young receiving the greatest measure of blessing. They break out into prayer, praise, testimony and exhortation.

> 20th . . . I cannot leave the building until 12 and even 1 o'clock in the morning—I closed the service several times and yet it would break out again quite beyond control of human power.

> 21st. Yes, several souls . . . they are not drunkards or open sinners, but are members of the visible church not grafted into the true Vine . . . the joy is intense.

22nd. We held another remarkable meeting tonight. Group after group came out to the front, seeking the 'full assurance of faith.'

23rd. I am of the opinion that forty conversions took place this week. I also think that those seeking assurance may be fairly counted as converts, for they had never received Jesus as personal Saviour before.

Seth Joshua thanked God for the time of real blessing to his own soul, feeling saturated, melted and made soft as willing clay in the hands of a potter.[17] A week of unparalleled services ended, with less than four hours' sleep, he was on his way to Newcastle Emlyn. There the work moved slowly, but a number of the students at the Academy were stirred, among them Sidney Evans, Evan Roberts's roommate. The students attended the next series, Blaenannerch.

At Bwlchymynydd in Loughor, near Gorseinson, close to the Glamorgan-Carmarthenshire border, Evan John Roberts was born on 8th July 1878.[18] His was a devout family, Bible reading, family worship and Sunday School playing a large part in his life. When his father was injured in the mine, he (as a big boy) began to work there before his twelfth birthday. A year or so later, he became a communicant in the Moriah Church of the Welsh Calvinistic Methodist denomination.

Evan Roberts worked at first as a door-boy in the pits, opening and closing metal doors for tunnel traffic. When he was nineteen, a pit explosion scorched his Bible, but his life and health were spared. He became superintendent of the Sunday School at Pisgah, Moriah's mission church.

As a young teenager, Evan Roberts was challenged by the remark of an elder[19] at the seiat or fellowship meeting: 'Remember to be faithful. What if the Spirit descended and you absent? Remember Thomas! What a loss he had!' Evan Roberts resolved to attend faithfully the means of grace; he attended prayer meeting Monday, youth meeting Tuesday, congregational meeting Wednesday, temperance meeting Thursday, and class meeting Friday. It was his life.[20]

His greatest passion was interest in revival, a subject that obsessed him from his youth up. He wrote to a friend:

For ten or eleven years, I have prayed for a revival. I could sit up all night to read or talk about revivals. It was the Spirit that moved me to think about a revival.

Most people would have dismissed the young Roberts as a visionary. None can gainsay that his visions came true in the most startling way.

After twelve years in the mines, Roberts became a black-smith. More and more constrained, he offered himself for the ministry in 1903. He sat for denominational examinations, preparing thereby to enter the Newcastle Emlyn Academy. Before he entered, he had an extraordinary experience of a mystical nature, and nightly after that he slept until 1 a.m., awakened for communion with God, returning to sleep.[21]

Evan Roberts's greatest fear in going back to school was not academic inexperience but fear of losing his fellowship with God under pressure of study. But at Newcastle Emlyn he attended a meeting conducted by Seth Joshua. Next night, he accompanied the other young people to prepare the way at Blaenannerch. There he waited, saying 'The altar is built, the wood is in place, and the offering is ready.'

On Thursday morning, Seth Joshua closed his meeeting with a moving prayer, crying out in Welsh, 'Lord . . . bend us.' Evan Roberts went to the front to kneel, crying in great agony: 'Lord, bend me.' Seth Joshua made a note in his diary, remarking upon the prayer of the young man.

Joseph Jenkins and John Thickens, however, were dis-turbed by Evan Roberts's intensity. They feared that such free expression would produce, not a quiet Keswick-style meeting but a spiritual uproar; they were afraid that young Roberts was a spiritual neurotic.[22]

Evan Roberts knew that he had reached the crisis of his spiritual experience. He was moved to pray publicly, but waited till one and another had prayed. He felt compelled to pray, yet still he waited.[23]

> ... when a few more had prayed, I felt a living power pervading my bosom. It took my breath away ...

His face was bathed in perspiration. He cried out, 'Bend me!' He was overwhelmed by the verse, 'God commendeth His love toward us . . .' Then a wave of peace flooded his soul. He became concerned about others.

> I felt ablaze with a desire to go through the length and breadth of Wales to tell of the Saviour; and had that been possible, I was willing to pay God for doing so.

A modern critic has pointed out that mostly wome were in attendance at the meeting in Blaenannerch when Roberts entered into his ecstatic experience. This observation would be miscostrued if it were not explained that the meeting referred to was held in mid-morning for those who were not at school or business, hence house-keepers were bound to predominate, along with the contingent of students of whom

Evan Roberts was one. It was conceded, however, that in Evan Roberts's own meetings, in very many cases, men outnumbered women in attendance.

Joseph Jenkins and his nephew proceeded to prepare for further Keswick conferences, and Seth Joshua to continue in Forward Movement ministry. Unwittingly, all were to be caught up in the Revival. But, for Evan Roberts, it was the most terrible and most sublime day of his life, for he knew without doubt that an extraordinary work was beginning.[24]

Evan Roberts returned to Newcastle Emlyn, to pray for his first team: Sidney Evans, himself and the young women of New Quay. He withdrew all his life savings of £200 for their support. The two men spent their time in prayer and reading, finding the study of Greek very distracting. Even so, they met with no opposition at the Newcastle Emlyn Academy. Principal Phillips was moved, saying later:[25]

> Evan Roberts was like a particle of radium in our midst. Its fire was consuming and felt abroad as something which took away sleep, cleared the channel of tears and sped the golden wheels of prayer throughout the area.

Evan Roberts wrote home to his brother Dan in Loughor:[26]

> The wheels of the gospel chariot are to turn swiftly before long, and it is a privilege to give a hand in the work. I do not know whether you possess the joy of the Gospel... but if you are to have it, you must be willing to do the Spirit's bidding... You must put yourself entirely at the Spirit's disposal.

Sidney Evans, who afterwards married the sister of Evan Roberts, was told by the young prophet, 'I have a vision of all Wales being lifted up to heaven. We are going to see the mightiest revival that Wales has ever known—and the Holy Spirit is coming soon, so we must get ready. We must have a little band and go all over the country preaching.' Roberts asked Evans directly, 'Do you believe that God can give us a hundred thousand souls now?' Sidney Evans never forgot the piercing look on the face of Evan Roberts, nor did other folk who saw such a look on his face—including the writer.

Roberts returned home by train on 31st October, 1904. On the way, he wrote to a deeply spiritual young lady from Cardigan, Mary Cerevig Evans by name:[27]

> Just a line to let you know that I am on my way home for a week to work with our young people. The reason for this is the command of the Holy Spirit. He gave the command last night at the meeting. I could not concen-

trate my thoughts on the work of the service. I prayed and prayed so that I could follow the service, but to no avail. My thoughts were wandering, my mind rivetted on our young folk at Moriah. There seemed a voice as if it said, 'You must go, you must go!'

I then told Mr Phillips about it and I asked whether it was the Devil or the Spirit. He answered, 'No, no. The Devil does not give such thoughts. It was the voice of the Holy Spirit.' Therefore I have decided to obey, and I feel as if the Spirit testifies of a blessed future. The main object of this note is to ask you and your friends to pray for us. I ask in the Saviour's name, to be bold at the Throne of Grace, and endeavour to impress this indelibly on the mind of your friends the importance of prayer, especially on this occasion.

I have written to New Quay and asked them to do the same. I pray God that He will ere long pour His Spirit abundantly on your young folk.

Although Evan Roberts planned to use a team of young evangelists, he went to Loughor alone. His alone was the task of convincing his family and his family church of his mission to the people.

The Roberts family, consisting of his parents, sisters Mary, Sarah and Catherine, and his brother Dan, welcomed Evan home, but they were disturbed. Why had he left his usual studies? What was this strange experience he reported? How could he conduct a week of meetings for the youth of the congregation? They were made uneasy by his utter confidence and felt confused by his certainty; he laughed easily in his assurance of a promised awakening, but he wept as easily when he spoke of his country's need.

Evan Roberts went to see the ministers of the Moriah congregation in Loughor and its daughter church in Gorseinon. The first, Daniel Jones, immediately gave his permission for meetings in the Moriah Church and its chapel, Pisgah. The other minister, Thomas Francis, moved in spirit also, added his permission.[28]

Evan Roberts, encouraged by the friendliness of the two ministers who knew him best, and not discouraged by the bewilderment of his family, commenced his mission in an aftermeeting on Monday night, seventeen only being present. It is an established fact that he believed this to be the beginning of a movement which would win a hundred thousand people to a vital Christian faith, in the little principality of Wales alone—not to mention its impact farther afield.

2

THE OUTBREAK OF REVIVAL

With his pastor's permission, Evan Roberts conducted a youth meeting on the evening of 31st October 1904, after the regular prayer meeting. He told the seventeen people who lingered of his experiences and visions of the past few days, and invited them to declare their Christian faith in public. The people first were unresponsive. It was a local peculiarity to be reluctant in proclaiming assurance of faith. Eventually, all of them gave testimony. It was ten p.m. when the Revivalist, as he was soon to be called, returned home with the satisfaction that his three sisters and brother had made open confession of Christ.[1] A first result was the reinstitution of family worship in the home.

The next meeting was held in Pisgah, a chapel of Moriah congregation closer to Roberts's home. On Tuesday evening, to an augmented audience, Evan Roberts spoke upon the importance of being filled with the Spirit. The meeting lasted three hours, from seven until ten p.m.

At Libanus Church in Gorseinon, Wednesday, Roberts enjoyed rapt attention, and many came to a youth meeting at the Loughor sister church. At the Moriah Church, the young prophet first made use of the 'four points': [2]

1. You must put away any unconfessed sin.
2. You must put away any doubtful habit.
3. You must obey the Spirit promptly.
4. You must confess Christ publicly.

At the meeting of 3rd November, he taught the children to pray,[3] 'Send the Holy Spirit to Moriah, for Jesus' sake.' That evening, he spoke upon the test, 'Ask, and it shall be given you.' With terrible earnestness, he told them: 'These things must be believed, if the work is to succeed. We must believe that God is willing and able to answer our prayers.' It is significant that on Friday 4th November, Evan Roberts wrote to the editor of a Sunday newspaper to ask for an estimate for printing notepaper, adding 'We are on the eve of a great and grand revival, the greatest the world has ever seen. Do not think that the writer is a madman.' [4]

8

On Saturday night, Evan Roberts spoke to a crowded chapel on the subject, 'Be not drunk with wine, wherein is excess, but be filled with the Spirit.' The meeting, lasting five hours, had been announced for 'young people,' but many parents attended, so radical was the change in the youth. Now Evan Roberts had to face his decision, to return to Newcastle Emlyn and studies, or continue in Gorseinon at the pastor's invitation.[5]

On Sunday, 6th November, an ordained minister from another town occupied the pulpit—as previously arranged. Evan Roberts sat quietly listening to the message, awaiting the aftermeeting. That evening, the subject of the young lay-man was 'the Importance of Obedience,' the meeting lasting until after midnight. The churchpeople in the locality were deeply moved by a sense of Divine awe and the turning point in the series of meetings had seemingly arrived.[6]

On the 7th November, the ordinary Monday evening's prayer meeting, announced for 7 p.m. as usual, attracted such crowds that the Moriah Chapel was filled to capacity— a new thing for the prayer meeting. At eight o'clock, the Revivalist arrived and opened his Bible to read the last chapter of the prophecy of Malachi. His hearers all were astonished by the holy boldness with which he insisted that this Scripture was about to be fulfilled in their midst in Loughor.[7] At midnight, the meeting was overflowing with power and three hours passed before it could be closed.

Tuesday evening's meeting, on 8th November, was cold by contrast. The young prophet and his helpers agonized fervently in prayer, together pleading the love of God. Three hours after the tolling of midnight, some intercessors left the chapel for home, among them the mother of Evan Roberts. Evan Roberts could not bear to leave the door open to the intrusion of the sounds of an indifferent world, so he followed his mother to close the door. He asked her:

'Are you going home now, Mother?' 'Yes,' said she.

He said, in a quiet rebuke, 'It is better for you to come back. The Spirit is coming nearer now.'

But Mrs. Roberts protested that the townsfolk all were asleep and would soon be rising to go to work, so she went home, grieving over the hardness of the meeting and puzzled by the strange conduct of her son. Dan and Evan Roberts arrived home before dawn and went to bed, but a couple of hours later Evan Roberts was wakened by the sound of his mother in sore distress. He comforted her, and they prayed.

The weekly organ of the Keswick movement, published in London, carried in the columns of its issue of 9th November 1904 a report that a cloud 'no bigger than a man's hand' had arisen in Wales.[8] Its writer, Jessie Penn-Lewis, gave the main facts of a letter from Seth Joshua.[9]

In Gorseinon, the tide was turning. Soon the bustle of the crowds of young people going to the early morning prayer meetings was awakening others not so inclined. Evan Roberts preached at the Brynteg Congregational Chapel on the 9th, the same day that an English-language newspaper back in Cardiff carried a brief account of the stirrings of revival in west Glamorgan.[10]

GREAT CROWDS OF PEOPLE
DRAWN TO LOUGHOR

Congregation Stays till 2.30 in the Morning

A remarkable religious revival is now taking place in Loughor. For some days a young man named Evan Roberts, a native of Loughor, has been causing great surprise at Moriah Chapel. The place has been besieged by dense crowds of people unable to obtain admission. Such excitement has prevailed that the road on which the chapel is situated has been lined with people from end to end. Roberts, who speaks in Welsh, opens his discourse by saying that he does not know what he is going to say but that when he is in communion with the Holy Spirit, the Holy Spirit will speak, and he will simply be the medium of His wisdom. The preacher soon after launches into a fervent and at times impassioned oration. His statements have had the most stirring effects upon his listeners. Many who have disbelieved Christianity for years are returning to the fold of their younger days. One night, so great was the enthusiasm invoked by the young revivalist that, after his sermon which lasted two hours, the vast congregation remained praying and singing until two-thirty in the morning. Shopkeepers are closing early in order to get a place in the chapel, and tin and steel workers throng the place in working clothes.

On 11th November, the Moriah Church was again overcrowded with eight hundred or more people, overflowing into the old chapel. Many were on their knees for a long time on account of their distress and agony of soul. By now a newspaper reporter from Cardiff had arrived, and he was amazed at what he saw. His report was given the widest circulation in Wales and beyond:[11]

Instead of the set order of proceedings . . . everything
was left to the spontaneous impulse of the moment . . .

at 4.25 a.m., the gathering dispersed. But even at that
hour, the people did not make their way home. When I
left to walk back to Llanelly, I left dozens of them about
the road still discussing what is now the chief subject
of their lives.

'I felt that this was no ordinary gathering,' he added.
All the next day, Friday, prayer meetings in the homes of
the people were held to intercede for the salvation of their
friends and kinsfolk.   The Friday evening service again
disregarded time, yet the spiritual excitement kept the folk
from awareness of hunger or fatigue.[12]

By early afternoon, Saturday 12th November, wagons and
carts were driven into town from the surrounding countryside. Shops in the town were cleared of all provisions by folk
who had come long distances. The meeting houses were overcrowded hours before the time for which services had been
announced.[13] Sidney Evans preached in one chapel and Evan
Roberts in the other. Day broke before the people dispersed,
to their homes first and to Sunday services afterwards.

A local minister reported that the community had been
converted into a praying multitude. The lives of hundreds
of coal-miners and tin-plate workers were transformed,
men going straight from the mills and pit-heads to chapel,
leaving the taverns practically empty.[14]

The only theme of conversation among all classes and
sects is 'Evan Roberts.' Even the tap-rooms of the
public houses are given over to discussion on the origin
of the powers possessed by him.

Evan Roberts enjoyed no sleep on Saturday night, but
early on Sunday morning, driven by a Loughor layman and
accompanied by five young singers, he arrived in Swansea
to catch a train for Aberdare. The opening meetings in this
town were disappointing. There was criticism by the local
Christians of the visiting team of girl singers.

On Monday 14th November, the great Ebenezer Chapel
in Aberdare (Congregationalist) was crowded by a thousand
eager people.[15] There was no sign of anything unusual in
either the Sunday or the Monday service. On Tuesday, the
early morning prayer meeting was crowded, people remain-
ing at home rather than going to work. The meeting lasted
four hours. There the young prophet announced that a great
awakening was coming to all of Wales.

Assisted by W. W. Lewis, W. S. Jones and others, Joseph Jenkins conducted a fourth convention on the Keswick pattern in Tregaron.[16] There teaching was planned, but the local people soon broke out into the 'freedom' of an open meeting and experienced 'much blessing in it.'

In the town of Carmarthen, there had been held a special series of meetings in early 1904, conducted by Mr. Reader Harris, King's Counsel; and other special efforts followed until, in November, the Rev. R. B. Jones came fresh from a great awakening in Rhos and shared ministry with Mrs. Jessie Penn-Lewis in a conference. Before the end of the year, Joseph Jenkins and his friends were enjoying the full effect of the revival there.[17]

Sidney Evans, occupied in revival meetings in Cardigan churches, returned to the Gorseinon area just before Evan Roberts left to visit Aberdare. Joined by the New Quay girls, he led the services in the Libanus Church with increasing attendances and augmented spiritual power.[18]

In Pembroke, 'little England beyond Wales,' the movement was felt strongly before the end of 1904.[19] One minister told of admitting to the membership of his church one Sunday 44 people of all ages, from an old man of 80 to a child of 10.

Nantlais Williams,[20] minister at Ammanford, instituted prayer meetings nightly in November before the arrival of Joseph Jenkins, in whose ministry the expectation increased. After his departure, the prayer meetings continued, one of them lasting till 2.30 a.m. Later in that month, Seth Joshua arrived. Of the Ammanford meetings, he wrote in his diary for November:[21]

> 20th. This has been one of the most remarkable days of my life. Even in the morning a number were led to embrace the Saviour. In the afternoon, the blessing fell on scores of young people. The crush was very great to get into the chapel. At 7 o'clock, a surging mass filled the Christian Temple and crowds were unable to gain entrance; the Holy Spirit was indeeed among the people. Numbers confessed Jesus but it is impossible to count.

The impression made at Ammanford was a lasting one. Bibles were sold out; swearing in the mines gave place to praise; the taverns were emptied of rowdy customers; and within a decade the Ammanford Convention for Deepening of the Spiritual Life[22] was established by Nantlais Williams, who traced his conversion to the time of the Revival—even though already an active, sympathetic, ordained minister.

Seth Joshua, Keri Evans and other itinerants exercised a steadying influence, Keri Evans saying that conviction was not conversion, that awakening was not repentance;[23] far too little attention has been paid to their teaching contribution.

After Aberdare, Evan Roberts went to Pontycymmer to speak in a Congregational chapel; the results were the same: fervent zeal in all the meetings, and outright conversion of notorious sinners. In one place, because of weariness he failed to show up but this did not diminish local enthusiasm.

In Porth, every chapel was filled. The movement swept the Rhondda Valley like a tidal wave.[24] The Revivalist proceeded to Caerphilly, but the work went on in the Rhondda, as in Gorseinon, long after the Revivalist left.[25]

An American visitor told a packed church in Tylortown: 'Some people think that this revival is the fizz of a bottle of pop. No, no! It is the fizz of a fuse, and dynamite is at the end of it!'[26]

Roberts declined to campaign in the Welsh metropolis, but extraordinary scenes were witnessed there in Cardiff. In the Baptist Tabernacle, a New Year's Eve service ran on until 1 a.m. on Sunday morning, thirty-three converts bringing the total of professions of faith to 260.[27]

Evan Roberts returned to his home in Loughor to spend Christmas with his family.[28] He declined to be interviewed. On Christmas evening, he attended regular Sunday service in Moriah Chapel and 'a large number' professed conversion. After Christmas, Evan Roberts continued his ministry in the Swansea Valley, drawing crowds of 2500 to 3000 again and again, filling a big chapel in Morriston.[29]

By the end of 1904, the main movement of the Revival had continued for two months.[30] Returns from incomplete lists of churches in South Wales and Monmouth indicated gains in membership of 34,131—a total not including North Wales.

In Rhos, near Wrexham in North Wales, the revival had begun early in 1904 with Rosina Davies. In mid-year, there were further stirrings. But on 8th November, the Rev. R. B. Jones began a ten-day mission, in which simultaneous prayer overwhelmed preacher and audience.[31] The closing meeting ran on and on from 10 am. till 10 pm. More than a hundred converts were counted in this phase of the movement, but four months later there were 2267.[32]

In the second week of December 1904, the local press reported that the religious revival was spreading rapidly throughout North Wales, beginning in town after town with interdenominational prayer meetings, generally followed by preaching services, developing into open meetings; the results were the same, the quickening of church members, the conversion of outsiders, and the virtual elimination of drunkenness and swearing.[33]

In North Wales, the Rev. Hugh Hughes, a local Methodist, preached at Bethesda for the Free Churches. An hour's 'open' prayer meeting preceded each service, which was succeeded by a young people's prayer meeting sometimes lasting for three hours. By December, one of the local ministers was rejoicing that the police were unemployed, the streets being so quiet, and he observed that the district council was quite willing to support them even if they were doing nothing. Feuds and quarrels inherited from a bitter strike recently past were settled.[34] The whole community was uplifted.

In the historic college town of Bangor, North Wales, there were many occasions when the crowded congregation at large would be praying audibly,[35] individually and simultaneously. This also occurred when Joseph Jenkins of New Quay had visited Bethesda in the Revival, and in the youth meetings extraordinary things were witnessed. Two months later, Evan Roberts in person visited the town.[36]

A visit to Talysarn by Joseph Jenkins and the New Quay girls resulted in an extraordinary stir, when a quarryman-turned-teacher, Evan Lloyd-Jones, received a call to an immediate ministry.[37] Evan Lloyd-Jones became almost as famous in North Wales as Evan Roberts was in the South.

A political rally arranged at Pwllheli for the Member of Parliament (later Prime Minister) David Lloyd-George was itself transformed into a revival meeting in which a clergyman opened in devotions, the audience sang a hymn with the greatest enthusiasm, and a blind man led in prayer, the two political speakers scarcely being noticed.[38]

The Baptist preacher, R. B. Jones, conducted missions in Anglesey in January 1905 with great response.[39] Most encouraging numbers of people were flocking into the churches all over North Wales at this time.[40]

Visitors flocked to Wales from all the English-speaking countries and the Continent to observe the Revival.[41] More often they visited the scenes of Revival in South Wales. Dr. F. B. Meyer, who visited the localities of the Revival, commented that 'No money was spent on advertising the Revival meetings,' and that there was no need of posters on hoardings.[22] The late Lord Pontypridd likewise commented that the Welsh Revival advertised and financed itself. 'There are no bills, no hired halls, no salaries.' Neither cursory reading nor detailed study of the secular press and religious journals[43] reveal the use of funds to advertise the meetings, conversations with leaders and converts after thirty years confirming this fact to the author.[44]

Throughout Wales, it was to keep an appointment with the Lord that people came to the meetings. More often than not, they crowded the chapels to overflowing, not knowing whether the Revivalist would be there or not. On occasion, Evan Roberts would arrive at the door of a church, make his way forward, sit on the front seat and say nothing for three hours. Then he would stand up, offer an exhortation or prayer, thus speaking for ten or fifteen minutes only, then sit down.

Dr. F. B. Meyer observed:[45] 'He will not go in front of the Divine Spirit, but is willing to stand aside and remain in the background unless he is perfectly sure that the Spirit of God is moving him. It is a profound lesson.' The people in the congregation continued the extraordinary work—in praying, testifying, praising, singing and exhorting, with no tiring of spirit.

A veteran Welsh preacher told the writer that he was only seven when the Revival reached the Rhondda. His father was a coal-miner. He came home from the early shift, washed off the coal-dust, put on his best clothes and took his wife and children to the nearby chapel, which was packed at four in the afternoon.[46] Evan Roberts arrived about seven, made his way to the front of the big church, climbed over the knees of the people sitting around the pulpit, stood up and uttered but one word in Welsh, 'Let us pray.' Immediately, prayer burst forth audibly and simultaneously from the vast crowd; but Evan Roberts took no further part in the extraordinary proceedings, making his way out about ten p.m. to pray all night in the quiet of his room. The meeting was continuing in full power at two a.m., when the family made its way out. The children were put to bed, but the miner dozed in the big chair by the fire till daybreak, went to work, returned home, took a bath, put on his best clothes, and took his family back to the chapel at four to the same meeting still going strong.

Gipsy Smith described a meeting at Maesteg where Evan Roberts appeared after two-and-a-half hours of spontaneous prayer and praise and exhortation.[47] 'Anybody would sing, even a little child. There was no speechmaking.' Even Evan Roberts did not take part in audible speech.

A little chapel in Llansamlet near Neath was packed out with six hundred people. There were two young mockers in the audience, and Evan Roberts became aware of their presence, calling on them both to yield to Divine influence. They both refused, hence a hurricane of audible prayer tore through the place, an agony of entreaty.[48] It was customary for the congregation to concentrate its prayers thus.

Campbell Morgan affirmed paradoxically that everywhere 'in what seemed supreme confusion, one was conscious of splendid order.'[49]

An eye-witness, the Rev. A. F. Williamson, read a paper before a company of Philadelphians, commenting upon the simplicity of organization and lack of anything superfluous or mechanical in the conduct of the meetings in Wales, the only leader recognized being the Holy Spirit, even the most sceptical being compelled to believe it as genuine. There was a spontaneity of participation in the services, no solos, no duets, no quartets, no choir, yet the singing was a special feature of every meeting, the whole congregation singing. There was a oneness of spirit, as at Pentecost. Prominence was given to prayer and a passionate love of the Bible was demonstrated.[50]

An English Baptist pastor, the late Rev. H. J. Galley of Bath, told the writer (in the 1930s) that, reading an account of the Welsh Revival in the London newspapers, he journeyed by train to South Wales and met at a local station a former classmate from Spurgeon's College.

The Welshman was full of joy. The Englishman told him: 'I have come a long way, and I would like to hear Evan Roberts preach. Where is he preaching?' He was taken aback when his friend professed ignorance of the Revivalist's movements. 'He does not tell people where to expect him. He tells them that they need the Lord Jesus Christ, and that they will find Him in the nearest church.' Galley must have looked disappointed, for his Welsh friend added: 'Look. I can not promise that Evan Roberts will be in my church tonight, but the Spirit of God will be there in mighty power.' And he proceeded to amaze his London visitor by claiming that every church in town was filled each evening until midnight, and that lesser meetings went on all day from daybreak.[51]

The outstanding feature of the Welsh Revival was utter spontaneity. The understandable fear of the ministers that the meetings would get out of control was met by the trust that the Spirit moving the people would rebuke deviation.

3

THE IMPACT OF REVIVAL

By the New Year of 1905, the Welsh Revival had reached its greatest power and extent. All classes, all ages and every denomination shared in the general awakening. Totals of converts added to the churches were published in local newspapers, 70,000 in two months, 85,000 in five, and more than a hundred thousand in half a year.[1] Eighty thousand were still in the membership of the Welsh churches in 1914, in spite of leakage to mission halls and emigration overseas.

Miners' Associations refused to hold meetings on licensed premises, hitherto the local custom. After the 1905 New Year, the Swansea County Police Court announced to the public that there had not been a single charge for drunkenness over the holiday weekend, an all-time record.[2]

In the Welsh metropolis, the Cardiff police reported a 60% decrease in drunkenness and 40% fewer people in jail at the New Year.[3] Figures released by Cardiff's Chief Constable four years after the outbreak of the Revival showed totals of convictions for drunkenness in Glamorgan:[4]

| 1902 | 9,298 | 1903 | 10,528 | 1904 | 11,282 |
| 1905 | 8,164 | 1906 | 5,490 | 1907 | 5,615 |

David Lloyd-George, a master of rhetoric, compared the Revival to an earthquake and to a tornado, predicting far-reaching social changes. At a public gathering in Scotland, he spoke of a town in his constituency where the total takings on a Saturday night in the local tavern amounted to fourpence-ha'penny—nine cents, on the drinking night of the week.[5]

The great wave of sobriety which swept over the country caused severe financial losses to men in the liquor trade, and closed many of the taverns.[6] A great improvement in public morals resulted in turn from the closures.

Stocks of Welsh and English Bibles were sold out. Prayer meetings were held in coal mines, in trains and trams and places of business. The works managers bore testimony of the change of conduct of their employees. The magistrates were presented with white gloves in several places, signifying that there were utterly no cases to try.[7]

The life of the coal pits was transformed. Not only did workers and management engage in prayer meetings on the company's time, which was being put to such good use in the ordinary hours of activity, but the pits themselves showed silent indicators of the new spirit—with texts chalked upon ventilitating doors for all to see who passed that way.

Cursing and profanity were so diminished that it was reported that a strike was provoked in the coal mines—so many men gave up using foul language that the pit ponies dragging the coal trucks in the mine tunnels did not understand what was being said to them and stood still, confused.

It was noted in London that the Poor Law Guardians (who administered relief) in Swansea were commenting upon an unusual happening in Wales, working people taking their aged parents home from the workhouse to which they had been inconsiderately assigned.

And there were striking cases of restitution made. At Maesteg, a tradesman received a live pig in payment of a debt which had been outstanding since 1898, and other striking instances of open restitution were reported.[8]

The police rejoiced in the Revival. One day in Holyhead, in the island county of Anglesey, the solemnity of court proceedings was broken by songs of praise in Welsh.[9] The police guard outside hurried in, but stayed to add his bass.

Many were the evidences of the Spirit of God working in Wales. Long standing debts were paid, stolen goods returned, while pugilists and gamblers were converted.[10]

Revival in Wales affected the university colleges. For example, in a student lounge at University College in Bangor, an undergraduate started to sing an old Welsh hymn; another student prayed and an unbroken succession of hymns, prayers, and testimonies followed.[11] Lectures were cut, as three hundred or more gathered for afternoon prayer, while in the evening the students marched en masse to the Tabernacle, which was crowded. There were similar scenes in other academic communities.

During the Revival, children held meetings of their own in homes, barns, and (in some cases) even in empty pigsties. The records are full of instances of young children taking part in public meetings, in prayer or song or exhortation.[12]

The four major Nonconformist denominations were reported to have gained eighty thousand in the months of the Revival, Anglicans proportionately less in the Revival period, but more in the aftermath of the Awakening.[13]

D. E. Richards, of the Baptist Union of Wales, wrote:[14]

> The Moderator of the Union, the professors of our
> colleges, the pastors of our churches and our students
> are surcharged with Divine fire; the Holy Spirit seems
> to have possessed our pulpit completely; the Church
> has wakened and has put on the beautiful garments of
> her glory. The people repent and the thousands are
> baptized in the name of Jesus for forgiveness of sins
> and the gift of the Holy Spirit.

The Welsh Presbyterians (known then as the Calvinistic
Methodists) fully supported the 1904 Revival, Evan Roberts
and other leaders[15] being affiliated with their organization.
Congregationalist leaders supported the movement, though
there were some who questioned Evan Roberts. The Wesleyan
Methodists also supported the revival throughout Wales, by
word of mouth and by pen.[16] Quaker reactions to the Revival
in Wales were shown in their journal in 1905 — 'What we have
seen in Wales is Quakerism rebaptized!' It was said that
their largest chapel in Wales, seating 2000, was packed out
at 10.30 a.m., 2.30 p.m. and at 6.30 p.m. on occasion.[17] 'The
iron in our Welsh valleys is hot. Let us strike before it cools.'

Even when controversy began, editors of the leading Anglo-
Catholic journal in Britain supported the Revival in Wales,
while the Roman Catholic organ published a sympathetic review, declaring that 'the Revivalist is infinitely nearer to us
than the indifferent or the sceptic.'[18]

Anglican reaction to the Revival in Wales was sympathetic.
In their pastoral letters, the South Wales Bishop of St. David's
and the North Wales Bishop of Bangor made 'wise and sympathetic' comments,[19] the latter finding in the movement 'convincing evidence that it is a manifestation of the Spirit of God.'
There seemed to be no Anglican opinion to the contrary.

The Bishop of Dorking spent three days in the valleys of
Wales, reporting incognito visits to mining villages, finding
four chapels of different affiliations filled nightly, the time
occupied by prayer and praise, testimony and exhortation,
but without preaching.[20] The Rev. and Hon. W. Talbot Rice
participated in Anglican services in Upper Loughor in which
there were spontaneous outbursts of prayer and praise.[21] The
redoubtable Anglican evangelist, Canon Hay Aitken, later conducted a preaching mission at the Swansea Parish Church,
New Year 1905.[22] Archdeacon Wilberforce, in Westminster
Abbey, declared that the Revival had done more in Wales in
two months than had the temperance laws in two years.[23]

The Welsh Revival, an American authority noted,[24] was on the whole a movement among the people. The meetings consisted almost entirely by prayer and praise and were under the direct control of the Spirit of God. 'There is in this a very profound lesson. The average (American) church regards revival as impossible without evangelists. As a matter of fact, there can be one wherever there are united Christian people ready for it. God sends the power in every case, just as He has in Wales.'

Dr. G. Campbell Morgan, Westminster pastor, asked the question: [25]

> What is the character of this revival? It is a church revival. I do not mean by that merely a revival among church members ... meetings are held in the chapels, all up and down the valleys, and it began among church members; and when it touches the outside man, it makes him a church member at once. . It is a movement in the church and of the church, a movement in which the true functions and forces of the church are being exercised and fulfilled.

There is a paradox in the proceedings of meetings in Evangelical Revivals, and Campbell Morgan commented: 'It was a meeting characterized by a perpetual series of interruptions and disorderliness; it was a meeting characterized by a great continuity and an absolute order.'

The sovereignty of the Holy Spirit in all His operations, the possibility of Spirit-filled assembly, confidence in the inspired Word of God, the power of earnest, united prayer, and the power of sacred song—these were the marks of the Revival.[26] Another observer summarized them: '1. Honour to the Holy Spirit as a presiding presence. 2. The plain preaching of Christ and of sound gospel doctrine. 3. The prominence given to prayer, individual and united. 4. The dependence upon God, rather than upon men. 5. The absence of stereotyped programme and set method. 6. The readiness for blessing by a willingness to remove obstacles. 7. The direct dealing with the unconverted.' [27]

Confession of sin was particular and specific, according to Vyrnwy Morgan,[28] while Campbell Morgan reported:[29]

> The movement is characterized by the most remarkable confessions of sin, confessions that must be costly. I heard some of them who have been members of the church and officers of the church, confessing hidden sin in their hearts, impurity committed and condoned, and seeking prayer for its putting away.

Professor J. Morris Jones of the University College of North Wales commented that the great Revival had brought a strange fluency to common folk, ploughboys having been known to burst into a flow of language in chaste and classic Welsh.[30] Even children in the meetings were affected by this spirit, leading in prayer, and exhorting and singing, with conviction and power.

That the Keswick Conventions exercised an influence on the lives of many about to become the heralds and prophets of the Welsh Revival is undoubted.[31] But the movement had little or no influence upon the preparation of Evan Roberts. Indeed, there was a hint of claiming too much on the part of some proponents, and this was repudiated.

Dr. F. B. Meyer was reported in the Welsh press as having claimed instrumentality in the outbreak of the Revival of 1904. This was true as far as six young ministers were concerned, but was repudiated regarding Evan Roberts by Dr. Cynddylan Jones in the Cardiff press;[32] there is no record of Dr. Meyer being offended, and he continued a lifelong friend.

But trouble was brewing in another quarter. Evan Roberts was 'clairvoyant and clairaudient,' said some experts, while others insisted that he possessed the charismatic gift of discernment.[33] Before the outbreak of revival, Evan Roberts had seen visions and heard voices. His manner in meetings was so unusual that he became a prime target for criticism on the part of sceptics.

There occurred in his Liverpool meetings an uncanny demonstration of Evan Roberts's gift of discernment, as reported by the national journalist and social reformer, W. T. Stead. The voluntary workers had met to discuss their house-to-house visitation aimed at enlisting attendance at the meetings. Each was reporting upon his assignment to a particular street. One young man modestly told of calling at every house in a certain street, when the Welsh prophet fixed his piercing gaze upon him and contradicted him. The young man stammered in confusion and admitted that he had not performed all that he had claimed. He trembled like a leaf and burst into tears when Evan Roberts told him that his deceitful ways had followed his forging of a signature on an earlier occasion.[34]

Evan Roberts also rebuked some ministers on the Sun Hall platform for secret opposition to the work. In the local press, two sponsoring ministers humbly confessed that his discernment of their spirit was correct: they apologized.[35]

During the Welsh Revival, nobody was more shy of publicity than the popular Revivalist himself. He avoided publicity. He dreaded newspaper reporters.[36] He feared the adulation of the masses. When he felt that the people were coming to see and hear him only, he withdrew himself. As soon as he became aware of the fact that the people were making him the focus of attraction, he pleaded in serious words and agonized tones that they would look away to Christ and Him alone, lest the Spirit withdraw Himself from the whole movement. Within weeks, Evan Roberts had become the world's most publicized preacher, far more than Torrey or any other, yet he refused repeatedly to give interviews to newspaper men from every part of the United Kingdom, from nearby Europe, and from far overseas, who came to see him and (of course) to record the happenings. Evan Roberts firmly refused to be photographed except by his own family.[37]

The Welsh people, who understood him better, were not suprised when the Revivalist sat among the people, praying silently, and then left without saying a single word. Strangers from the other parts of Britain and overseas were astounded to witness exciting ministry in crowded meetings where the people sang and prayed and testified without the young prophet of God being there, or if there, without taking part.

Evan Roberts was sometimes accompanied by the young women from New Quay and Gorseinon who sang spiritual solos or duets in the meetings, or who exhorted penitents of their own sex. There was no hint of scandal in this association. Womenfolk commonly respond warmly to spiritual leaders and this was the case with Evan Roberts, as it was with his Master centuries before. Critics have often read into situations their own inclinations or experiences, and some of them refused to believe that platonic rather than romantic, spiritual rather than carnal, friendship existed. Scandal was sought for, in vain; the worst that was verified was that the young women workers had on an occasion washed Roberts's socks, but even that caused a clucking among the hens.[38] And Evan Roberts remained free of entanglement or scandal.

There was an inevitable attempt to pin some financial indiscretion or pecuniary motivation on Evan Roberts. In this, the critics were unsuccessful. A £200 thankoffering, given after the Cwmavon meetings, was given to the Pisgah mission church, liquidating their debt. Evan Roberts gave his £200 savings, which he had drawn for the use of a team of young evangelists, to the Moriah congregation, and thereafter lived from day to day, month to month, and (even in his long retirement) from year to year through the ministration of friends, as did his Master long before. (This I know)[39]

The Revivalist commenced his mission in the town of Dowlais on Sunday 22nd January 1905.[40] The various chapels were crowded that morning, but in the afternoon meeting in a Congregational Church, Roberts declared: 'There is something wrong in this meeting.' That night, in another chapel of the same affiliation, he complained of the coldness of spirit and, asking the crowd to sing a hymn, put on his coat and retired from the meeting.

Half-a-dozen churches were well-filled for services on Monday morning, and, long before commencement, a huge crowd packed out the Bethania Chapel in Dowlais. An overflow was arranged in the schoolroom, and hundreds were turned away.[41] On Tuesday morning, 2000 people crowded Bethania again. But it seemed that some of the ministers and officers were offended.

At the end of January, Cardiff papers carried a letter signed by the minister of the Bethania Congregational Chapel:

Peter Price, (B.A. Hons.)

Mental and Moral Sciences Tripos,

late of Queen's College, Cambridge.[42]

It was a bitter attack on Evan Roberts. The gist of the Rev. Peter Price's argument was that there were two revival movements going on in Wales, the real and the sham. He affirmed that in the six months past, his church had experienced something of the true revival, with hundreds of conversions. But he did not hesitate to identify the other revival, 'a sham Revival, a mockery, a blasphemous travesty of the real thing,' as the work of its 'chief figure,' Evan Roberts.

Mr. Price accused Evan Roberts of using the language of Deity, asking if the lay-preacher were the fourth person of the Godhead. He urged Evan Roberts 'and his girl-companions' to withdraw, examine themselves and learn a little more of the meaning of Christianity. He insisted that, in Dowlais, there were scores of young colliers who exceeded Evan Roberts in intellectual capability or in spiritual power. He denounced the 'mock Revival' as 'exhibition,' 'froth,' 'vain trumpery,' 'false fire,' an 'utterly sacrilegious' and 'bogus' performance.

The editor of the Cardiff newspaper replied in person to the attack of Peter Price.[43] Evan Roberts was asked about it and said, 'Let him alone. I have my work to do.' [44]

A storm of protest and controversy ensued, in which Evan Roberts answered not a word further. Peter Price's friend, Dr. J. Vyrnwy Morgan, who in 1909 published his account of the Welsh Religious Revival as 'a retrospect and a criticism,' detailed a selection of abusive postcards and letters received from angered Roberts supporters together with some of the choicest items from Price's friends and admirers.[45] This device failed to convince people that Evan Roberts's supporters were all nasty, while supporters of Peter Price were all nice. The public reacted overwhelmingly in supporting Evan Roberts, according to the evidence.

In his 1968 treatise, Dr. Eifion Evans has pointed out that neither Peter Price's supporters nor Evan Roberts's defenders seriously treated the points at issue: an individual claim to be under the immediate control of the Spirit, and a general charge that excesses were marring the Revival. From apostolic days, claims were made of individuals being under such control, and the Church at large sustained these only if warranted by the results of their ministry. Likewise there were counterfeit accompaniments manifested even in the days of the Apostles.[46]

While Evan Roberts remained silent, he was hurt. Early in February, he followed medical advice to rest after 'nervous prostration.' Late in February, he postponed a Briton Ferry series and retired for seven days' silence. More and more, he became aware of obstacles in meetings and this in turn led to unhappy incidents.[47] Professor Henri Blois, a French author publishing observations of the Revival said:[48]

> Roberts ignored the attacks, but they had their effect on him, for he became passionately concerned about the immediate revelation from the Holy Spirit. This came to a head with an extraordinary incident at Cwmavon, on February 21. During the meeting, Roberts cried out in agony that a soul present was damned; the congregation began to pray, but Roberts stopped them, saying there was no point in praying, for this soul was finally damned.

Entirely apart from Evan Roberts, there was a flood of emotion in the Welsh Revival.[49] There were those who attributed the movement to the 'blind hysterics of the Celt.' But Gwilym O. Griffith[50] affirmed that the 1904 Revival in Wales was the least emotional of all the Welsh Revivals on record.

There were always those who objected to the emotion shown in the meetings. To some, 'life with exuberance' was more to be dreaded than 'death with composure.' For fully half a century, anti-Evangelicals dismissed the Awakening as a wind of emotion, and some even blamed upon it the ineffectiveness of the Welsh Churches in the 1950s, a charge refuted by Ambrose Bebb in 1954.[51] Emotion is not emotionalism, the 'calculated exploitation of feeling for unworthy ends.'

It is interesting that William James published in 1902 a series of lectures on the subject of the varieties of religious experience.[52] His thesis—that experience of 'conversion' is produced by sub-conscious emotional excitement, altogether subjectively without any objective Divine element—became a popular scholarly view.

There were attempts by writers in the organ of the British Medical Association to explain away the power of the Revival in Wales.[53] Another in a contemporary medical magazine contended that the human will is rendered 'weak by emotion.' This surely was a strange conclusion, to explain why men for years enslaved by alcoholic and other appetites should suddenly become so weak in will through strong emotion that they thereupon resolved to quit the habit, and succeeded. Modern psychology has taught that emotion, the stronger the greater, strengthens the will. Indifference sabotages it.[54]

Medical experts reported a slight increase in the number of patients admitted to mental hospitals in Wales in the early months of the Revival, but pointed out that this was due to the relapse of former patients or the breakdown of patients with a family history of mental instability.[55] The highest expert consulted affirmed that he could not cite a single instance of religious mania caused by the Revival. It was admitted that the excitement of the movement had an unsettling effect upon a few people already diagnosed as mentally unstable.

In March 1905, there came reports that the health of Evan Roberts had begun to be affected. The strain of incessant travel, irregular meals and long hours in meetings, added their quota to the toll on his health.[56]

It must not be thought that only Evan Roberts suffered from the strain of working a sixteen to twenty hour day. It was reported that Sidney Evans and Samuel Jenkins were likewise temporarily incapacitated by nervous prostration. Evan Roberts's friends in Liverpool insisted that he should consult medical opinion. His examiners stated:[57]

> We find him mentally and physically quite sound. He is suffering from the effects of overwork, and we consider it advisable that he should have a period of rest.

The four medical men who had signed Evan Roberts's certificate of physical and mental health were James Barr, M.D., F.R.C.P.; William Williams, M.D., F.R.C.P.; Thomas Bickerton, M.R.C.S.; and William McAfee, M.D.[58] Some folk hooted that Evan Roberts was the only evangelist on record with a certificate of sanity—a jibe which lost its punch when applied to professionals other than evangelists.

Dr. Forbes Winslow,[59] a mental specialist, intemperately declared: 'I would have men like Evan Roberts locked up as common felons, and their meetings prohibited like those of socialists and anarchists as being dangerous to the public.' Of course, Dr Winslow had examined Roberts telepathically only before reaching his professional opinion.

The Revivalist rested for a few weeks, then wrote to his personal friends:[60]

> The mountains are high—my hope is higher;
> The moutains are strong—my faith is stronger;
> The mountains will depart—my God, never.

Then he returned to his preaching.

Evan Roberts's health never fully recovered from the strain it suffered during the assault on his ministry by Peter Price. He kept working in 1905 and into 1906, but retired in April that year to the shelter of the home of the Penn-Lewises in Leicester, where he was hidden from a prying public. His recovery was intermittent and slow, lasting many months, and was followed by a long period of convalescence.[61]

For half his lifetime, Evan Roberts adamantly refused to take part in any ministry in public, refused almost all callers, and lived the life of a recluse, devoting his time to intercession.[62] His post-Revival activity was regarded as a strange mystery by the Christian public.

The author of this treatise met Evan Roberts thirty years after the outbreak of the 1904 Welsh Revival.[63] At that time, the Revivalist was living as a recluse at the home of friends on Bettws-y-Coed Road in the Cyncoed suburb of Cardiff. His health was poor, so he had a good reason to shield himself from visitors. But his mind was alert—and the whole household held him in awe as a saint.

The decline of the ministry of Evan Roberts did not mean the end of the Welsh Revival. Other men, in whom the press was less interested, faced an ever-increasing demand as preachers or teachers. The phenomenal phase of the Welsh Revival gave way to one of building up converts and extending the outreach to other parts.

There were many outstanding evangelists in the Welsh Revival—Joseph Jenkins, R. B. Jones, W. W. Lewis, Seth Joshua, W. S. Jones, Keri Evans—all of them busy from morn until night. The many famous preachers coming to Wales to see the Revival demonstrated no spirit of envy or competition, rather one of humble awe. Gipsy Smith, John McNeill, William Booth, Campbell Morgan, and others of like fame visited the scenes of Divine visitation, but were themselves content to offer brief prayers or say a few words, or to sit quietly in the meetings while old men dreamed dreams, young men prophesied and even children prayed and sang and testified in the Spirit.[64] But both Welsh evangelists and English-speaking or foreign ministers played a significant role in promoting extraordinary meetings in countries overseas.

Throughout 1905, the spiritual tides were high throughout Wales, evangelists and pastors busy. Gipsy Smith conducted an evangelistic series in Pontypridd in the Glamorgan valleys, with an unusual measure of blessing and unusual manifestation of power.[65] In the extreme southwest of Wales, 'extraordinary meetings' were conducted by Seth Joshua, with as many as twelve hundred upon their knees,[66] praying simultaneously. What in normal times was extraordinary was no longer considered 'news' in Wales, hence reports that told of steady evangelism went unnoticed.

In 1906, Evan Roberts shared in a three-hour service in an Anglican Church in Aberdaron and 'former pentecostal scenes'[67] were noted in Loughor, Pontcymmer and Trecynon. But, Seth Joshua commented, there was no great blaze of revival enthusiasm now in Wales, just a steady glow in many places north and south.[68] 'The fire has been partly extinguished among the young converts in many places by officialdom suppressing their testimony as to the assurance of salvation; this opposition is peculiar to Welsh theology.'

It was said that some had grown weary and some had gone back, but not in any large proportion. The life of the churches had been distinctly and permanently quickened.[69] 'After the storm, the calm—not of stagnation, but of settled conviction: not so much ecstasy, but much peace.'

In 1907, a 'noticeable reaction' following the Welsh Revival was reported, but A. T. Pierson[70] contradicted the report, quoting Keri Evans as saying that only the form had changed. The four major Nonconformist denominations, which had added twenty percent to their membership, lost two-and-a-half percent,[71] some possibly gained by the Anglican Church and others by independent mission halls   from which the emerging Pentecostal churches drew their strength.

One of the strongest criticisms of the Revival was made by Vyrnwy Morgan in pointing out that four Nonconformist Churches had gained 80,000 in the Revival, and lost 20,000 in the aftermath.[72] Conceding that even three stood of each four who made public profession of faith is establishing a record that neither 20th nor 19th nor 18th nor 17th century pastor or evangelist would care to claim for his evangelism.

As early as January of 1905, Evan Roberts was reported as declaring that the Awakening begun in Wales would sweep the British Isles and the rest of the world.[73]

The famous explorer and military man, Sir Francis E. Younghusband, returned to Britain in 1905 and came down to Wales to investigate the Revival. After failing to see Evan Roberts, he asked Dan Roberts whether the Welsh Revival would spread, and the latter, speaking for his brother in all certainty, said that it would spread all over the world.[74]

Sixty years after the Revival, it was said by historians of Evan Roberts, 'without him, the revival faded away.' This is a common fallacy.[75] The extreme excitement of the Revival had already passed when Evan Roberts retired from public ministry, but the movement kept the churches of Wales filled for a couple of years to come; and the Awakening swept the rest of Britain, Scandinavia, parts of Europe, North America, the missionfields of India and the Orient, Africa and Latin America. It was not dependent upon Evan Roberts, but rather seemed initiated and sustained by the Spirit to Whom Evan Roberts submitted his will.

The vision of Evan Roberts, that a hundred thousand people would be won to the Churches in Wales was fully realised in a matter of months. At the time, the Revival united the denominations as one body, filled the chapels nightly, renewed family ties, changed life in mines and factories, often crowded streets with huge processions, abated the social vices and diminished crime.[76] Gomer Roberts asked:[77]

> Who can give an account of the lasting blessings of the 1904-5 Revival? Is it possible to tabulate a sum total of family bliss, peace of conscience, brotherly love, and holy conversation? What of the debts that were paid and the enemies reconciled to one another? What of the drunkards who became sober and the prodigals who were restored? Is there a balance that can weigh the burden of sins that was thrown at the foot of the Cross?

4

THE IRISH AND SCOTTISH AWAKENINGS

Northern Ireland, with its memory of the 1859 Revival fresh in the conversation of its oldsters, welcomed news of the awakening in Wales.[1] The resultant movement affected all classes in the North,[2] metropolis and country town alike, and was effective also in the Dublin Pale where a fifth of the population was Protestant.

Official Presbyterianism in Ireland first evinced a dour caution regarding the manifestations of the Awakening in Wales. Whispers of religious mania caused a questioning rather than condemnation, but by the turn of the New Year of 1905 all editorial comment had become well-disposed.

In January, articles on the Welsh Revival appeared each week in the journal[3] which served the Irish Presbyterians, the most numerous denomination of Ulster Protestants. A Call to Prayer was issued that month by the officials of the General Assembly. Irish Episcopalians likewise showed an interest,[4] while a sudden enthusiasm developed among the Methodists, Congregationalists, Baptists, and Brethren.

Down in Dublin, a Day of Prayer for Ireland was held on St. Patrick's Day, the Metropolitan Hall being host to great crowds of intercessors.[5] Similar meetings were conducted in several of the great halls in Belfast. In April, two young Dubliners, Frederick and Arthur Wood, packed the Wellington Hall of the City Y.M.C.A. nightly, and hundreds of inquirers were instructed.[6] At the same time, the attention of local presbyteries was called to 'the widespread desire in the congregations for reviving.'[7] Noonday and evening prayer meetings multiplied and attracted encouraging attendances in Belfast and the country towns.[8]

Meetings for the reviving of Christians and the winning of outsiders were held in series in congregation after congregation all over the North of Ireland.[9] A 'spirit of grace and supplication' in an unusual degree was noted by Irish Methodists,[10] also prevailing in other denominations. These meetings for prayer were followed by successful evangelistic campaigns—too common to deserve individual reporting.

The Methodists in Lurgan commenced a series of revival meetings in that bustling market town.[11] Extraordinary zeal was manifested, communicated to the larger congregations of the Presbyterian denomination. First Presbyterian Church was packed nightly with more than a thousand people, while the Methodist Church was crowded for weeks on end.[12] The Irish General Assembly acknowledged that the awakening had begun among the Methodists, had filled the churches of the town, had largely emptied the taverns, and had added fifty per cent to communicant rolls. Several new Christian Endeavour societies were formed to care for the converts, and older societies were increased in membership.[13] It was reported to General Assembly that the meetings attracted habitual non-churchgoers, resulted in children's conversion, displayed an absence of emotionalism, and emphasized the simple teaching of the truths of Scripture. Among the Lurgan evangelists were J.J. Mackay of Hull and the local preachers, Spence and Dixon.

News of the Lurgan Awakening spread rapidly in Ulster and the rest of Ireland.[14] Before long, local awakenings were occurring in Antrim, Armagh, Derry, Down, Fermanagh, and Tyrone, notably in Newtownards, Portadown and other market towns. In Newtownards, a single church reported the enrolling of 1300 inquirers.[15]

Meanwhile Belfast, the northern metropolis was swept by evangelistic activity. Seth Joshua, as Welsh Presbyterian commissioner of evangelism, addressed the Irish General Assembly on the Welsh Revival.[16] The beautiful and capacious Assembly Hall had been completed, and there the Scottish evangelist John McNeill preached the Word to multiplied thousands, with lasting results.[17] The rougher-tongued Billy Spence harvested the crop in the Albert Hall on Shankill Road, open declarations of new-found faith there numbering 700, pledges of total abstinence a thousand. On every hand, evangelists were busy in the city and suburbs.[18]

Much more surprising was the outbreak of enthusiasm in tiny Protestant congregations of the South, where 'a glorious revival'[19] was reported in the towns in the hinterland of Cork. There were also movements in Clones[20] and Sligo,[21] 'border towns,' and in villages with a substantial Protestant church minority.

Not only Presbyterians and Methodists were affected by the revival. Among the Ulster Quakers, there were unusual manifestations of spiritual power at Moyallon,[22] and a layman there afterward helped to found the Irish Keswick Convention at Portstewart on the north coast.[23] The Salvation Army reported revival in corps after corps.[24] The Baptists, never a numerous folk, experienced an upsurge. So did Moravians and Congregationalists.

J. Stuart Holden, an Evangelical Anglican, crossed to the Irish counties and missioned for the Church of Ireland.[25] The Irish Episcopalians reported record responses everywhere in their parish campaigns:[26]

> We do unfeignedly thank God for the many signs of a revival of true religion which the Church of Ireland is showing just now . . . not only amid the populous and Protestant north but also in many parishes in the south.

An interdenominational spirit of cooperation prevailed. Despite the competitive activities of past generations, two Presbyterian and one Baptist congregation cooperated in a series of meetings in the town of Clough, County Antrim. Meetings in Cloughmills continued for more than ten weeks, and hundreds professed conversion in that district.[27]

In Dublin, fervent enthusiasm greeted the ministry in the visit of Henry Montgomery in April 1905.[28] Meetings in the Rotunda produced more than three hundred converts. It was at this time that the religious press began to notice the evangelistic ministry of the young Dubliners, Frederick and Arthur Wood, who emerged into a national usefulness in the evangelistic field, founding the National Young Life Campaign of Great Britain. The annual Dublin Christian Convention was overcrowded in the autumn of 1905.

A Report on the State of Religion presented to General Assembly in those years told the Presbyterians:[29]

> The Assembly records its devout thankfulness to the God of all grace for the many tokens of blessing bestowed on the Church as a whole, and several parts in particular, which remind us in some measure of the marvellous year of Grace, 1859. In these places, the Spirit of God has been exercising His gracious agency in deepening the religious life of the people of God: in bringing to open decision the anxious and the inquiring; and in quickening the careless and godless. It is believed that no such spirit of earnestness has been manifested since the Revival of '59.

Typical of the local awakenings in Ulster was one which occurred in Tobermore, County Londonderry, in the wake of the Welsh Revival.

The Rev. Fred C. Gibson accepted a call to the First Presbyterian Church in Tobermore. Gibson felt that this little town was morally and spiritually dead, so he made a covenant with God to seek revival, signed it, and started to preach and to pray accordingly. There was much resistance to the message.[30]

But special meetings lengthened to six weeks; six good men and true (five of whom became Moderators of General Assembly) came to minister. The rector of the Episcopal parish was friendly; the Baptist minister George Marshall cooperated heartily. An intense conviction of sin replaced the indifference of the people. There were extraordinary conversions of hardened sinners. All the meetings were held in local churches, and their schedule of accustomed services was followed as closely as possible. The converts in turn were integrated into the congregations smoothly. One of them became an outstanding missionary in India. Another was a woman whose life was a reproach to the community, but she became a most respected citizen.

The Awakening of 1905 in Ireland proved to be much less startling than its predecessor of 1859. But it had a lasting effect upon the Churches. It maintained the high spiritual standards of church life which Ulster had inherited from the Revival of 1859; it commissioned a host of candidates for the ministry and the missionfield; and it prepared a people for the trauma of World War I, which on a single day brought mourning to almost every family in Ulster.[31]

    *   *   *   *

In the Isle of Man, the self-governing island in the Irish Sea, an awakening[32] spread through the villages and farms. Not only were the Free Churches involved, but the Bishop of Sodor and Man, Bishop Stratton, and his clergy were most generous in commending the movement.[33]

    *   *   *   *

The news of the Revival in Wales was spread through Scotland far and near, from the end of 1904 onwards. By early 1905, the press was reporting awakenings throughout the northern kingdom, the Baptists affirming that 'revival has already begun in many of our churches,' as part of 'a gracious movement' proceeding all over the country,[34] the Presbyterians reporting that the awakening was spreading to even the remotest places in Scotland, while the churches of other denominations noted the unusual spiritual interest in all their congregations.[35]

Some of the first reports of local awakenings bespoke of dormant interest, as in a remarkable work in Cockenzie, sparked by veterans of the 1859 Revival, in which a newly-opened church had already proved to be too small for the crowds attending nightly,[36] or in Blairgowrie, where all the churches were packed in turn, including St. Andrew's which seated fourteen hundred.[37]

The news of the Revival in Wales first created extra-ordinary expectancy and unusual meetings for prayer. The Christians flocked to their own churches and to interdenominational gatherings devoted to intercession. Only a spark seemed necessary to strike fire, and a shower of sparks was provided by the visit of a team of Welsh enthusiasts who invaded Glasgow and the industrial heartland of Scotland.[38]

A great movement in Motherwell began in the Christian Institute, an interdenominational hall, but the local ministers soon opened their churches to the crowds of seekers after God.[39] It was reported that the streets in Motherwell were crowded wall to wall. As the excitement subsided, eight churches and three public halls were filled nightly, while ministers told of 100 here, 120 there, added to the churches.

J. J. Thomas was one of the Welsh visitors to Motherwell, and the influence of the Welsh Revival was seen in the fact that on some nights there was practically no preaching, the crowded gatherings becoming huge, spontaneous testimony meetings resulting in the winning of numerous outsiders or lapsed church members to vital faith.[40]

The awakening spread to Cambuslang[41] from Motherwell, renewing demonstrations of Divine power witnessed in both the eighteenth and nineteenth century awakenings.[42] A very 'remarkable work of grace' occurred in Falkirk,[43] while all the churches in Stirling were filled and hundreds professed conversion.[44] An evangelist, Harry Turner of Alva,[45] moved Inverkeithing as 'never before for thirty years.' The total of accessions in Coatbridge was the largest in the history of the church reporting.[46] From Motherwell, revival spread to Bellshill and Mossend, Holytown and Clydesdale. As in Hamilton, the movement was everywhere marked by a most cordial interdenominational cooperation.[47]

Before long, an awakening 'similar in form to Wales' was reported from the city of Glasgow, whose civic motto fitted the phenomenon, 'Let Glasgow flourish by the preaching of the Word and the praising of His Name.' The party of Welshmen provided the spark which ignited the fuel.[48]

In Glasgow itself,[49] central halls and suburban churches were packed to capacity.[50] The visiting Welsh party provoked unlimited enthusiasm, and in the midst of the spontaneous movement no less than five hundred converts professed faith publicly; even the afternoon prayer meetings attracted twelve hundred intercessors.[51] The capacious Tent Hall was filled nightly for months on end, and five thousand inquirers were instructed there.[52] From Glasgow, awakenings spread to suburbs and satellite towns.[53]

In Dumbarton and in Clydebank, there began a striking prayer movement among believers and an aggressive open-air witness to outsiders.[54] In Kinning Park, the churches experienced an extraordinary renewal: and twelve months later, a Presbyterian congregation reported a year of revival in which professed conversions numbered 140, increasing to 142 added to membership.[55] Nor was the awakening only in churches: Methodists reported 2000 packing the Lyceum in Govan.[56] In Govanhill, four weeks of ministry by Maggie Coudie of Dowlais produced 'strong crying and tears.'[57] A great awakening began in Paisley, where Josiah Nix led a 'wonderful' movement.[58] The greatest enthusiasm filled the churches. A Baptist congregation experienced a quickening which lasted for months and added 240 to the membership.

In Leith,[59] the port of Edinburgh, evangelistic meetings were packed nightly for twelve weeks. And as in Wales, the meetings were marked by a great spontaneity, the extraordinary praying producing many instantaneous conversions. Edinburgh and its suburbs shared in the general movement of religious revival.

Joseph Kemp, pastor of Charlotte Chapel in Edinburgh, visited Wales in late 1904, and returned to Edinburgh to experience a recurring revival in his own congregation. Beginning with a watchnight service,[60] on New Year's Eve 1905, extraordinary zeal in prayer gave way to deepened conviction of sin.[61] The local press chronicled the progress of the movement, which by spring and summer had developed into marches along Princes Street and evangelistic rallies in the church.[62] A thousand inquirers were given counsel in the movement. On 22nd January of 1906, a meeting begun at 3:30 p.m. continued until 12 midnight.[63] The awakening was renewed in 1907, when the organ of Scottish Baptists carried a lengthy article on the Charlotte Chapel revivals, dubbing them spontaneous, of Divine origin, not transient and with no sign of abatement two years after the initial outbreak.[64]

A younger Baptist deeply affected by that revival was W. Graham Scroggie, who became a famous Bible teacher. His brother, F. John Scroggie, became a well-known evangelist, while Joseph Kemp became pastor of a renowned church in New Zealand.

J. J. Thomas of Wales visited the border country south of Edinburgh, where the ministers of Hawick reported that 'the revival has come.' A similar movement developed in the town of Galashiels, reported as an 'undoubted revival,' which eight weeks later was still in full swing, continuing 'informal and open' in character.[65]

The awakening spread to the northeast. In Fifeshire, the converts of the awakening were baptized in the Daft Mill Burn during a snowfall, before a thousand people gathered under wintry skies.[66] In Dundee, the revival movement lasted three full months without let-up. In Arbroath, the meetings were remarkably well attended.[67] A 'winter of blessing' was reported from Aberdeen, showing no sign of abatement after several months.[68] The movement in the granite city followed an account of the Welsh Revival given by J. J. Smith, and the work increased until Gipsy Smith harvested the crop in a great crusade in Aberdeen in 1906.

From Perth to Inverness, the awakening swept over the congregations in the Highlands. A revival started in each church in Thurso, on the northern tip of Scotland, among the Scots of Norse blood.[69] Further north, in the Orkneys, 'a gracious visitation' occurred,[70] 'no movement like it, in the memory of any one living.' There were stirrings in the Shetlands too.[71] Even in little islands on the west, such as Tiree, there was marked blessing.[72]

Although the 1905 Awakening in Scotland seemed to fall short of the widespread Pentecost experienced in 1859,[73] it is undoubted that the wave of revival affected the churches of Scotland from the Border to the Outer Islands, either in phenomenal revivals of church members, or in an effective evangelism of outsiders, or both.

Reuben Archer Torrey, accompanied by his song-leader, Charles Alexander, campaigned throughout Scotland in huge mass meetings,[74] Edinburgh, Aberdeen, Glasgow and Dundee, with encouraging attendances and response. His campaign did not make the impact made a generation before by D. L. Moody, but it certainly gave opportunity to the churches to harness the evangelistic zeal of their members, and it was successful in winning thousands to the Christian faith.

5

THE AWAKENING IN ENGLAND

In Britain, the Welsh Revival of 1904 has been regarded as a peculiarly Welsh phenomenon, a passing event unrelated to any other country. As a capable biographer has written: 'The Welsh Revival subsided, like all revivals since the days following Pentecost, leaving a clear mark on Wales and its people. England did not blaze.'[1] Even Welshmen who had been active in the movement seemed to share this idea. In November 1968, a Welsh magazine carried an article by a Welsh veteran of the Revival, in which it was stated that —with rare exceptions—the churches of England were untouched.[2] This is far from the truth of the matter. But the Welsh Revival so surpassed resultant movements in Britain that reports of the latter were not considered newsworthy, and World War I overshadowed happenings of the previous decade in the memory of the generation that survived.

Because of the proximity of North Wales and the presence of so many Welsh immigrants on Merseyside, the phenomenon of Revival soon became a burning theme of conversation in Liverpool and Manchester, and prayer meetings multiplied in the Lancashire cities and towns.[3]

Results were soon forthcoming. In Stockport nearby, a local awakening began in the New Year of 1905.[4] Methodists reported 'a marvellous awakening' in Bootle,[5] the circuits boasting of 700 additions to their membership. A national Methodist weekly announced the town of Wigan 'aflame,' the Holy Spirit descending on crowds of more than five thousand in the greatest movement ever known in the town,[6] described by other correspondents as 'tides of the Spirit in Wigan.' This was followed by a movement in Accrington, gathering congregations bigger than ever before.[7] In Liverpool proper, the Welsh phenomenon of simultaneous audible prayer occurred in revival meetings.[8] Two famous Nonconformist preachers, Dr. John Clifford and Dr. J. H. Jowett, were deeply moved in the movement in Manchester, where (as in Liverpool also) there was revival in the churches and evangelism outside their walls.[9] Gipsy Smith, fresh from his successful tour of

South Africa, held a series of meetings culminating in a great midnight meeting for drinkers and drunkards. Farther north, in Blackpool, Charles E. Barraclough led a movement in the resort town.[10] In Barrow-in-Furness, the awakening began in January and ran unabated through February, hundreds being converted.[11] In Birkenhead also, an awakening occurred.

Evan Roberts campaigned only once outside Wales, and when he did he used the Welsh tongue for the Welsh community resident in Liverpool.[12] The series was beset with peculiar difficulties. The organizers of the meetings, conditioned to think of planned evangelism, were frustrated by the Welsh prophet's reluctance to commit himself to dates. So sensational had been the reports of the English press that reporters were falling over one another in their pursuit of the spectacular. Once Evan Roberts stopped the service in Sun Hall abruptly before thousands of people to announce: 'There is an English friend in this meeting who is trying to hypnotize me this very moment. Will you leave the building at once or ask the Lord to forgive you? God is not mocked.' The metropolitan audience was taken aback, but a hypnotist appearing at the Lyric Theatre later acknowledged publicly the truth of the odd assertion. Walford Bodie, M.D., D.D.S. (U.S.A.), F.S.Sc. (London), known also as the British Edison, took the blame for trying to hypnotize Evan Roberts there.

Evan Roberts's Liverpool Campaign stirred up hostile reactions in some Merseysiders. Besides enthusiastic Welsh immigrants, there were the scornful scoffers, supercilious cynics and curious critics; there were painful silences on the part of the evangelist, interruptions and incidents. Still, secular journalists were impressed by the man and by his message.

Over the Pennines in Yorkshire, young people's societies promoted an interest in revival in Kingston-upon-Hull.[13] An awakening developed in Hull, 'not in magnitude but in power equal to the Welsh Revival,' such sights never seen in twenty years. By March, enthusiasm in Hull had so increased that the Methodists called it 'a converting furnace,' averring that there was a fire burning in Hull, fed by pentecostal power and holy enthusiasm. Extraordinary awakenings began in Halifax and Sheffield,[14] it being said that 'the city of steel has caught the flame.'[15] As many as two thousand attended a single prayer meeting in the manufacturing city of Bradford;[16] a great movement of the Spirit began, with blessings unknown since Wesley's time, it was said: good news of drunkards converted, bad news for purveyors of strong drink, who suffered financial loss. Guiseley, near Bradford and Leeds, witnessed a movement in which a tenth of the population professed conversion.[17] There were similar results in the city of Leeds, where Samuel Chadwick reported that his church was never empty all day, as in Wales—a remarkable work of grace, where the awakening transformed the life of a factory.[18] In Huddersfield also the revival swept the churches and the awakening moved the masses.[19] In York, the cathedral city, the population was stirred by the fiery preaching of Edgar Geil, an American evangelist.[20] In Middlesborough-on-Tees, the awakening began with noon prayer meetings, followed by fourteen weeks of united evangelistic gatherings.

Farther to the north, phenomenal awakenings occurred in Durham and Northumberland.[21] In the colliery town of Hirst, in England's most northerly county, the meetings were crowded, and hundreds of outsiders were converted in the gatherings which manifested the peculiarities of the movement in the Welsh colliery towns, including some trances. Geil led a great campaign in the city of Newcastle-on-Tyne, attracting 700 inquirers. As many as a thousand professed conversion in a single week in the Tyneside capital.[22]

The movement spread rapidly through the towns and mining villages.[23] In a tiny Durham village, 450 professed conversions were reported. In Bishop Auckland, there was such a gathering that both the Town Hall and the Drill Hall were overcrowded, followed by 'glorious aftermeetings' in the churches, in which inquirers were given counsel and instruction, W. E. Geil again being the evangelist. In Wheatly Hill, an awakening began among the people. In South Shields, four hundred people professed conversion in the gatherings. John McNeill enjoyed 'standing room only' at the ancient city of Durham. Spencer Walton found Sunderland 'ripe for blessing'—and it later became a Pentecostal rallying point in the succeeding decades.

There was an awakening likewise in Cumberland. In the town of Ellenborough, 279 adults and 128 young people were professedly converted, representing a third of the town's population.[24] The ancient city of Carlisle experienced quite a revival movement also. Both Anglican clergy and Free Church ministers of Westmorland were convened in special session to discuss the Revival. In the town of Kirkby Stephen, a political meeting was given up on account of meetings for prayer and praise.[25]

News of the Welsh Revival provoked many Christians in the English Midlands to prayer, not least in the great city of Birmingham.[26] In January a simultaneous mission was begun by the Birmingham churches. By March, Methodist journalists were reporting a great awakening in Birmingham and the Midlands, a movement which affected all denominations— 'Signs of springtime in the Church,' observed Ian Maclaren. It was also described as 'Wales in Birmingham.' In Rocky Lane Chapel, the movement was unprecedented, with 300 inquirers enrolled. The theological college at Handsworth was moved by a spirit of prayer, confession and dedication, all regular classes abandoned.

Nuneaton provided sensation.[27] A week of united prayer meetings culminated in a 'glorious revival,' utterly unlike any previous experience in the town. R. M. Redward, a local supply minister stirred by the Welsh Revival, electrified the town. Following 'wonderful outpourings' and 'remarkable scenes' in the churches, the Prince's Theatre was packed each Sunday night after church with 1500 praying saints and seeking sinners. During a great blizzard, there were 826 conversions. Special trains were run to Nuneaton prayer meetings, provoking a periodical to quote Zechariah: 'The inhabitants of one city shall go to another saying, "Let us go at once to entreat the favour of the Lord.' "

The awakening began in Nottingham with 'no leadership, no advertising, no missions, simply fellowship, praise, prayer, testimony and opportunity for decisions.' The whole city felt the glow. Nearby, in Bulwell, many of the most degraded drunkards of the town were converted in a movement which produced 386 converts in eight weeks, 376 of them marching in public witness.[28] Likewise, in Ashby-de-la-Zouch, in a densely packed meeting which lasted three hours, there was simultaneous audible prayer, with no sense of confusion.[29]

The local newspaper reported that Worcester was shaken in a movement in which there was 'little advertising, little preaching, little order,' with prolonged meetings, a densely packed mass of men, women and children who had come despite the Arctic weather which afflicted the country.[30]

Charles Taylor and Andrew Forbes, cousins, stirred the Bedfordshire villages and towns, all nights of prayer preparing the way for powerful evangelism. The soloist of these extraordinary meetings was but five years of age—Charles Forbes Taylor, afterwards an American Baptist evangelist. In Stamford, the various revival phenomena occurred.[31]

Awakenings occurred in Bedford,[32] Grantham,[33] Hereford,[34] Hinckley,[35] Kettering,[36] Kidderminster,[37] Leicester,[38] Loughborough,[39] Northampton,[40] Rugby,[41] Stratford-upon-Avon,[42] and Wellington,[43] and in places without number where the unusual outpouring of the Spirit no longer made special news.

In the Midlands, Gipsy Smith experienced a great awakening in the churches of Hanley where hundreds filled the inquiry rooms.[44] With very few exceptions, the two thousand professed converts became members of local churches. It was said: 'This great movement in Wales is whetting the appetite and making men examine things.'

Monmouth, a Welsh county within English jurisdiction, had been mightily moved by the Revival in late 1904, so it was not long before the impact was felt across the Severn.

Prayer meetings multiplied in the churches of Gloucester, bringing about an eager desire on the part of church folk to evangelize their towns-folk, and on the part of nominal Christians and non-churched folk to hear the message. The movement swept the town. Matters reached a climax when an enthusiastic procession of thousands of singing people was invaded from the local taverns by a mob, inflamed by drink and hate, resulting in an ugly situation. This did not at all prevent the crowds of interested people from packing a church with 1500, a nearby school hall with 600, while the roadway was blocked by a dense crowd unable to get in.[45]

In the city of Bristol, united prayer meetings held in early January soon resulted in an evangelistic drive.[46] Soon the news of 'revival in Bristol' was reaching the far ends of the United Kingdom, as 'remarkable scenes' were witnessed throughout the historic city. A local daily newspaper carried a column on the 'phases of the Revival.' Apparently, the first outbreak of revival phenomena occurred in Bedminster, in which the churches united in prayer and witness.

Kingswood, where a spirit of conviction had been manifested five generations before under Whitefield and Wesley, became the scene of spiritual impact unknown since the days of the great evangelists, according to the American Congregational pastor of the Kingswood Hill Church. That the Rev. F. Hugh Smith was not merely carried away by the enthusiasm of the moment may be noted in his report of 900 professed conversions in five weeks, 300 of whom already joining his congregation. More than three thousand professing conversion in that district since the movement began were being followed up by a committee of 73 ministers and laymen.[47]

Nearby, the Baptist and Methodist ministers of Hanham affirmed that, of 250 known converts there, only one had relapsed. The Rev. A. E. Bray of St. George's reported that the Jolly Boys Society, a gang of roughs who had terrorized the district, had broken up, its converted members trebling his Bible class in numbers.

A secular correspondent in the daily press in Bristol noted that in East Bristol it was now rare to meet an inebriated man. Instead, the pedestrian was more likely to encounter street demonstrations led by brass bands, followed by six or seven hundred people marching to a revival meeting. That the movement in Bristol was not ephemeral was seen in the reports of the Wesleyan Methodist Quarterly Meetings from March onwards. The ministers were busy caring for an influx of trial members.[48] An Anglo-Catholic parish priest pointed out that if it had not been for the Church of England maintaining its witness down the centuries, the other chapels would be enjoying no revivals whatsoever.

Evan Roberts visited Bristol later in 1905, and his address was greeted by a great outburst of spontaneous prayer and testimony.[49] The 'tides of the Spirit' remained high.

Other parts of the West Country were moved.[50] Swindon, a railway community by no means large, enjoyed a spiritual awakening, with crowds ranging from 2500 to 3000 in attendance.[51] Weymouth and other Wiltshire towns were affected also.[52] Bath, in Somerset, was stirred by the revival.[53]

It was not long before 'the tides of the Spirit' reached the Devon communities.[54] An extraordinary awakening began in Torrington, a 'gracious work of grace'; and in Barnstaple 'a truly wonderful work' was wrought. By March, the movement begun in Bideford had reached 'floodtide.'

Exeter was moved, with other places in South Devon. In Falmouth, a wonderful revival was reported by the churches, followed by 750 professed conversions, while hundreds of converts were taken into the churches at Devonport and Plymouth, where the revival was felt early in the year. Not only were the towns of Devonshire stirred, but the rural countryside also, thanks to the preaching of 'anointed farmers.'

Cornwall, inhabited by Celtic kith and kin of the Welsh, was deeply moved by the Awakening of 1905.[55] Rhys Harries told of the Welsh Revival, his visit heralding a remarkable revival in most of the churches. At Newquay, in Cornwall, a pastor's strength failed after fifteen nights in a packed church, but the awakening went on. A great revival began in the parish of St. Just, whole families professing conversion. Redruth was stirred in the summer. The British press noted that the 1905 Awakening had reached Land's End, where a movement stirred the Salvation Army corps in Penzance, early in January, 200 converts in the town's congregations increasing as the weeks went by. It was in the Cornish Revival of 1905 that Harold St. John, a famous Brethren evangelist, emerged into a useful world ministry.[56]

By February,[57] the movement in Southampton had become so powerful that an observer was reporting that 'Christians had never seen anything like it for many years past.' That awakening was felt in Hampshire[58] and the Isle of Wight.[59] In Southampton, the Vicar of Shirley, while fearing 'emotion,' agreed with his leading workers to invite Frederick and Arthur Wood for a mission. Soon the hall was overcrowded, and two services were held nightly. The amazed vicar noted:

> How thankful I am for this, I cannot say. The absence of excitement and the energy of the flesh were marked features of every service. We know of at least 500 inquirers, so we praise God and trust him to extend this wave of spiritual blessing to other parts of this great town; and we feel moved prayerfully to arrange for another mission in a tent seating 1500 next summer.[60]

After a winter of missions in various towns, in all of which there was unusual blessing, the Brothers Wood returned to Southampton for the Tent Mission of 1905. Again there was success. In 1906, the Philharmonic Hall was engaged by a representative committee and again the larger place was overcrowded. In 1907, the enterprising vicar and ministerial colleagues took the Skating Rink and the Hippodrome Theatre (seating 3000) and again the evangelists reaped a harvest.

Throughout Sussex, the movement spread, Hastings being touched in March.[61] In Berkshire, St. Mary's Church and the Baptist chapels in Reading in particular reported unusual blessing.[62] In Woking,[63] there were 200 converts of a series, and the streets echoed with the tramp of feet in a torchlight procession at midnight. The awakening moved Watford[64] also. Great success was reported from Tunbridge Wells[65] in Kent. In Deptford, 190 members in 1903 became 729 in 1905, with another 327 on trial—in one Methodist circuit.

In Essex, there was a movement in Colchester which followed the pattern of the Welsh Revival, with midnight rallies of evangelistic nature.[66] Percy Hicks visited Southend and witnessed an outpouring of the Holy Spirit. In Suffolk,

Ipswich was touched by the Awakening. Days of prayer built up an energy for witness, between 800 and 900 gathering in prayer meetings. A torchlight procession of witness filled the streets, and the churches reaped a harvest.[67] A great work began in Lowestoft, and it brought the churches a great ingathering. Notable conversions followed a 'remarkable outpouring of the Holy Spirit.' King's Lynn, among other places in Norfolk, reported the beginning of an awakening.[68]

In the world's greatest city, the metropolis of London, the New Year 1905 began with remarkable united prayer meetings, Aldersgate Street in the City and Exeter Hall in Westminster being overcrowded with intercessors, and 200 other meetings throughout the United Kingdom reported the best attendance at the Week of Prayer for years.[69] There were early signs of an awakening in the metropolis. At Christ Church, south of Westminster Bridge, Dr. F. B. Meyer welcomed a great gathering of ministers and leaders to discuss the Revival, in which the singing of praise often overwhelmed the programmed speakers.[70] There followed all sorts of prayer meetings, one in which attendance on thirty nights rose from 130 to 550. The evangelistic phase in London included the huge Torrey-Alexander Campaign as well as the preaching missions of the Bishop of London.

Typical of the movements[71] in the suburbs of London was that in East Finchley, where prayer meetings led to midnight marches of witness, and to an evangelistic harvest. There was a similar movement in South Woodford. Gipsy Smith conducted a great evangelistic campaign in Islington. The East End of London felt the impact of the awakening. In the eastern suburbs, Gipsy Smith campaigned on the crest of a revival wave in Leyton, and won 800 converts. In Ilford, there was 'unparalleled blessing' which prolonged the meetings week after week, with hundreds of inquirers. In Mile End Road, visited by workers from Cardiff, one English minister literally jumped for joy on beholding the results. Three Welsh girls visited a Welsh chapel near the Elephant and Castle crossroads in South London, with huge success. A great wave of spiritual blessing was felt in all the western suburbs of London, particularly in Ealing. Church after church promoted prayer meetings. In one of these, a timid little girl shyly asked for prayer of a leader, who said: 'O Lord, there is a little girl here who does not want her name known... save her soul.' In the sympathetic silence, a little voice piped up: 'Please, it's me, Jesus—it's me.'

6

THE IMPACT ON ENGLAND

It can be shown that the Awakening of 1905 affected each of the counties of England, making it a nation-wide movement. While it is true that happenings in England sometimes matched but never exceeded the explosive manifestations reported from Wales, they were certainly far from ordinary.

A deputation of three hundred Welshmen went to the 1905 Keswick Convention.[1] Such men as R. B. Jones, the Welsh expositor, and Charles Inwood, the Irish evangelist, had challenged the larger-than-usual crowds to pray that the 1905 Convention might be the means of communicating a Revival as profound as the Welsh Revival to all of England.

Dr. A. T. Pierson directed a midnight prayer meeting on Wednesday.[2] He reported 'nothing like this had ever before been seen at Keswick; it was like one of the Welsh meetings on a far larger scale.' Young people especially were impressed. Every one of the Oxford and Cambridge house-parties made his commitment to God. 'In less than a week, the Convention had become a revival. . .' On Friday, open confession swept the Keswick assembly. It was regarded unanimously as a time of revival.[3]

Yet the impression has lingered in England that Keswick Convention somehow quenched the flow of the revival.[4] This may in part have been due to the meeting of 1906, when Evan Roberts was invited to address the huge gathering but remained silent on the platform.[5] Later, Roberts apologized, saying that he had feared men more than God in this matter. Diverse currents were noticed in the meeting. Some desired an 'open meeting,' while others feared 'false fire.'

In England, highly effective church missions multiplied among Anglicans and all other denominations.[6] The famous Scottish evangelist, John McNeill, was at his busiest, saying: 'Audiences are easier to get together than ever they were, during the twelve years of which I can testify.'

He further explained the success of Torrey and Alexander in Britain by saying that they had 'benefitted by the sough in the air produced by the Revival in Wales.' He added:[7]

> All evangelists know that in previous years, even with large meetings and the gracious accompaniment of conversions, restorations from backsliding and Christians stimulated, we failed to get the churches to carry on the work after we left. The experience is different today. Churches . . . visited are working every night.

John Wood, secretary of the Evangelization Society, noted that 'from all parts of the country, testimony reached the office of "times of refreshing" to God's people, and large numbers of conversions.' [8] Evangelistic agencies reported extraordinary opportunities and results, and the churches of all denominations shared in the movement.

The Torrey-Alexander Mission in Cardiff had preceded the revival outbreak in Wales so that it was easy to suppose a connection. This was denied by those who knew: [9]

> About six weeks ago, the Torrey-Alexander Mission closed in Cardiff. Great preparations were made, and much money spent. Great crowds were gathered. Those who visited Cardiff on that occasion from the valleys were disappointed and the condition of the valleys was absolutely unaffected. No one connects the present movement with that mission.

Charles M. Alexander was quick to point out the difference between mass evangelism and spontaneous revival. He noted the size of the biggest of the packed-out churches as against the size of the huge mass meetings, and observed that such spontaneous outbursts would be impossible in huge meetings. [10]

As an evangelist of the conventional type, Torrey was a success. Assisted by Charles M. Alexander as his singer, Torrey preached in cities with an aggregate population of fifteen millions, in Edinburgh, Aberdeen, Glasgow, Dundee, Belfast and Dublin, in Birmingham, Liverpool, Manchester and London. [11] In each place, his success was unprecedented since the days of Moody. In each city, large auditoriums seating many thousands were filled, and inquirers were registered in equally great numbers, about eight thousand in Birmingham, and fifteen thousand in London. A few years later, Alexander teamed up with Dr. J. Wilbur Chapman, repeating the British series with similar results. [12]

In 1905, 454 new 'Societies of Christian Endeavour' were organized, bringing up the total to 5012 in Great Britain and Ireland, with more than a quarter of a million members. Ten thousand associate members became active members and seventeen thousand joined the churches in 1905. [13]

The British and Foreign Bible Society reported an unprecedented demand for Bibles in 1905.[14] There was also an extraordinary revival of missionary giving in Anglican and Free Church and interdenominational societies.[15]

As far away as the hills of Kentucky,[16] it was reported that the Lord was reviving His people in Wales, except the Anglicans. The records simply disprove this, for Anglican congregations experienced a quickening, and the Bishops in Wales commended the movement. What of the Bishops in England? In March 1905, the Archbishop of Canterbury held a conference of clergy to discuss the Welsh Revival,[17] and found unanimous support. At Whitsun, the Archbishop then preached on the Paraclete, and issued a Call to Prayer for an outpouring of the Holy Spirit on the whole kingdom.[18]

Thirty English bishops met in conference to discuss the Revival.[19] Their colleagues in the Welsh episcopate had reported approvingly,[20] while the Bishop of St. Asaph told of a confirmation of 950 in a parish church near Oswestry.[21] The leading organ of the Anglo-Catholics sustained its approval of the Revival.[22] The leading organ of Evangelical Anglicans carried an editorial in January 1905, entitled 'England and the Revival,' and thereafter featured news of the Awakening catering to widespread Anglican interest in every diocese.[23]

As early as March 1905, a prayer for revival was issued for general use by intercessors in Anglican congregations:[24]

> Revive, O Lord, we humbly beseech Thee, the work of Thy saving grace in the Church Universal, in our Church of England, in our diocese . . . in this parish wherein we dwell and in our own hearts . . . to the conviction and conversion of forgetful souls, to the quickening of Thy true disciples in life and witness, and for the glory of Thy Holy name: through our Lord and Saviour Jesus Christ.

Dr. Cosmo Lang, Bishop of Stepney, later Archbishop of Canterbury,[25] in a remarkable sermon delivered in Saint Paul's Cathedral in February 1905, deplored the loss of spiritual power in the Church of England, and urged one and all to seek 'oil for their lamps.' The Bishop of Bath and Wells and the Bishop of Manchester adopted a friendly attitude,[26] while the Bishops of Litchfield and Peterborough recognized 'the evident blessing of God.'[27]

The Bishop of Rochester convened a meeting of 150 clergy at St. Augustine's, Clapham, a notable gathering which gave vent to its feelings in singing 'Revive Thy work, O Lord,' continuing crowded out.[28] The Bishop of Dorking,[29] who had

visited the scenes of the Revival in Wales incognito, wrote
to his former parishioners in Barrow-in-Furness, telling
of his finding all the churches full, of three hundred miners
engaged in a prayer meeting at the coal face in the pit, of
police with nothing to do.   Revival in Furness followed.

The Bishop of London,[30] who spoke of the Revival in Wales
with elation, laid aside his mitre, cope and staff (to quote an
Anglican journal),[31] and preached in the West End churches,
beginning in Lancaster Gate with 2000 people,[32] continuing in
St. Paul's Church in Onslow Square, where his ministry was
followed up by the ardent Anglican missionary, Barclay
Buxton, and by the local rector, Prebendary Webb-Peploe.
Hundreds were turned away from the meetings.[33]

Not all Anglicans were in sympathy with the results of the
Awakening. The Dean of Manchester declared himself averse
to sudden conversion,[34] saying 'early ripe, early rotten,' a
maxim scarcely borne out by the perseverance of converts.

Despite the tensions which had arisen between Anglicans
and Free Churches over an Education Bill, a new friendliness
developed between them. Clergy and parishioners supported
the campaigns of Gipsy Smith, Free Church evangelist.[35]

In 1905, the Church Missionary Society undertook a bold
experiment, that of holding its annual meeting in the Royal
Albert Hall, where multiplied thousands of eager missionary
supporters packed the vast auditorium.[36]

In the five years between 1903 and 1908, the Baptists
increased from 336,789 to 400,348—an almost twenty per
cent increase. The Congregationalists increased from 418,
461 to 459,147—an almost ten per cent increase. The Presbyterians, including the Welsh Calvinistic Methodists, increased from 241,904 to 271,709—an increase of more than
twelve per cent, gained very largely in the principality. The
Methodist connexions, in the five years from 1903 to 1908,
increased from 945,621 to 1,004,073, an increase of eight per
cent.[37] The membership of the Free Churches increased from
2,010,834 to 2,178,221, an increase of more than eight per
cent, total membership having passed the total of Church of
England communicants.   Many converts of the Awakening
were already members of Anglican parish churches.

The Baptists wholeheartedly welcomed the Awakening.
The Baptist Union Assembly devoted its third session to the
discussion of Religious Revival.[38] All over England, and in
Scotland and Ireland as well as Wales, the Baptist pastors
and people displayed genuine enthusiasm for the 1905 Revival.

Membership climbed from 388,357 in 1903 to 394,811 in 1904, a gain of 6,454; to 426,563 in 1905, a fivefold gain of 31,752.

There was a movement of revival in the Metropolitan Tabernacle, where Thomas Spurgeon was pastor. By the end of March, 720 had professed conversion. Midnight meetings went on until three in the morning, and the whole district around about was canvassed for inquirers.[39]

There was no recorded opposition among Congregationalists to the Awakening of 1905, though undoubtedly there were those who had reservations about aspects of the movement. Leaders in London, Birmingham and Manchester and other cities shared in the general movement as it reached their congregations.[40] Early in the year, the journal most read by Congregationalists adopted a weekly headline for its news: 'The Revival in England.'

The Quakers welcomed the movement, to judge from their literature. Early in the year, General William Booth proclaimed a day of confession, humiliation and prayer.[41] He told officers: 'You have heard the glad tidings of the remarkable spiritual awakenings both outside and inside our land . . . the ball is at your feet!' The Salvation Army responded happily, as the headlines in their journal indicated: 'Spread of the Revival Spirit'; 'Many Corps Aflame with Revival Fervour'; ending with '1905—A Memorable Year: Notable Advances.'

Throughout the 1905 Awakening in England, apparently no opposition to the movement occurred among Methodists. Revivals appeared throughout the churches of the Bible Christian Connexion,[42] and all other branches of Methodism. The Primitive Methodists gained thousands of new members. The Wesleyan Methodist denomination reaped the greatest of results.[43] Three London districts, with a membership of 54,785, added 1784 immediately and welcomed to probation more than five thousand. It was reported to Conference that 50,021 had been welcomed to full membership in 1905, 56,549 in 1906, a hundred thousand additions which would have included some of the 46,271 on trial in 1905, but none of the 38,148 on trial in 1906.[44]

The Methodist journals welcomed the Awakening, as a glance at their news columns indicated: 'Drunkenness and Blasphemy Disappear'; 'Ministers' Meetings for Prayer'; 'Revival Missions Column'; 'The Revival: More and More It Spreads and Grows'; 'The Revival Shakes the Trembling Gates of Hell'; 'The Spread of the Revival'; and the like.[45] Not an instance of adverse criticism appeared.

Wesleyan Methodist Conference met in 1905 in Bristol, where Wesley began his evangelistic ministry and where the circuits had just experienced another outpouring of the Holy Spirit. There was 'a spirit of expectation of great spiritual good . . .' and the proceedings were often interrupted by spontaneous outbursts of singing.[46] It was a time for praise. An editorial in an official denominational journal claimed:[47]

> Happily there is no longer any need to use the comparatively restricted phrase 'the Revival in Wales.' There is spiritual movement in the churches all along the line ... London, the Midlands, in the North and the West...

Early in February, an editorial in the official Wesleyan Methodist magazine declared of the Revival:[48]

> Tried by every test, thus far it stands. There have been elements of excitement which caused many sober people to shake their heads, but results have proved that the emotion was deep and true. The imprint which all can read is the high ethical character of the movement.

The impact of the Revival upon drunkenness and profane language as social vices was plain for everyone to observe. Inevitably, some critics of the emotional impact of Evangelical Awakenings have suggested that the Revival produced an increase of sexual laxity. The register of illegitimate births at Somerset House in London showed a decrease of illegitimate births when measured against the one per cent increase of population,[49] this being true of not only England but the other parts of the United Kingdom.

But, undoubtedly, the major effect of the Awakening told first upon the Church as a body of believers and witnesses. By April 1905, qualified editors recognized the 'manpower' contributions of the movement, which was recruiting human resources for ministry at home and abroad:[50]

> The fresh tide of spiritual life which is renewing the Churches is in a notable degree uplifting the ministers.
>
> ... Mr. J. R. Mott is infusing renewed energy into the Student Federation movement and the provision of well-educated and enthusiastic young ministers for the work in foreign fields.

In the light of all this unanimity of rejoicing, it seemed a thing incredible to the historian that, within a generation, the churches and people had forgotten the extent of the Awakening of 1905 in Britain, outside Wales. Much research by others ought to follow this pioneer presentation of the facts before a proper analysis of the movement can be made.

7

AWAKENING IN SCANDINAVIA

News of the Welsh Revival stirred Christians to pray for an awakening in the Scandinavian kingdoms. When the answer came, it was long remembered by friends of the writer. Dr. Eivind Berggrav, the worthy Bishop of Oslo, once in his home at Gamlebyen told the writer that the most stirring awakening he had ever witnessed was the 1905 Revival in Norway under the preaching of Albert Gustav Lunde.

The preparation for the awakening in Scandinavia began in a movement of prayer long before the Welsh Revival occurred. As early as 1900, Count Moltke of Denmark invited friends from various evangelical denominations to his home to unite in prayer, among them Pastor H. P. Möllerup.

The following year, a similar meeting was held, with such overflowing blessing that it was resolved to conduct public meetings for prayer instead of private gatherings. Leaders in the State Church and the Methodist, Reformed and Baptist denominations arranged for such rallies.[1] In 1902, hundreds of thousands of cards were distributed, soliciting daily prayer: 'Lord, send a revival and start with me.' Similar mobilization of prayer occurred in Norway and Sweden.

A week of prayer for young people brought a 'rich harvest' in Stockholm in 1903. Many of those awakened joined themselves to different denominational congregations near their place of work or residence. The great Rosenius congregation, Betlehemskyrkan, enrolled 219 of them that year, and more than fifty youth groups joined De Ungas Förbund, the youth league of Evangeliska Fosterlands Stiftelsen, the Church of Sweden's autonomous National Evangelical Foundation.[2]

In Norway, at that time sharing a dual monarch with Sweden but striving for independence, there were many intercessors for an awakening, among them a lay preacher, Albert Lunde, and a city missioner, T. B. Barratt.[3]

All of Scandinavia, predominantly Lutheran, had been much influenced by Anglo-American Evangelical Christianity, which during the nineteenth century had eclipsed German rationalist interest in the Nordic countries.

50

Many of the outstanding Evangelical leaders in Great Britain and United States possessed a vast audience in Scandinavia for their utterances. The religious literature, for example, that was most popular in Norway (the writings of Carl Olof Rosenius of Sweden being the single exception) was translated from the British Baptists, C. H. Spurgeon and F. B. Meyer, and the American Congregationalists, R. A. Torrey and D. L. Moody.[4] A Norwegian edition of Ira D. Sankey's hymnal sold 129,000 copies in 1899. Without a doubt, Anglo-American Evangelicalism played a great part in redirecting Scandinavian Protestantism.

Norway was in ferment in 1905. Norwegians, separated from Denmark ninety years earlier, had found themselves reluctantly united to the Swedish Crown. Growing nationalism demanded a separate consular service, and on this issue the dual monarchy was dissolved. War between the two countries was narrowly avoided as the people flocked to church to pray. A plebiscite decided Norwegian independence.[5]

There was also a theological controversy in Norway, chiefly between modernists supporting a German theology and orthodox maintaining the Scriptures[6] and the Confessions. Because of the controversy, the number of students in training for the ministry had declined and the attendance at services had dwindled. It was said that the theological controversy, in which the press of the whole country participated, led the people back to consideration of the Bible[7] and its message, a factor in preparing for the ministry of Albert Lunde.

There was also an outcry against the use of intoxicating beverages.[8] Although consumption of alcohol had decreased 40 percent in fifty years while population had increased 60 percent, many spiritual leaders were dissatisfied.[9]

The reaction of State Church Lutherans to the reports from Wales was mixed. The evangelistic clergy and laity were encouraged, the liberal and sacramentarian critical, for different reasons.

One official, commenting on Evan Roberts's gift of discernment,[10] deemed it impossible: and another Lutheran reacted against emotion in religious preaching,[11] saying that 'religion at the boiling point is as capable of harm as religion at the freezing point.' It was stated that the steady preaching of the Law and the Gospel[12] was what could bring men to see their need of a Saviour, yet a Welshman had said that his kinsfolk were saturated in Law and Gospel and needed to cry out: 'Men and brethren, what shall we do?'

Lutheran formalists have often stressed as the ordained 'means of grace' the preaching of the Word and the sacrament of Communion; and procedures which do not give equal stress have usually been suspect. A Lutheran writer conceded that in the Welsh Revival there had been sustained interest as well as a great number of conversions, in spite of the lack of preaching, but 'God's Word preached ... by men who are in intense earnest, and the Holy Sacrament administered to broken-hearted sinners ... is God's method; and twenty centuries of experience has convinced the Lutheran Church ... that the Spirit of God ... is a stranger to methods in which the means of grace play a subordinate role.'[13]

The apostolic order is clearly stated: doctrine and fellowship, communion and prayers; doctrine and communion are incomplete without apostolic sharing and apostolic praying.

Strange to relate, an earthquake occurred in Norway on 23rd October 1904, striking fear in the hearts of the people. And in the New Year of 1905, the phenomenon of a 'rushing mighty wind' was reported there. Prayer meetings became more and more numerous, and a spirit of confession of sins was manifested among Christians. A prophet emerged.

Bishop Berggrav was not alone in attributing the Revival of 1905 (humanly speaking) to Lunde.[14] Albert Gustav Lunde was born in Vanse in South Norway in 1877. As a lad of 18, he became a sailor, crossed the Atlantic and worked in the United States, later as a Customs official. He was converted in a Salvation Army meeting in Chicago, came under the influence of D. L. Moody,[15] and at first preached to Norwegian settlers in the Dakotas.

Lunde became concerned about the spiritual condition of sailors, ministered to them in New York and studied for ordination. He returned to Norway in 1901 and journeyed all over the country.[16] He returned from a short American visit in 1904 and devoted his time wholly to prayer for revival and preaching a message of awakening. The news of the unusual happenings in Wales accelerated his efforts.

Albert Lunde began preaching in a Bedehus in Oslo (then Christiania), but the attendances forced him to move to the Tivoli Theatre.[17] By 1905, he was preaching nightly in the Calmeyersgate Mission House (Lutheran Inner Mission Hall) with more than five thousand in attendance. The Minister of Ecclesiastical Affairs, Dean Knudsen, lent his support; and Lunde preached in churches as aristocratic as Uranienborg as well as to the masses.

Lunde was not alone in the Oslo Revival. The evangelists Paul Sand and Modalsli exercised a great influence for good. Observers were quick to compare Lunde with Evan Roberts of Wales, but his was a very different temperament:[18]

> The bishop of the city has taken a deep interest in his work. Ministers of the State Church generally have welcomed his revival services and invited personal workers who have seen something of such meetings abroad to come and aid in a work which, strange as it appears to them, they feel to be of God. The young sailor, Lunde, is as simple in his ways and speech as Evan Roberts . . . nothing outside of Wales compares with the work which is still in progress in Norway.

Unlike the Welsh movement, the Norwegian Revival was not charged with sensationalism. Lunde avoided affront to the State Church, and its leaders showed reciprocal sympathy. Otto Jensen, a high official, and the bishop and clergy of Trondheim gave Lunde permission to preach in the churches of the old northern capital.[19]

The awakening spread all over Norway. It was effective in State Church parishes, Inner Mission prayer halls, and Free Church congregations. In its general phase, it was interdenominational and singularly free of partisan reactions. Less than three percent of the population were associated with the Free Churches, but these 50,000 were as active in the Revival as the corps of the most convinced Lutherans. Soon they were reporting that 'the Awakening in the Land of the Midnight Sun, under Albert Lunde, has had no parallel within a hundred years'—which comparison took it back to the days of Hans Nielsen Hauge in Napoleonic times.

The Norwegian press, which generally ignored religious gatherings and movements, was devoting much space to the Awakening and its beneficial results among all classes. Its converts were found in every grade, except the upper class. Old debts were settled and conscience money was paid-up: misappropriated articles were restored, intoxication was abandoned by many, and a purer moral atmosphere was noted by observers of social conditions.[20]

The Revival was the theme of conversation generally for months. City ministers had taken part regularly in the great meetings; evangelists and workers had no let-up in their exertions nor any desire for a rest, for the results were so numerous, striking and blessed. The Awakening reached even jails, where convicts and warders professed conversion.

In the midst of such activity, it was recognized that Lunde maintained his passion to 'win souls,' his burning zeal, his message on the death and resurrection of Christ, his trust in the power of the Word, and his reliance upon prayer.

Various reforms were proposed in the wake of the Revival. A University professor advocated separation of church and state, which was opposed by his rationalist colleagues. Two bishops and a number of pastors and laymen supported the opening of a free seminary to educate young men for the ministry according to church standards: Menighetsfakultet outgrew the university school of theology.[21]

In other ways, the Church was restructured. The clergy of Oslo discussed in conference what could be done to make the Revival of lasting benefit to the individual believers and entire Church. The Awakening had shown that parish churches were incapable of seating all those interested, for several parish churches served 20,000 residents.[22]

Bishop Bang, noting the increased activity of laymen in the Awakening, proposed measures to make it easier for them to speak in church. Lay preachers agitated for permission to conduct communion services in private circles, and the Storting expunged penalties against such practices.[23]

Social welfare action increased. One church in Oslo had twenty-two societies so engaged.[24] A Norwegian concern for the Lapps revived, and interest in foreign missions increased. Gifts to missions were brought by folk attending funerals and weddings.[25] In 1905, Norway passed the other more populous Scandinavian kingdoms in giving to missions.[26] A great Student Volunteer missionary rally was held in Oslo in 1906.

The main vehicle of the Awakening in Denmark in 1905 was the Danish Lutheran Inner Mission.[27] In the 1900s, the Inner Mission had more than 150 missioners, but suffered from a lack of funds and the indifference of 'unbelieving' clergy. Vilhelm Beck, veteran of earlier Danish awakenings, criticized those clergy who indulged in strong drink and in sexual immorality; but at the same time, meetings for the deepening of the spiritual life began to multiply, though with differences of opinion on the terminology of sanctification.[28]

In 1902, significant revivals occurred on the peninsula of Jylland and the island of Sjælland, Denmark's two most populous sections.[29] In 1903 and 1904, 'a landslide' of young people began to fill the prayer halls. In 1905, only one in fifty of the young people who wished to attend a national Youth Rally could be accommodated.[30]

With the news of the Welsh Revival, the Danish movement reached full force. A great awakening began in the autumn of 1905 and continued through the winter into the following year. The director of the Inner Mission declared in 1906:[31]

> I will not mention separate parishes, villages or persons or relate stories of what happened. I want only to say that we have had a marvellous winter this year. One worker said to me 'There has not been a winter like it in Denmark since Christianity came to our country.'

In the Danish' capital, Pastor Möllerup was preaching nightly in Copenhagen's largest hall, utterly overcrowded. Throughout the rest of the country,[32] as a Lutheran leader declared: 'The pentecostal winds are blowing over Denmark . . . revivals every where, in many places great revivals.' The streets of Copenhagen were filled with the echoes of Revival hymns then sweeping the world, 'The Glory Song,' 'There is Sunshine in my Soul Today,' and the like. In many Danish towns, the tramp of marching feet was heard, as the Christians demonstrated in the streets.

The Lutheran leaders complained of 'a certain measure of tiredness' after the Revival, but this did not hinder more than three thousand young folk gathering in May 1907 at the national Christian Youth Rally in Aarhus in Jylland.[33]

The non-Lutheran denominations shared in all the aspects of the Awakening.[34] Count Moltke reported to London, 1907:

> The first three days in the week (January) the different denominations had prayers in their own churches or halls at 8 in the evening, but at 12 o'clock the same day the leaders and some few others came together for prayer. The next three days, we all came together in the large hall of the Y.M.C.A., crowded. Sunday evening, we had taken the largest hall, the Concert Palace, and half an hour before the fixed time every seat was taken, and many had to come again, finding no room. It was the most blessed meeting the Alliance has ever had. Nearly all the different leaders spoke... Pastor Möllerup spoke with very great power.

By 1908, the Awakening had run its course. The Inner Mission leaders noticed a pause, 'a stillness,' in spite of sporadic local revivals. But, they hastened to add, 'we are not going backwards; a gracious congregational life prevails in so many parts of our beloved land.' A great, deep hunger for the Word of God was manifest, but 1908-1909 did not compare with 1905-1906, though better work indeed was done in the 'dead spots' hitherto missed by the Revival.[35]

Among the contributory factors in the Revival in Denmark in the 1900s was the fact that the British and Foreign Bible Society in fifty years, through its Danish Auxiliary, had distributed a million Danish Bibles, at almost no charge.

It is astounding that standard Danish Church histories, while indicating knowledge of newer organizations (such as the Danish Young People's Society, a country-wide work) springing up in the first decade of the century, have not a word to say about the occurrence of a nation-wide, internationally related Evangelical Awakening.

It is curious to note that a volume of monthly papers published by the Danish Clergy Association in 1906-07 carried many articles by clergy upon ministers' salaries, farming for priests, financial rights, liturgy, ecclesiastical law and the like,[36] but not a word about the Revival, rather confirming the conclusion that the Awakening was fully accepted by the Danish Lutheran Inner Mission and not by the higher State Church clergy, who ignored it.[37]

Early in 1905, 'signs of revival' were seen in Sweden, whose people had 'heard of the great blessings' in Wales. Before long, awakenings became general in Sweden.[38]

Despite the political tension between Norway and Sweden, the Swedish Christians rejoiced in the news of the Norwegian Awakening, and were eager to welcome the Norwegian Lunde. By request, Albert Lunde proceeded to the Swedish capital in May 1905 and was welcomed by nobility and gentry, bishops and clergy, as well as vast throngs of the common people. His most ardent supporter was Prince Oscar Bernadotte.[39]

The Blasieholmskyrkan, seating more than two thousand, was packed out early, and Lunde preached a simple sermon on the words of Peter: 'Lord, save me; I perish.' There was an immediate response.[40]

International correspondents reported: 'Soon a revival commenced in Sweden, and both countries are being swept by the fire of a glorious revival.'[41] The same description was applied to a movement which began in November 1905 in the Philadelphia Chapel in Stockholm.[42] Throughout 1906, missions were held in places far apart, an unusual time of refreshing (that lasted over the winter) occurring in Storvik. State Churches, Free Churches and voluntary organizations all enjoyed the blessing throughout the country.

Prayer meetings were held by the ministers of Stockholm, the Evangelical Ministers Union there comprising a hundred serving Lutheran, Mission Covenant, Baptist and Methodist congregations. A Week of Prayer, as two generations earlier in the 1860 Awakening onward, proved to be a special time of blessing—for the Christians as well as for the converts. The churches rejoiced in their spiritual well-being.[43]

The preaching of Lunde and the general awakening affected every class in Swedish life.[44] In 1908, King Gustav V Adolf (recently succeeded to the throne) in a proclamation declared 'The most important change, the most necessary improvement is a universal turning to God . . . In spite of the great hostility against the Gospel, however, we see that it brings blessed results among ourselves and also among the heathen in these days.'

Missionary interest in Sweden boomed in the years following the Revival. Nearly a thousand Swedish schoolteachers formed a mission union with interests in Lapland, China and South Africa. Other societies prospered.

The Baptists[45] and the Methodists[46] increased in Sweden until they numbered (in 1913) 53,087 and 17,637 respectively. Not only these folk, but the Evangelical Foundation and the Mission Covenant reaped a harvest, as did also those more essentially State Church organizations. A Young People's Church League, founded in 1902, grew to six thousand in membership in the year of the Awakening.[47]

The Swedish-speaking part of Finland was moved in the Awakening, particularly the Åland Islands and the Swedish enclaves on both coasts.[48] Among the Finns, a movement of prayer became manifest. In Helsinki, intercessors of various denominations gathered continually for prayer. In Lutheran Churches, there was an evident awakening, the obvious instrument being the Finnish Mission, Suomen Lähetysseura. The awakening spread to Viipuri, Turku and other towns, outstanding results being recorded in Kuopio where long preparation of prayer had preceded revival.[49]

Frans Hannula, a missionary, toured Finland in mission meetings, young people in particular being drawn to them. The movement became known as Hannula's Revival, and for a while it tended to independence of the State Church, but with careful handling it was merged with the establishment. Sixty years later, the impact of the 1905 Revival was stressed by State Church rectors.[50]

Surviving witnesses recalled the scenes of the awakenings of 1905 onwards in Finland, when 'the Spirit of God worked powerfully in the churches, so that men cried for mercy, down on the floor in an agony of conviction.'[51]

8

THE EUROPEAN CONTINENT

German Protestantism had been profoundly influenced by the Anglo-American Awakenings of the latter half of the nineteenth century. Not only did the great movement of prayer of 1858-1859 in the United States and the United Kingdom make a deep impression on German leaders, but succeeding movements developed German counterparts.[1]

Out of the Second Gnadau Conference (1890), a German Committee for Promoting Evangelical Fellowship and Evangelism grew, lending aid to various local organizations.[2] It was stated that 3170 Germans were candidates in 1890 for theological training but only one to be an evangelist.[3] The friends of evangelism started out to remedy this situation.

Out of Jakob Vetter's concern for evangelism grew the German Tent Mission.[4] A student at St. Chrischona, he was burdened with the problem of reaching the masses. The success of tent ministry in England moved him to commence a similar work in Germany. The first tent was dedicated in 1902. Thereafter the work grew rapidly.[5]

In 1905, Dr. Reuben Torrey was invited to address the Blankenburg Convention in Germany.[6] He found the people agog with interest in the Welsh Revival and its repercussions. After Reuben Torrey and Charles Inwood had delivered their messages at the Blankenburg Conference and departed for London, General von Viebahn[7] directed the conference, 'humbly and wisely' yielding to the Spirit's guidance.[8]

> At last we came to prayer. One prayed and another. Suddenly, the Spirit fell upon us and numbers were praying at once. There was no disorder. It was all harmonious, like the advance of a wave. Prayer merged into praise, into song . . . I have never been in a meeting like it. If it was like Wales, it was because the same Spirit was present.

In this conference of Christians for the Deepening of the Spiritual Life, the spontaneous work of the Holy Spirit led to the salvation of those unconverted in the meeting, sixty inquirers being confirmed in faith, including striking cases.

58

At the turn of the century, Pastor Jonathan Paul gave up his pastorate at Ravenstein in the Pomeranian country, and became an evangelist working with the Tent Mission. In 1904, evangelist Paul testified of a personal quickening of heart.[9]

Ten years before the Welsh Revival, the C. E. Societies had gained a foothold in Germany. In 1905, extraordinary revival was reported from Berlin meetings of the organization.[10] Within a decade the societies numbered 600, with 12,000 members active in German churches.

Jakob Vetter visited Wales in early 1905, and there saw spiritual power beyond his experience.[11] He returned to Germany, and shared with Pastor Ernst Modersohn in an extraordinary awakening in Mülheim in the Ruhr.[12] Ernst Modersohn happily observed (in his autobiography) that from olden time there rested a blessing of prayer upon Mülheim, the influence of Gerhard Tersteegen lingering there. News of the wonderful Welsh Revival gathered united prayer meetings, beginning on Ascension Day, attracting a thousand, and continuing until Pentecost, effective not only in prayer but in outright evangelism. It was an interdenominational effort—as customary in such awakenings.

Such blessing was manifested that it was decided to continue meetings into the summer. The German Tent Mission provided a 'big-top' with seats for 3000, but up to 4000 attended and as many as 200 professed faith nightly. Prince Salm-Horstmar visited the Mülheim regiment and arranged a meeting for the military addressed by General Georg von Viebahn, in which many soldiers professed conversion.

In March 1905, an awakening had occurred in Hanover. In July,[13] the Rev. F. S. Webster reported from Germany unusual revival, with outbreaks of simultaneous prayer. As in Mülheim, extraordinary awakening began in Breslau.

A great Tent Mission was held, July to September 1905, in Berlin. Those moved by happenings in Wales or Keswick testified of what they had seen or experienced. On several occasions, the great crowds under the 'big top' were moved in much the same way, as 'their prayers and praises mingled with testimonies and tears.'[14]

The general awakening throughout Germany resulted in the formation of many new societies to supplement the work of older associations also revived. Societies of Christian technologists, miners, merchants and manufacturers, police officers, farmers, butchers and bakers and barbers—to name a few—were formed in the wake of the Revival.[15]

An unusually large number of the nobility participated zealously in revival movements of the first decade of the twentieth century.[16] The continued cooperation of the nobility in evangelism was attributed to the earlier Pietist revivals which had influenced both royalty and nobility.

In the autumn of 1903, the Protestant Church Council of Prussia announced that evangelistic committees had been established in seven of the German provinces, and three provincial synods granted annual support for evangelism. Several of their choicest pastors dedicated themselves to the evangelistic ministry. Tension between the independent evangelists and parish ministers notably lessened. Yet, in spite of all this, there remained such a variance between evangelists and the parish system that evangelism remained a specialty of the fellowship groups.[17]

German hymnology was affected by the Welsh Revival, and its songs of praise were adopted into German hymnals along with many new German songs.[18]

By the New Year of 1906, German Evangelicals reported gladly to their London contacts that, while Germany had not yet experienced a religious awakening as powerful as the one in Wales, a great increase of spiritual religion had already occurred.[19] All through Germany, an ingathering of converts into 'gemenschaften' (groups) was going on.[20]

An extraordinary awakening began in Silesia, in Austrian Poland, the mining district of Teschen being particularly moved.[21] A survivor, Karel Kaleta, recalled the outbreak of revival in the Teschen district, later incorporated into the Czechoslovak Republic.[22] The most active evangelist was a Lutheran minister, Karel Kulish, who stressed the new birth by the Holy Spirit. Young People's Societies (C. E.) waxed particularly strong in the Silesian churches.

In Bohemia, news of the Welsh Revival stirred the Czech Evangelicals. Though no great awakening followed, the Welsh revival hymns were translated into Czech and are sung until this present time. In Moravia, it was the same. In Slovakia, the news of the Welsh Revival stirred Slovak Christians, in particular the evangelistic-missionary organization, Blue Cross, being encouraged. Several hymns of the Revival, including the Glory Song, entered Slovak hymnbooks, and are sung today without recollection of their origin.

The indefatigable, peripatetic Dr. Baedeker reported an extraordinary movement of the Spirit in Slovakia, marked by prayer, confession, pardon and reconciliation.[23]

In the summer of 1905, news was received of awakenings in various parts of the Magyar kingdom.[24] A revival of the same type as Wales was experienced in the town of Tard, and stirrings were noted in other parts of greater Hungary. Later in the autumn, it was reported that 'the spirit of revival' had been manifesting itself in a surprising fashion, with prayer, confession, pardon, reconciliation, and praise going on in meetings lasting five hours, with conversions of outsiders added to the reviving of believers.[25] Lutheran and Reformed denominations reaped a harvest, and gains were made by the minorities of Baptists and Brethren.

American Congregationalists and American Methodists were busy in the Balkans, where the national Orthodox Churches predominated. In 1905, 'widespread awakening' was experienced in the tiny evangelical communities of Bulgaria, with congregations of 500 crowding tiny churches. The same was true in other Balkan countries.[26]

Lutheran churches of the Baltic countries of Estonia and Latvia, together with Baptist and other evangelical minorities, were moved by the same winds that were blowing in the west. A German evangelist, Herr von Gerdtell, shared in a great awakening in Riga (in Latvia) in the summer of 1905, on one occasion packing the Guild Hall with eleven hundred men, hundreds more being turned away. It was described as a downpour of spiritual rain.[27]

Persecution of Evangelical Christians had increased in the Russian Empire at the turn of the century. There the Stundists, the Mennonites, the Baptists, and the Evangelical Christians all felt the heavy hand of the state-church autocracy.[28] Then came the Russo-Japanese war of 1904. The reaction resulted in a measure of liberty, and not only were the evangelical bodies recognized, but the revival of believers and eager evangelism combined to multiply their numbers.

The Baptist World Alliance in 1911 recognized that significant things were happening in Russia.[29] It summed up the situation by saying that before 1905 there was persecution, after 1905 toleration. The edicts of the Czar Nicholas II of 17 April 1905 and 17 October 1906 legalized the Evangelicals, whose ablest leader was Ivan S. Prokhanoff, an engineer.

Prokhanoff became the leader of the Evangelical groups which had multiplied through the ministry of Lord Radstock and Dr. Baedeker. These included many aristocrats, such as Princess Lieven. They were Baptistic in practice, though not then calling themselves Baptists.

In 1908, the first Baptistic church was granted legal recognition in St. Petersburg. In 1909, a talented Lettish graduate of a Baptist college in London arrived in St. Petersburg.[30] He was welcomed by these Evangelical Christians. Staying on, William Fetler (in later life known as Basil Maloff) decided to build another Baptist church there, thus founding Dom Evangelia. Fetler transmitted the dynamic of the Welsh Revival to the Russian Empire, he himself having witnessed the movement in Cardiff and in Spurgeon's church in London. He was an outstanding evangelist in Russia until driven out by the Revolution. Then he established a greater work in the capital of Latvia, Riga.

Meanwhile, I. S. Prokhanoff continued his work with the Evangelical Christians, the Baptists being stronger in the Ukraine. (Pentecostalism[31] arrived from Germany before World War I, a Russian-American reinforcing that work from Odessa in the post-Revolutionary years of toleration.) All three movements, Baptists, Evangelical Christians and Pentecostalists, combined later in the all-Union Council of Evangelical Christian-Baptists—Mennonite Brethren later, creating the second largest national aggregation of Baptists.

Despite their preoccupation with theological and political disputes, the people of the Netherlands experienced some measure of spiritual awakening in the first decade of the twentieth century. Already, by January of 1905, the Dutch periodicals carried news of the Welsh Revival. Some Dutch leaders took time off to organize prayer meetings in the various provinces. It was reported that the Welsh Revival, which from the beginning had been followed with interest by 'religious enthusiasts' at 's Gravenhage, had found some effective supporters willing to promote the work.[32]

> Meetings have been held in several places in the industrial district of Twenthe in the province of Overijssel, and others are announced in which Calvinist preachers and dominies will address congregations.

'Conferenties a la Wales' were conducted in the various parts of the Netherlands. Ds. B. Klein Wassink, an editor of an evangelical weekly, a Hervormde minister from the locality of Leeuwarden, reported on three days of Welsh-style meetings, running on morning, afternoon and night. An impact was made on groups of Christians throughout Friesland. These conferences continued into 1906.[33]

The Awakening in the Netherlands took the form of an anticipated multiplication of prayer meetings and increased activity in evangelism in the cities and the country towns. The period of the Awakening coincided with an important development in the political life of the Netherlands.[34] The Calvinist party, led by the able Reformed minister, Abraham Kuyper, in alliance with politically active Roman Catholics, provided Holland with a government of Christian principles.

The Dutch Calvinists were divided into many parties, from near-rationalist to hyper-Calvinist, but there was a significant body of believers both evangelical in doctrine and evangelistic in practice. They, and the denominational minorities such as the Baptists and the Christian Brethren, were greatly stimulated by the news from Wales.

Neither the Confessional Union nor the Liberal Union constituencies in Dutch Reformed circles displayed much affinity with the dynamic movement in Wales. There was more sympathy in the Evangelisch Vereeniging within the Hervormde Kerk, and a real enthusiasm in the minority groups, such as the Baptists.

Much more surprising was the reaction in Belgium, where the Protestant minority was a tiny fraction of the population. The Synod of the Belgian Christian Missionary Church, which had an active work among the coal-miners, altered its 1905 agenda to discuss the revival in Wales. A local awakening was reported from Charleroi in the Walloon section of Belgium.[35] Within ten years, membership in this Reformed body had grown to twelve thousand, and most of its membership represented converts from either the Roman Catholic or free-thinking sectors of the Belgian population, which in the main continued in the faith of its fathers.

Strange to say,[36] the Welsh Revival had a most significant effect upon France.[37] Two thirds of a million Frenchmen professed some form of the Protestant faith, the majority of them Reformed of various parties from liberal to conservative, 80,000 Lutherans, and a number of Methodists, Baptists and Plymouth Brethren, sometimes called Darbistes.

In the records of the Welsh Revival, one is struck by the recurring mention of visitors from France, participating, observing and returning to tell the story. In an extraordinary meeting in Aberdulais, two visiting French leaders kneeled and fervently prayed for another Réveil in France to repeat the triumphs of sixty years before.[38] The chorus of vocal support testified to the rapport of the Welsh with their Celtic cousins in Britanny. Caradoc Jones devoted his lifetime to ministry in Britanny.

In early 1905, an awakening was reported from Cannes, a resort town on the Riviera.[39] Within six months, revivals were occurring in various parts of the Republic. An awakening began in the north of France where a united meeting of pastors had gathered at Henin-Liètard, the French correspondents declaring: 'It would fill a volume to recount the marvellous things we saw.' [40]

The Free Church reported an extraordinary revival at Valentigny, where 'bitterness, remorse, tears, confessions and repentance' preceded an outbreak of spiritual power.[41] Not only among the Reformed, but among the Methodists and Baptists was the Awakening felt.

The McCall Mission, founded in France by a visiting English minister, and drawing its support from interested Evangelicals in Britain and the States as well as from French Protestants, reaped a harvest during this second Réveil. The evangelist Reuben Saillens, himself extremely busy, told of revival meetings all over France.[42] Saillens, who had visited the Revival in Wales, became a great Evangelical leader, if one may judge from his lasting enterprises.

Thus the Welsh Revival produced a marked effect upon the French Evangelical Churches. The year 1905 was characterized by persevering prayer, conventions for the deepening of the spiritual life, and tours of revival and evangelism. French workers were happy and busy.[43]

French Protestantism had been severely fragmentized, tensions disrupting fellowship. The second Réveil was so effective in so many major fellowships and minor groups that ways of cooperating across the lines that divided them were found. A tentative Protestant Federation was set up in 1905, and fully accomplished in 1907, and it embraced the great majority of French Protestants.[44] The year 1905 was also the year of ecclesiastical disestablishment in France.

French-speaking Switzerland shared in the awakening affecting France, and German revival movements had their repercussions in German-speaking cantons. The ten years before the outbreak of World War I were years of evangelical well-being and goodwill, as in most of Europe.

It is worthy of comment that phenomenal awakenings of the Welsh pattern were reported from mining areas, as far apart and different as Silesian Teschen and Belgian Wallonie. This was also noticeable in Great Britain, awakenings being reported in mining communities in the Midlands and North of England, as well as in the Scottish coalfields.

9

NORTH AMERICAN EXPECTATIONS

At the beginning of the twentieth century,[1] immigrants were pouring into the United States at the rate of a million a year, chiefly from the countries of southern and eastern Europe rather than northwestern Europe, hitherto the main source. The vast majority of these immigrants were Roman Catholic by upbringing. In the decade after the turn of the century, less than two and a half million were won by that Church—out of five million originating in Roman Catholic countries.[2]

The immigrants of Roman Catholic stock had little or no acquaintance with Evangelical Awakenings or with Protestant evangelism. It was most likely that they would affiliate with the Roman Catholic Church in the United States, or drift away from organized religion. As it was, a considerable number of them were absorbed into the mainline Protestant denominations, because of (it will be seen) another Revival.

Meanwhile, the urbanization of the American population was proceeding apace. In 1890, a third of the population lived in towns of four thousand or more; in 1900, two-fifths. The forces of Evangelical Protestantism were taking the challenge of urbanization seriously, through evangelistic campaigns, through institutionalized churches, through voluntary societies such as the Y.M.C.A. and the City Missions, and in a hundred different ways. Not least was the almost universal custom of Baptist, Congregational, Disciples, Methodist and Presbyterian churches holding annual evangelistic efforts.

Dwight Lyman Moody had dominated the evangelistic scene for a generation. But there were others who managed to attract either national or regional attention despite Moody's near monopoly of the great campaigns. Among them were John Wilbur Chapman, Benjamin Fay Mills and Samuel Porter Jones. Moody himself thought of Chapman[3] as 'the greatest evangelist in the country' in 1895; Mills[4] was regarded by some as more efficient in campaigning than Moody; while Jones[5] was known as 'the Moody of the South.' None of them compared with Moody in the general esteem of the churches, nor exceeded him in total commitment to the Cause.

Chapman, born in 1859, began his education for the gospel ministry at Oberlin College and finished it at Lane Seminary. He professed conversion under Moody's ministry in 1878, and three years later he was licensed to preach by an Ohio presbytery.[6] For ten years or more, Chapman served in the pulpit of Presbyterian churches, then entered the evangelistic ministry, first helping Moody, then organizing his own work.

Benjamin Fay Mills had been a successful evangelist in the 1890s, using a combination plan for city-wide evangelism that was organized to a high degree.[7] In his first five years, he gave out a simple gospel message, but later was converted to the concept of social Christianity. He spoke stirringly on Christianity and Socialism. His emphasis was known as 'the new evangelism.' Soon few but the Unitarians backed his ministry. In 1899, he gave up evangelism and became pastor of a Unitarian Church in California.

Samuel Porter Jones had been converted at the age of 25 in Georgia in 1872. He became an itinerant preacher for the Georgia Methodists. He began to campaign in cities such as Louisville, Memphis, Chattanooga and the like in the 1880s, making an occasional foray into the country outside the South, but he preferred Southern audiences, who seemed to relish his 'home-spun humor' and preaching. Sam Jones directed his most fiery denunciations against the social evils of strong drink and the like. His brand of evangelism left much to be desired, but it was credited with increasing the church membership rolls in the Southern States.[8]

It seems very clear from all the records that Christians in the United States of America regarded the Awakening of 1858 as the outstanding event of the latter half of the nineteenth century, the awakening against whose achievements all subsequent movements were measured.

As early as winter 1900, the Methodists were reporting an increasing number of conversions in evangelistic campaigns throughout the country. In Muncie, Indiana, there were 2162 conversions in local meetings,[9] with 'the work widening and deepening.' Across the nation, Methodists were engaged in a Twentieth Century Forward Movement. Its objective was the winning of two million souls, and twenty million dollars were needed for the project. An editorial on the subject stated:[10]

> It was believed that with better knowledge of how to work and a feeling that it was a Church-wide movement, a great religious awakening might be secured at the opening of the twentieth century.

As expected, Baptists (North and South) were likewise full of hope and prayer for a twentieth century awakening, and Presbyterians lent their support, one saying whimsically 'Theoretically, we are opposed to revivals and in favor of an even and uninterrupted growth of the Churches, but unfortunately, the facts are against us.' One-half of the membership of the Presbyterian Churches and an equal proportion of their ministry had 'decided' during some revival.[11]

An Evangelistic Commission was formed at the General Assembly of the Presbyterian Church (U.S.A.) in May 1901. Dr. J. Wilbur Chapman was the recognized leader. In 1902, there were 56 Presbyterian evangelists ranging the States, and, in 1903, twelve hundred Presbyterian pastors united in a circle of prayer for Revival.[12]

Special evangelistic services were held in 1285 Presbyterian churches, and 1580 ministers reported decisions in excess of the usual. From 1904 onwards, Chapman gave his whole time to simultaneous evangelistic campaigns not only Presbyterian but generally interdenominational, for interdenominational cooperation increased, as usual in times of evangelical awakening. The Baptists and Methodists praised their Presbyterian colleagues for their initiative.

Throughout these years, 1900-1904, the press reported 'revivals' here and there, generally using this term to describe local evangelistic efforts, not only good or successful series, but dynamic campaigns that evidenced much revival. They were not compared with a spontaneous and general movement of the Spirit in all the churches, as in 1858.

As the nineteenth century came to an end, and the twentieth century approached, so full of promise, yet so unexpectedly disastrous, the minds of Christians turned toward the need of another outpouring of the Holy Spirit.

The annual Week of Prayer at Moody Church and Moody Bible Institute in Chicago in 1898 had been so fraught with blessing that greater things were experienced in 1899. And in 1899, just before he died in harness, D. L. Moody opened up his heart on the subject of Revival:[13]

> Now the question is, 'Shall we have a great and mighty harvest, or shall we go on discussing our differences? As far as I am concerned, I am terribly tired of it, and I would like before I go hence to see the whole Church of God quickened as it was in '57, and a wave going from Maine to California that shall sweep thousands into the Kingdom of God.

Within a year of the Welsh Revival, Moody's friends at the Moody Bible Institute were able to say: 'This desire was not gratified in the flesh, but the Revival has come.'

In 1905, the news of the extraordinary Welsh Revival burst upon the pages of religious journals. The press was so full of it that it is unnecessary to cite instances. Every denomination appeared to be stimulated. What was happening in Wales could not be related to local evangelistic effort, even though designated 'revivals' in American parlance. It recalled rather what was remembered of the '58 Revival.

The organ of Anglo-Catholic Episcopalians in the United States reflected the friendly opinions of its Anglo-Catholic correspondents in England concerning the wholesomeness of the Welsh Revival, brought about 'by the strong breath of God's Holy Spirit.' It recognized the Awakening as unique in that it was a lay movement.[14] Before long, Dr. G. W. Shinn was writing on 'The Verge of Revival?' and an editorial considered 'The Revival in Religion.'

The Baptists were moved to say,[15] 'Let us cease talking about revivalism, and get on our knees and pray for a revival.' Throughout the North and West, prayer was thus mobilized. In one of the most influential of the Southern Baptist state periodicals, read far beyond its boundaries, it was asked:[16]

> Will the revival be repeated in this country? To answer the question, we are as usual doing the inconsistent thing. We read that the Welsh Revival grew out of prayer and has no machinery, and then we set to work to get all our machinery in motion.

A widely read Lutheran journal reported the Welsh 1904 Revival with obvious approval, designating it 'a marvelous spiritual movement.'[17] A more cautious contemporary also voiced approval, but added in editorial opinion that it had 'never said, nor would it have the courage to say that revivals are a thing of the past, though it could heartily wish that that which goes by that name were a thing of the past ...' obviously referring to promoted revivalism, not revival.[18]

The Methodists, carefully considering the evidence, said simply: 'The evidences of the coming of a general religious revival, which shall move the whole country from border to border, are accumulating . . . there is something more this year.'[19]

The Presbyterians were quick to observe that throughout the United States, 'all the land seems to be on the lookout for a great outpouring of the Holy Spirit.'[20]

A widely-read interdenominational magazine published an editorial entitled 'The Coming Revival,'[21] and stated: 'From various parts of the country, the welcome news comes of an earnest and deep-seated desire for a revival of religion. The beginning of the movement may be small.' Francis E. Clark, in an editorial in the New Year of 1905, noted that the Welsh Revival had actually begun in a local Young People's Society meeting in New Quay.[22] He filled his vast, interdenominational constituency of American young people with the hope of an awakening in the United States: 'If such a revival can shake Wales, why not America? If the Welsh Awakening began in a Christian Endeavor meeting, why should not the American?' Don O. Shelton supplied a trenchant challenge on 'Young People and a Great Spiritual Awakening,' and Clark himself added another on 'The National Importance of a Revival of Religion.' Instructions were given for 'Revival Consecration Meetings' by the thousands, and Young People's Society prayer circles multiplied all over the United States and Canada, headquarters exulting that the circle of prayer was widening, the revival spirit deepening.

In the District of Columbia, the united prayer meetings and local congregational services of intercession became so numerously attended that it was reported that 'there has never been such a concerted movement in Washington as now, reaching out for better things.'

An important meeting, representing practically all of the Protestant churches of New York was held in the Marble Collegiate Church, and ministers and laymen prayed fervently there for a sweeping revival in the city and country.[23]

A similar meeting was held in Chicago for ministers, including there Bishop W. F. McDowell, President Charles J. Little, the Revs. J. H. McDonald and John Thompson, Drs. W. E. Tilroe and P. H. Swift—outstanding leaders.[24]

Conferences on Revival were held in the cities and towns throughout the States and in Canada. Wherever ministers of the gospel gathered, the topic of discussion was Revival, and rarely did the meeting end without earnest intercession. So many agreed with Reuben Torrey's hope for 1905:[25]

> I have longed in the past that it had been my lot to live in the time of Wesley and Whitefield. But indeed I feel it is a greater thing to be living in 1905. This year and the years that follow will bring manifestations of God's saving power such as the world has never known. I see no great man looming up, and I am glad I do not.

10

THE 1905 AMERICAN AWAKENING

Thousands of Welsh folk had settled in the central and western valleys of Pennsylvania,[1] and a majority of them had become members of Welsh-speaking or bilingual churches. An awakening in Wilkes-Barré began suddenly in December 1904, the Rev. J. D. Roberts having been moved by news received directly from Wales by Welsh Pennsylvanians.[2] In a month, he instructed 123 converts, about half of them men. Large congregations gathered in the Scranton district, and a spirit of revival was manifest in all the churches. Town after town, city after city, the tide of interest flooded the churches, reviving members and converting outsiders.[3] An unusual awakening was reported from New Castle, western Pennsylvania, 'the city moved to its center.'[4] In Pittsburgh, city and satellites, the churches experienced a reviving.

The leading Baptist periodical in Pennsylvania devoted a whole issue during the first week of March 1905 to reports of awakening in Pennsylvania and throughout the country.[5] It was loaded with items of interest. President E. Y. Mullins, of Southern Baptist Theological Seminary,[6] visited the state in February of 1905, and found revival interest everywhere.

By early spring, the Methodists alone in Philadelphia were claiming ten thousand converts, their total membership increasing by 567 to 76,236, with 6,101 on probation, while their Sunday Schools had increased their number of pupils by 1813 to reach a total of 95,519.[7] One commented that 'newspapers and some church leaders are talking about Coming Revival . . . some do not know such a thing when it is at hand.'[8]

Of the Philadelphia Awakening, they added that it was the greatest ingathering since 1880, a quarter of a century ago. And they claimed that a greater number of the converts had been received into church membership than during the Moody and Sankey meetings of the previous century.

In the state of New Jersey, 240 'Young Peoples' Societies of Christian Endeavor' added an average of more than 10% to their memberships, individual societies gaining from 10% to 300%, 120 Intermediate and Junior Societies likewise.[9]

On the Jersey coast, there was such a revival in Atlantic City that (it was claimed) not more than fifty unconverted people remained in a population of 60,000.[10] Town after town in New Jersey experienced a reviving of church life. And in November 1905, a great awakening was reported in Newark, New Jersey, in which 'Pentecost was literally repeated . . . during the height of the revival, with its strange spectacle of spacious churches crowded to overflowing and great processions passing through the streets.'[11]

In 1904, in Schenectady, New York, the local Ministerial Association heard reports of the great revival in Wales and united all evangelical denominations in meetings for prayer and in evangelistic rallies.[12] Before long, the interest was so extraordinary that the Rev. George Lunn of the Reformed Church emerged as the main evangelist. Baptist, Congregational, Dutch Reformed, Lutheran, Methodist and Presbyterian churches cooperated in the movement. Emmanuel Baptist Church was packed afternoons with more than 600 women and State Street Methodist Church nightly with more than 1200 people. Between 800 and 1100 people waited for aftermeetings. By Sunday 22nd January, all the evangelical churches in town had been moved, with packed congregations in each, and the movement continued for months on end.

The secular press of Schenectady offered a couple of columns daily to keep the public informed of progress— 'The Power of Prayer,' 'Great Moral Uplift,' 'The Fires of Pentecost,' 'Yesterday's Conversions,' and like headlines.

In Schenectady, the women meeting in the overcrowded afternoon meetings developed an evangelistic zeal of their own, formed teams of witness and visited the local saloons where they were 'treated with every courtesy and respect' by the saloon patrons, though correspondence in the press from saloon-keepers deplored the idea of treating tavern-owners any differently than any other businessmen.[13]

The Awakening made such an impact upon the churches of Troy, in upper New York State, that it was said that no such unanimous and spontaneous movement had been known in the city for a generation.[14] The movement began with the January Week of Prayer, held in the Second Presbyterian Church, but developed into a revival of church members of six Baptist, ten Methodist, seven Presbyterian, one Christian, one Congregational and one Episcopal churches. Awakenings occurred also in Utica, Syracuse, and other Mohawk cities, and throughout New York State.

When the Awakening reached Calvary Methodist Episcopal Church in New York City, it produced 'a sight never duplicated.' Before two thousand two hundred packing the church, 364 were received into membership on 2nd February 1905, of whom 286 were on probation, an indication of more recent conversion. Of the total, 217 were adults, 134 were men, and 60 were heads of families. Of the approximate membership of 2000, a thousand partook of Holy Communion.[15]

When the 'cleansing wave' reached the Baptist Temple in Brooklyn in January 1905, five hundred people waited behind, to receive prayerful counsel from the pastor, Dr. Cortland Myers.[16] Other Long Island churches were stirred.

In New York's smaller towns, pastors engaged in ardent evangelism, a typical instance being Gloversville, Fulton County, where Chester Ralston embarked on January 15 on special meetings, continuing for four weeks. In Gloversville, the converts included 'the infidel, the drinker, the moralist, white and black, American, Italian, Swede, father, mother, young men and women'—a typical cross-section.[17]

The Baptists in New England, in an editorial entitled 'The Present Revival,' observed in May 1905: [18]

> As the news continues to come from the churches, the conviction is confirmed that additions to the churches in New England during the month of April were larger than during any one month for many years.

Despite the lack of any large evangelistic campaign, the churches were obviously in the midst of a revival of greater power and extent than New England had known since 1858, they said. The movement was characterized by an intense sensation of the presence of God in the congregations, as in the Welsh Revival. Despite the lack of organization, either in meetings or follow-up, the movement was deemed most effective compared with organized evangelistic campaigns. Churches large and small, here and there, were affected.

Daniel Shepardson, Ph.D., the 'wheel-chair evangelist,' conducted meetings in Danbury, Connecticut, which resulted in an awakening of the townsfolk.[19] His host-pastor expected to baptize candidates every Sunday for two months to add the converts to the active membership of his congregation. Town after town in Connecticut experienced the movement of the people towards the churches. It was reported that the revival at East Lyme, Connecticut (for example) continued with unabated force, 'men who have not been inside a church for years ... coming out and confessing Jesus.' [20]

By March of 1905, the Awakening was stirring churches in Providence,[21] and local revivals were felt in Rhode Island.

On a single Sunday, Dr. A. C. Dixon and his diaconate in Ruggles Street Baptist Church in Boston enrolled a hundred and fifty people professing conversion in the Boston Revival. In 1905, a British pastor-evangelist, W. J. Dawson, landed in Boston to engage in united evangelistic work in New England, where ministers declared that 'the present seemed like other great epochs when mighty revivals occurred.'

A summer revival began in Forest City, Maine, in 1905. The decline of the population there had brought about decline of the churches, which were closed for eight months of the year. Drunkenness was common and entire indifference to religion prevailed. The revival that resulted was thorough, for drunkards were transformed, and the influence of the awakening spread for miles around, over state borders.[22]

The 'Great Revival' reported from Rutland, in Vermont, began with a Y.M.C.A. director, F. B. Tibbitts. Union prayer meetings were faithfully supported by the Congregational, Baptist and Methodist pastors and people.[23] So great was the response that an urgent call for help was sent to the able Boston Baptist, the Rev. A. C. Dixon, who came post haste and preached in a vastly overcrowded auditorium. Within a week, 450 inquirers had been given instruction.

To Northfield Conference, founded by Moody, G. Campbell Morgan brought news of the Welsh Revival, personally observed. Len Broughton led some unusual meetings, overtaken by a wave of confession.[24] Correspondents averred that 'the scenes witnessed during the closing week almost defy description.' In summer conference after conference (including Winona Lake), a great catharsis of souls took place.

Late in 1904, the Atlanta newspapers reported that nearly a thousand businessmen had united in intercession for an outpouring of the Holy Spirit.[25] On 2nd November, with a unanimity unprecedented, stores, factories and offices closed in the middle of the day for prayer. The Supreme Court of Georgia adjourned; even saloons and places of amusement closed their doors to enable patrons to attend the united prayer meetings, turning the weekday into a veritable sabbath. Chapman and his team shared the opportunities.

The cause of Revival was greatly helped in the Southern Baptist Convention by the warm interest of its leading scholar in Louisville, Dr. E. Y. Mullins, who supplied the Baptist periodicals with a scholarly 'Study of Revivals.'[26]

Typical of the South, an awakening began in Louisville, Kentucky, with simultaneous meetings in which more than a thousand men confessed their faith in Christ.[27] Of 1500 inquirers, two-thirds joined the churches immediately.[28] As the movement continued, the press reported that the 'most remarkable revival ever known in the city is now interesting Louisville.[29] Conversions numbering 4000 have been recorded. . . . fifty-eight of the leading business firms of the city are closed at the noon hour' for prayer meetings. In March 1905, Henry Clay Morrison said of the Louisville Awakening:[30]

> The whole city is breathing a spiritual atmosphere . . .
> Everywhere in shop and store, in the mill and on the
> street, salvation is the one topic of conversation.

It was his opinion that a thousand had been added to the churches of the city, seven thousand instructed and twelve thousand interested enough to attend services further.

Before and after the Louisville 1905 Campaign, a spirit of revival gripped the Presbyterians of the state of Kentucky, the leading journal of the denomination carrying articles on 'the Spirit of Revival in the Synod of Kentucky,' 'the Presbyteries and the Revival,' and the like, as well as endless items concerning local awakenings.[31]

During the awakening at Danville, Kentucky, all houses of business were voluntarily closed on 1st February 1905, as employers and employees attended services in a body. It was reported that Danville's day of blessing had come.[32]

The city of Paducah, Kentucky, witnessed an awakening described by Southern Baptists as a 'great pentecostal revival within our own bounds.' The movement swept the city from November 1905 until March 1906.[33] One church alone, First Baptist, received into membership more than a thousand new members. Its pastor, Dr. J. J. Cheek, an old man, was laid to rest—'a glorious ending to a devoted ministry.'

The religious press of Virginia early featured articles on the Welsh Revival.[34] In February, a Norfolk pastor preached on 'the Coming of a Great Revival.' Next month, the Norfolk churches united in a series of intercessory and evangelistic services, and blessing overflowed the local congregations. In Richmond, the Rev. G. W. McDaniel and his congregation experienced a great reviving, and made a gift of $3000 for the work of the Southern Baptist Foreign Mission Board. In 1905, Baptists, Episcopalians, Methodists and Presbyterians cooperated in the movement in Norfolk.[35] Epworth Methodist Church added four hundred to its rolls in the awakening.

The pattern of the revival in many of the churches of the Southern Baptist Convention was revealed by a report of a pastor in Tennessee:[36]

> Last month we held revival services. I failed to get any one to assist me, so I had to do the preaching myself. We had a great meeting. There were sixty conversions and the church was greatly built up ... in a great outpouring of the Spirit and a great ingathering of souls.

Early in 1905, the state organ of South Carolina Baptists supplied its readers with articles on Evan Roberts and the Welsh Revival,[37] urging them to pray for a revival of Bible study, of believing prayer, and of grace in which multitudes of sinners would be converted. Before long, local movements were being reported from both the Carolinas and Georgia.

In Florida, revival meetings multiplied, 'part of the mighty movement the world over.' Prominent in the Florida awakening was an evangelist, Mordecai F. Ham, afterwards to win fame as the missioner who moved a teenager in Charlotte, Billy Graham, to profess his faith in Christ. Observers in Florida reported that the revival wave was 'still rolling' over the Christian communities of the peninsular state.[38]

The Awakening affected the states of the Deep South, and reports of revival were received from churches in Alabama, Mississippi and Louisiana. The Baptists and the Methodists of both races were affected, as elsewhere in the South.

In the northeast corner of Texas, a spiritual movement swept the churches of Paris. The pastors of the churches had been deeply concerned over the fact that local theatres were thronged while the churches were not. The Baptists, Congregationalists, Methodists and Presbyterians and others engaged in united prayer meetings, leading to evangelism of a most successful and spontaneous kind.[39]

The awakening reached the city of Houston in Texas in the spring, affecting chiefly the Baptists and the Methodists. 'A tidal wave of spirituality has rolled through the city,' it was said, resulting in not only the crowding of churches but in the closing of gambling dens and the ordering out of the gambling gentry.[40]

When the awakening reached Dallas,[41] Dr. George Truett of the First Baptist Church enlisted the help of Dr. F. C. McConnell as evangelist, and reaped the harvest he had sown. The churches of Waco were moved by the Revival of 1905, and the awakening stirred Baylor University also. Other towns in Texas were stirred.[42]

The Kansas City (1905) meetings of the Southern Baptist Convention noted the vast improvement of conditions in the churches as a result of the Awakening.[43]

> It is manifest to all that there has come about an awakened interest in the subject of evangelistic work. There is an atmosphere of evangelism . . . Scarcely a week passes but may be found in some of the public prints soulstirring articles from thoughtful pastors and others on evangelistic methods and preaching. Not only so, but the new books on this subject show that there is new interest and an increasing demand...

An outcome of the Awakening of 1905 in the Southern Baptist Convention was the appointment of Dr. W.W. Hamilton as the connexional evangelist.[44] No other major denomination became so committed to congregational campaigns.

The movement soon spread into Ohio.[45] In Dayton it stirred fifty churches, while the congregations of Cleveland rejoiced in seasons of blessing, the spiritual outlook 'never so bright.' In Columbus, Ohio, a spirit of extraordinary prayer fell on a congregation (simultaneous prayer) for two hours.[46]

The Michigan Baptists devoted the front page of their journal to Evan Roberts, the Welsh Revival, and mobilizing prayer for an awakening in Michigan. Already, they had reported that the town of Adrian had experienced an awakening unheard of for years. Soon it was noted that copious showers had fallen in Bay City, where never before had the churches been so greatly blessed in an evangelistic enterprise. Their front page was given to the subject, 'Lessons from the Welsh Revival,' by G. Campbell Morgan; and at the mid-year, head lines proclaimed that the revival spirit was widespread.[47]

The Methodists in Michigan reported as early as January 1905 that the Saginaw district was in the midst of 'a most gracious religious awakening,' unlike anything seen in those parts for many a year,[48] the unction of the Spirit outpoured. They were soon announcing 'many gracious revivals' and a thousand conversions in the Albany district, eleven hundred in Lansing, five hundred in Big Rapids, and then results too numerous to catalogue[49]—across Michigan,[50] district after district—in Owosso, the 'whole town was awakened'; in Tuscola, the church filled with 'pentecostal power for five weeks'; in Laurium, 'revival fires'; in Marquette, an outpouring of the Spirit on many charges. In Grand Rapids, one church received 118 on probation, its pastors reporting that 'the revival wave has certainly struck this city.'

Trimountain[51] reported 'the greatest revival in its history'; in Lansing, the Methodists claimed 700 conversions and 740 actual accessions—insisting that this was 'no guesswork'; in Ypsilanti, the churches reported a 'red-letter' day in March, and the movement continued with unabated interest. Second Street Methodist Episcopal Church in Grand Rapids was enjoying the 'greatest revival in its history.'[52]

In the spring,[53] the churches were still responding to the 'thrill of a vigorous, thoroughgoing revival triumph' which was continuing in Grand Rapids, while thousands had been converted in the Marquette district. Country districts were enjoying their uplift also, a Methodist church in Pentwater reaping sixty conversions during the visit of a Salvation Army 'revival brigade' under the direction of Adjutant George Bennard—who wrote the hymn, 'The Old Rugged Cross.'

Michigan Baptists shared in these benefits received by the Methodists, their annual convention reporting a greater number of baptisms (2575) than any year for a decade, a total membership for the state being 44,649, Saginaw and Detroit leading in numbers won. A year later, 2658 were added to raise the total to 45,709. An awakening in Sault Saint Marie had added five hundred to the local church.[54]

Meanwhile, Methodists announced that awakenings were spreading over their Northwestern jurisdiction, in Indiana, Illinois, Iowa, Minnesota and the Dakotas.[55] In one week in March, their Northwestern territory reported 632 converts, pacing Central's 947, Western's 1511 and Pittsburgh's 1529.

Once news of the Welsh Revival had reached Indiana, the ministers gathered for conference in Indianapolis and other Indiana towns, and prayer meetings for the reviving of the churches were begun in Indianapolis in all congregations. In the towns throughout the state, there was unabated interest, and in congregation after congregation the meetings multiplied, reviving the saints and converting the sinners, 'a great day for the Baptists,' it was said, though the Methodists and other evangelistic folk shared fully in the ingathering.[56]

Noonday prayer meetings were held in Chicago for a great awakening in the mid-western metropolis and hinterland.[57] A band of praying ministers of Chicago, hearing the reports of the Welsh Revival, decided to operate through the churches rather than engage in a mass evangelistic campaign:[58]

> The plan in Chicago has been to urge pastors to hold their own meetings in their own churches, to help each other as the needs suggest.

A central prayer meeting was held daily for ministers and lay workers, not a mass meeting; and in it they reported that the revival spirit had reached every denominational organization in the city, hundreds being added to the local churches in city and suburbs.

The C. E. Societies which were associated with so many of the denominations told of a great Awakening in Chicago, in which the churches of the various denominations were fully cooperating, in prayer and in evangelism. The interests of one church had become the interests of all the churches.[59]

> A determined effort has been made to reach the unsaved, and this is succeeding. Hundreds have already been baptized in the different churches. It has become almost commonplace in our ministerial gatherings for a pastor to rise and say: 'My church has never known such a blessing of salvation as we are now having.'

The movement in Dixon, Illinois, was described as a 'cyclonic revival,' the Baptist, Christian, Congregationalist, Evangelical, Lutheran, Methodist and Presbyterian churches cooperating, the evangelist being the renowned baseball star, William A. Sunday. His ministry was sensational. An outcome was the destruction by the proprietor of one gambling joint of his gambling wheels and tables.[60]

Reports from Iowa[61] showed that the Revival of 1905 and its evangelistic outreach were making great progress through many gracious ingatherings and many evangelistic crusades. In the city of Burlington,[62] every store and factory closed its operations between 10 and 11 a.m. to permit its employees to attend services for the revival of religion. Mason City in its turn shared in a great awakening under Billy Sunday.[63] In other Iowa cities and towns, there was spontaneous revival in the churches and awakenings among the masses.

The Awakening of 1905 spread from St. Louis throughout Missouri. A great revival was reported in Warrensburg. Sixty miles from St. Louis, strange phenomena occurred:[64]

> Everything reported as 'peculiar' in the Wales revival is found in the Lead Belt. Great throngs attend the services, and conversions take place at almost every meeting. I never heard such amazing prayer or such expression of conviction of sin.

Francis E. Clark's headquarters in Boston reported that 'Greater Kansas City has been passing through a season of spiritual awakening, and the Revival of 1905 will go down in history as a new spiritual epoch.'[65] Kansas like Missouri was stirred. Intercessory meetings began in Nebraska in New Year 1905, and by February the churches were reaping the results.[66] A church in Fairbury reported a great awakening in the town and more than 250 added to its congregation.

In Redwood Falls, Minnesota, the awakening brought out six hundred men, women and children to interdenominational meetings during temperatures of 22 degrees below zero.[67] A great wave of revival touched many of the churches of the Minneapolis area. W. B. Riley told of a movement in Spring Valley[68] where a sixth of the population professed conversion. The awakenings were felt in the Dakotas and Montana, the Baptists, Methodists, Presbyterians and others uniting in the movement, which in Anaconda won 165 converts.[69]

The Denver campaign began on 4th January 1905, with J. Wilbur Chapman, W. E. Biederwolf (afterwards missioner for the Federal Council of Churches), Henry Ostrom, and seven other evangelists sharing the ministry in city and in suburbs. Friday 20th January was declared a Day of Prayer. At 10 a.m., the cooperating churches were filled; at 11.30, almost all the stores were closed, at the Mayor's request, and four theatres were crowded for prayer at noon, 12,000 attending the services of intercession in all seriousness. A vote of the Colorado Legislature postponed business in order to attend the prayer meetings. Every school was closed, as a whole city engaged in intercession and in evangelism. And it was said months later that Denver 'has had a good winter. The influence of the great revival is still felt.' Most of the churches extended the work by local evangelism.[70]

In the simultaneous campaign in Los Angeles, a hundred churches cooperated.[71] The professional evangelism of the visiting team was undergirded by the spirit of revival in the California congregations and the awakening of the masses. Aggregate attendances were in excess of 180,000, and 4264 inquirers were registered, 787 of whom being children. One night, despite torrents of rain, four thousand marching people wended their way singing to the Grand Opera House, attracting a host of bleary-eyed brawlers, besotted drunkards and blatant scoffers to a midnight meeting, with not a few women of 'easy virtue' engaged in midnight street-walking.

The churches of Los Angeles received an encouraging number of additions to their congregational roll. Burdette, pastor of Temple Baptist Church, gave the right hand of fellowship to forty folk one Sunday morning; and McIntyre, pastor of First Methodist Church, the same day received fifty to full membership and fifty on probation. California's smaller towns, such as Redlands and Pomona, reaped a full harvest of converts. The Methodists in Southern California agreed that the churches there had enjoyed a remarkable spiritual awakening, the summer conference learning of many more conversions than known for several years past.[72]

In a report entitled 'Portland's Pentecost,'[73] describing religious enthusiasm in the Oregon metropolis, it was said:

> . . . for three hours a day, business was practically suspended, and from the crowds in the great department stores to the humblest clerk, from bank presidents to bootblacks, all abandoned money making for soul saving.

Upwards of 200 major stores signed an agreement to close between the hours of 11 and 2 to permit their customers and employees to attend prayer meetings. In connection with the simultaneous campaigns directed by Wilbur Chapman, there was a similar movement in Seattle. Towns throughout the Pacific Northwest experienced the general awakening.[74]

*   *   *

Churches in Canada were affected from coast to coast. An awakening began in a Baptist church in Wolfville, where large numbers were converted;[75] more than two thirds of those baptized were students from Acadia University there. Also in Nova Scotia, a great awakening occurred in the Cape Breton collieries. The evangelist most signally successful was Joseph Mackay. The Dominion Coal Company, however, forbade meetings in the machine-shops there.[76]

In early 1906, Dr. Reuben Torrey ministered in Toronto for a month.[77] Repercussions of Torrey-Alexander meetings affected Ontario churches. Two teenage lads journeyed from Embro to the big city, found the Massey Hall packed with 3400 people. Both lads professed conversion and both entered the ministry—Dr. Ernest Gilmour Smith of the United Church of Canada, and his zestful brother, Dr. Oswald J. Smith of the Peoples Church, Toronto, world-famed missions advocate.[78]

The expectancy of a general awakening reached Manitoba. First Baptist Church in Winnipeg was packing two thousand into its new sanctuary and turning two thousand away.[79] West, across the prairies, church after church was stirred. Deep revivings occurred in Vancouver and Victoria, and even on the faraway Skeena River, the Indians were awakened.[80]

The manifestations of the Awakening in Canada were the same as in the United States, prayer for revival, a concern for the outsider, ardent evangelism, remarkable response.

11

RESULTS IN NORTH AMERICA

In the 1900s, the Methodists were the largest Protestant denomination in the United States, accounting for a third of the total. A Methodist editor, in an official journal, stated:[1]

> A great revival is sweeping the United States. Its power is felt in every nook and corner of our broad land. The Holy Spirit is convincing the people 'of sin, of righteousness and of a judgment to come.'
>
> There is manifested a new degree of spiritual power in the churches. Pastors are crying out to God for help, and not a few of them are gratified to find that help right at hand. The regular prayer-meetings and public services seem to be surcharged with convicting power, so that cries of penitence and prayers for mercy have been heard in places unused to such demonstrations.
>
> In several of our Detroit churches great throngs have attended the meetings, and the converts have been so numerous that the membership rolls will be increased by hundreds. It is a real revival.

Less than a third were Baptists. The editor of a national Baptist journal wrote in 1905 of 'a spiritual renaissance': [2]

> The tidings of revival come from every side. There is a quickening of spiritual impulse and life in the churches and in our own educational institutions: evangelism is no longer in the air, it is in the active realm of Christian experience. There is a remarkable responsiveness to the presentation of the claims of Christ upon the hearts and consciences of men. . .

In 1905, there were sessions on evangelism in each Baptist state convention, and conferences on evangelism were held in the major cities, such as St. Louis, Omaha, Chicago and Indianapolis, and in areas other than the Middle West.

Early in January 1906, a Chicago Baptist journal published its annual survey of the condition of the denomination in 1905, and found it a hopeful, fruitful and promising year.[3]

Each of the New England state conventions reported good times. The Baptist cause in Massachusetts was never so hopeful, its second century opening with great promise. In each state, the reviving of congregations or evangelizing of the foreign born caused the greater rejoicing.

The cause of Christ in the state of New York was regarded as increasingly cheering. There was a higher appreciation of evangelism as essential to the continuance and growth of the churches, congregational as against professional effort. Other Middle Atlantic states reported similarly, New Jersey claiming the best year ever, numerically and financially.

In the Ohio valley, the outlook in West Virginia had never been brighter; in Ohio, the cause never looked better; in Michigan, a large number of baptisms and spirit of revival was significant; hopeful conditions prevailed in Indiana; in Illinois, it was more promising than for a dozen years; but in Iowa, observers reported it not very hopeful, the major emphasis being education and 'quality' rather than 'quantity.' In Wisconsin, Baptists were growing in influence; and in Minnesota, the most blessed event was Chapman's campaign. In Missouri, there were more than 10,000 believers baptized. Baptist interests in Nebraska were hopeful; in Kansas, they were brighter than ever before. Good conditions prevailed in the Dakotas and Montana. Colorado had added 10%, and Wyoming the same, while Utah was never in better condition.

Washington Baptists reported a hopeful cause, Oregon the most cheerful for twenty years, a 12% increase in baptisms. Throughout California, the outlook was good, in the southern half new churches organized and many new edifices built.

Optimism prevailed in Arizona and New Mexico. Texas claimed a year of notable advance; Oklahoma noted 5000 baptisms; Arkansas, Louisiana, Mississippi and Alabama reported great growth, Negro membership doubling. And in Georgia, membership reached a record for both races. In the Carolinas, revival was reported from every part, while Virginia, Kentucky and Tennessee claimed a healthy growth.

Methodist membership (North), noted in 1901 as 2,952,234, added an average of 35,000 annually for four years, then in 1905 more than doubled, adding 78,090 to make 3,148,211.[4]

> There is the beginning of a stir in our Methodist camp,
> and the spirit of evangelism spreads along our ranks.
> In 1903, we made very little gain in membership. In
> 1904, the net gain was 32,000. In 1905, it is not less than
> 60,000, one conference reporting an increase of 16%.

The increase in 1906, adding probationers of 1905,[5] doubled again to 119,000. Significantly, after three years' promotion, the same Methodists— aiming for two million accessions in three years—confessed very little gain in membership, rather emphasizing that human planning is incapable of such an avowed objective as 'securing' a great awakening. The awakening in North America followed the outpouring of the Holy Spirit in quite an unprogrammed way, provoking one Methodist missionary to comment that 'the Lord waited until our project was out of the way to bless the Methodists.'

Methodist editors agreed that 'the Revival is now here; it is on already; it is stirring America, not so much yet in the East as in the West, but coming everywhere.'[6] Thus, Methodist news items all throughout 1906 featured reports about congregational awakenings[7] too numerous to recount such as: 'Since the Rev. W. C. Wallace, pastor, began revival meetings in October, 247 have sought Jesus, and the good work still goes on with no sign of ceasing.' A regular column of news was entitled, 'Revival Notes from Near and Far.'

Methodism's second thoughts in 1906 about the Awakening affirmed that 'a genuine revival is the greatest blessing God can bestow on any church, village, town or city.'[8] Another editorial claimed that it had accelerated movement for union.

The Holiness Movement operating in the Wesleyan family of denominations welcomed the coming of the great revival, Henry Clay Morrison and his colleagues seeming only to slip into a higher gear when the Awakening overtook them.[9] And outside the Methodist Episcopal Church, the Holiness folk harnessed the enthusiasm of the 1905 Revival, and produced vigorous growth—the outstanding example being the Church of the Nazarene, an amalgamation in 1907 of several lesser groups, which in fifty years founded more than three thousand churches catering for a quarter of a million members.

The perennially evangelistic Baptists of the day rejoiced in the response of their Congregationalist colleagues:[10]

> We are glad to notice that our Congregational brethren are taking hold of the evangelistic movement with both hands. The strongest men among them, such as Drs. N. D. Hillis, Washington Gladden, F. E. Clark and F. W. Gunsaulus are arranging to give their services.

The Congregationalists gave their greatest measure of support to the ministry of W. J. Dawson, a London minister of liberal theology who had been galvanized into evangelistic action through participation in one of Gipsy Smith's forays into the slums of England. Later, Dawson worked alongside Wilbur Chapman in simultaneous campaigns, though holding occasional solo efforts.[11]

The Disciples of Christ denomination launched a four-year Crusade,[12] leading up to their 1909 Centenary Year.

Thirty thousand Disciples gathered in Pittsburgh for an enthusiastic commemoration of Thomas Campbell's 1809 Declaration and Address. They had grown in the century from some twenty people to a million and a half. Like the Southern Baptists, they faced a revolt from their exclusive right wing, but the first decade of the twentieth century was one of their best for growth also.

The attitude of Lutherans was as varied as their polities. Among the Scandinavian Lutheran groups, the tradition of revival was strong, and movements occurred among local congregations in Minnesota and adjoining states. The older Lutheran groups often cooperated in Chapman's and similar campaigns of evangelism, welcoming the interdenominational operation of the campaigns. The more strongly confessional synods went their own way, but gained from the nation-wide turning to God which drew so many to church.

A large sector of Lutheranism rejoiced to read that the revival 'wave seems to have crossed the seas and to be breaking upon our shores . . . from widely separated points come tidings of great spiritual awakenings.' And it was urged that participation in revival rallies was not in conflict with the Lutheran ideal of catechization.[13]

A more conservative editor, whose liturgical sensibilities had been offended, published a sarcastic report of a meeting of other denominations in a Pennsylvanian town, and in a following issue he reprinted a 'hard-shell' exclusivist Baptist report which questioned the value of Chapman's campaigns.

The same editor, T. E. Schmauk, expressed his approval of the British evangelist Dawson, and published generous praise of the Philadelphia awakening, insisting that 'the Catechism and the Revival are not a necessary and mutually exclusive antithesis,' and advocating not a high pressure revival system but rather the most proper methods of evangelizing the non-Christian world. 'Every congregation should be an evangelistic center,' he wrote.[14] He featured articles such as 'A Revival of Honesty' in which he acknowledged a distinct awakening of the public conscience. And at the end of the year, he described 1905 as a most eventful year, and its ethical movement as 'a wave of civic and commercial righteousness.' By the New Year of 1906, he was warmly defending Torrey for faithfully preaching the Word of God, though he could not refrain from suggesting that evangelism could be better done by weekly pastoral preaching. Torrey would not have disagreed.

A Missouri Synod journal likewise advocated pastoral evangelism, and attributed the success of the Welsh Revival to the solid and continuous work of local pastors.[15]

Of the four types of expression of the Awakening, it seemed that the unprogrammed meeting distressed some liturgists among the Lutherans; that the mass evangelistic campaign created mixed feelings and was judged on its merits; that the uniting of congregations interdenominationally to witness was generally supported; and that the spontaneous packing out of individual churches by eager crowds delighted the hearts of the pastors involved.

A leading Presbyterian periodical presented its readers with articles on Revival and Awakening throughout January, 1905. By early February, it carried a headline, 'The Present Revival,' and it noted that, throughout the country, the awakening power of the Holy Spirit was being widely felt, larger additions to the churches than usual being reported.[16]

By the mid-year in 1905, the Presbyterians rejoiced that 'a revival of genuine religion is now in progress throughout the country,' and reports from congregations, presbyteries and synods confirmed the news of nation-wide blessing.[17]

Other denominations readily paid compliments to the work of the Evangelistic Commission of the Presbyterian Church in the U.S.A., 'a vast work in awaking interest and adding numbers,' J. Wilbur Chapman rightly receiving credit.[18]

The Awakening of 1905 produced quite a movement among the Presbyterian laymen, outstanding being such as J. H. Converse of the Baldwin Locomotive Works. It was usual to expect such lay activity among Methodists and Baptists, but now the Presbyterians took the lead.[19]

From nation-wide reports, the Presbyterians judged that the evangelistic season in 1905 had been the most remarkable in so many respects ever witnessed in the United States— it was marked (an editorial entitled 'The Revival of 1905' stated) by four unusual characteristics: the unexpected interest of non-Christians, the desire of all classes to hear the Word of God, the ease and joy of interdenominational cooperation, and the abounding joy in participants as well as conviction and repentance among hearers.[20]

That Presbyterians became less confessional and more evangelistic in 1905 was suggested by a whimsical statement by Dr. J. B. Shaw: Our own Presbyterian Church has lately been forced by the times to put love into the Westminster Confession from which it had for centuries been absent.'[21]

Wilbur Chapman, upon whom the mantle of Moody had fallen, shared Moody's 'whosoever will' brand of evangelistic Calvinism. The older and harsher reprobationary kind was left to the hyper-Calvinistic minorities.

At the end of 1905, it was estimated that the Methodists had gained 102,000 members, the Baptists 72,667, the Lutherans 51,580, the Episcopalians 19,203, the Presbyterians 18,803, and the Disciples 15,000. At the end of 1906, the Methodists had gained 117,000, the Lutherans 116,087, the Baptists 93,152, the Presbyterians 48,006, the Disciples 29,464, and the Episcopalians 19,365.

The census estimates for New Year 1906 showed the following strengths of the major denominations in the U.S.A:

Roman Catholics	10,915,251
Methodists	6,429,815
Baptists	4,974,047
Lutherans	1,841,346
Presbyterians	1,723,871
Episcopalians	827,127
Reformed	405,026
United Brethren	274,012
Evangelicals	166,978
Quakers	120,415
Dunkards	116,311
Mennonites	61,437 [22]

At the New Year of 1907, the census estimates produced the following denominational totals:

Roman Catholics	11,143,455
Methodists	6,551,891
Baptists	5,140,770
Lutherans	1,957,433
Presbyterians	1,771,877
Episcopalians	846,492
Reformed	422,359
United Brethren	286,238
Evangelicals	179,339
Dunkards	121,194
Quakers	118,752
Mennonites	61,690 [23]

It will be seen from these statistics that the Protestant denominations in the United States in the year of the Revival grew 150% as fast as the Roman Catholic Church, despite the overwhelming advantage of heavy immigration, a million a year, three-quarters of them Roman Catholic.

There was an immediate impact of the Awakening of 1905 upon the student population of the United States and Canada, not only in the Christian colleges but in the secularized universities as well.

A Methodist editor observed that 'the Spirit of God is being graciously poured out in many places of our country, but not more anywhere than in our colleges . . .' A Baptist counterpart rejoiced in the quickening of spiritual impulse and life in Baptist educational institutions.[24]

The active membership in the state university Christian associations increased 200% in 1905, while attendance at voluntary Bible classes increased 130%. Great evangelistic meetings won thousands of converts in the universities of the country and of Canada.

The World's Student Christian Federation declared 12th February 1905 as a Day of Prayer for Students, and in local groups and special services the students responded. John R. Mott reported sympathetically on the Welsh Revival and the Y.M.C.A. proclaimed the rise of an unparalleled interest of men in spiritual things.[25]

Prof. Henry B. Wright begged Mott to campaign in Yale —he had never known a time when there were so many inquirers.[26] Bible study doubled in numbers at Bowdoin College, a typical New England college. This also happened at the campus of Cornell University in New York State. And at Princeton University, more than a thousand of the 1384 men registered there attended the weekly evangelistic meetings throughout the year. It was the same in nearby colleges, in the Middle Atlantic States.

'Marked spiritual awakenings' were reported from many Virginian campuses,[27] and 'a revival of very great power' swept the student body at Trinity College in Durham, North Carolina, a third of the two hundred men there professing conversion, leaving no more than twenty-five unconverted. Spontaneous revival occurred at Stetson University, Florida. It was the same in the other Southern States, and Baylor University in Texas enjoyed a sweeping movement, long remembered on the campus.[28]

Among the converts at the University of California at Berkeley were outstanding athletes and student leaders.[29] In McMinnville, Oregon, and in Seattle, Washington, there were revivals at the Baptist and Free Methodist colleges, forty students (out of a hundred and seventy-seven) at the former campus seeking baptism.[30]

Drake University in Des Moines, Iowa,[31] reported a Bible study enrollment of a third of the student body—300% increase. 'A spiritual awakening of real power' took place in many of the university colleges of Missouri. Two thirds the men at Northwestern University in Illinois enrolled in Bible classes and 2400 of the University of Michigan's 3600 men packed University Hall in Ann Arbor to hear the Word. This was a sampling of response in the Middle West.

There were awakenings in colleges for Red Indians and Negroes. All the students but two at Topeka Industrial School professed conversion, and a Christian Association was organized with every last Negro on campus enrolled.[32] Revival stirred the Canadian universities and colleges also, Mott's campaign at the University of Toronto being outstanding.

Evangelical life on college campus expressed itself in corporate college activities on many campuses where the administration and faculty were evangelical bodies. In the state universities and in the secularized historic colleges, the voluntary interdenominational associations were the vehicles of Christian life, a vast majority of them affiliated with the Collegiate Y.M.C.A. which alone collected nation-wide statistics.

In the two years before the 1905 Awakening, Collegiate Y.M.C.A. active membership increased one-half of one per cent, but fifteen per cent in the two years following 1905 or twenty per cent including that year also. Membership of the students in evangelical churches increased one-and-a-half per cent in the two years before 1905, three-and-a-half per cent in the two years following, but nearly twenty per cent including 1905 also, which indicated that considerable numbers of nominal church members were converted during the period of revival.[33]

In 1896, 2,000 students engaged in missionary studies, but in 1906, there were 11,000 so enrolled.[34] From the outbreak of the Awakening onward, 300 a year were sailing for foreign fields—many of them the choicest college people. So great was the response to the student volunteer call that a Laymen's Missionary Movement was founded in 1906 to undergird the newer missionary drive[35] focalized by the quadrennial convention of the Student Volunteers and by the centenary celebration of the Haystack Meeting at Williams College, the student beginning of the American missionary outreach abroad, with its significant by-products in social action—schools, hospitals, and responsible training.

In February, 1905, an extraordinary revival occurred at Asbury College and the tiny town of Wilmore in Kentucky. The school was 'practically closed' as its classes became services of prayer, confession, reconciliation, restitution and dedication, even of conversion.

A talented student from Maryland was completing studies at Asbury College at the time. He had a friendly disdain for those rougher raised Kentuckians and Tennesseeans who made up the majority of students there, and in particular he felt much superior to the 'shouting Methodists' whose feelings seemed to lie so close to the surface.[36]

This Jones boy was engaged one evening in an ordinary prayer meeting of a few fellows in a dormitory room. There was nothing unusual expected, but no doubt their friends were praying for the boys at college. Suddenly the Holy Spirit fell upon them, transforming their dutiful travail into a tryst with God upon the threshold of rapture. Young Jones himself was overcome by an emotion never hitherto expressed in private or public.

Next morning, he and his companions were amazed to find that the regular chapel service had given place to spontaneous intercession, spreading throughout the school and the town. In the midst of overwhelming feelings being vented by young and old, Jones was possessed by an uncanny sense of quiet. His storm had passed, and he heard the still, small voice of God. It showed him that emotion was not indispensable and that excitement was only incidental to real experience.

Subsequently, Jones was asked to address a missionary meeting on Africa, and, feeling utterly inadequate, sought the help of God. In prayer, he had an unshakable conviction that this, his first missionary plea, would issue in at least one hearer volunteering for mission service. He was tempted not to tell his fellow students of his conviction, but did. And when he had delivered his message, no one was more amazed than himself when the Voice told him, 'You are the one!' It was a clear call.

Upon graduation, Jones had the alternatives of teaching or evangelism placed before him, but volunteered for Africa, until the same Voice confirmed in like manner his call to India. There he walked with the Christ of the Indian Road, and it is no exaggeration to say that Dr. E. Stanley Jones became the best-known missionary of the twentieth century to India, one who held the affection of India's leaders, from Gandhi onwards.

At the same time, the witness of the campus Y.M.C.A. and Y.W.C.A. was supplemented by denominational appointment of student pastors to the universities to care for their students on secular campuses, outnumbering others at the traditional denominational colleges.[37] As Christian-founded colleges and universities became secular, and life on the university campus became more secular, increased efforts were made to reach the students therein.

Before the Awakening of 1905 was six months old, it was announced that 5495 new Young People's Societies (C. E.) had been organized. Dr. Francis E. Clark, in a triumphant vein, observed: [38]

> As the historian of a hundred years hence looks back to the earlier years of this twentieth century, he will describe it as a decade of revival, a revival of interest in spiritual things, a revival of missionary zeal, a revival of civic and corporate righteousness.

Sunday Schools were revitalized in the Awakening of 1905. In the decade of the Revival, their enrollment passed the fifteen million mark, their teachers numbering more than a million and a half, a predominantly lay movement in service. In 1907, the National Vacation Bible School Committee was formed, its developments supplementing the Sunday Schools throughout the United States and Canada.[39]

Throughout the Southern States, a spiritual awakening in power moved the Negro churches, James Wharton stirring a multitude of hearers in campaign after campaign.[40] In those days, the social life of Negro Americans was segregated, but movements among the whites were reproduced among the Negroes; now the proportion of Negroes in membership of churches approximated at last the white percentages. No end to racial discrimination was yet in sight, however: the theory being separate but equal, the practice but unequal.

The temper of today is such that many social activists would question the value of an Evangelical Awakening which did not immediately attempt to solve the race question. The impatience ignores or defies the lessons of history.

Pentecost did not provoke a Spartacist revolt, but its full effects made slavery impossible. The social conscience itself develops slowly, always leaving work for succeeding generations to do, and no one can predict a timetable for social reform, in which—as in eschatology—it is not for mere men to tell the times or the seasons in advance. The Lord of eternity is the master of time.

12

IMPACT ON CHURCH AND STATE

In 1906, the Christian press continued to report revivals here and there: 'blessed times of refreshing,' 'an unprecedented revival,' 'a happy united people,' 'the good work goes on,' 'the greatest revival for years,' and similar phrases. The Christian and Missionary Alliance, busy in evangelism as well as missions, summarized the year 1906 thus: 'It has been a year of revival, a year of the Holy Ghost.'[1]

The visit of Seth Joshua of Wales coincided with an outburst of the phenomenal type of revival that characterized the Welsh movement,[2] occurring in evangelical strongholds. The Moody Bible Institute was visited by an unusual awakening in the autumn of the year 1906, all classes given up, prayer groups continuing until 2 or 3 in the morning.[3] The Alliance school at Nyack suspended regular classes also in 'a profound spiritual movement' which went on for three weeks. That it was on the Welsh pattern was evident, for there was much confession. The awakening spread to the mother church, the Alliance Tabernacle in New York.[4]

In 1906, under the sponsorship of the Boston Evangelical Alliance,[5] Gipsy Rodney Smith (fresh from revival in Wales and evangelism in Africa) conducted an evangelistic campaign in Tremont Temple Baptist Church which in fifty meetings attracted more than a hundred thousand people. The same Gipsy Smith participated in a 'remarkable spiritual movement' in Portland, Maine, a campaign supported by all congregations of the Protestant denominations.[6] Gipsy Smith became an evangelist much in demand in the States.

In New York, the movement of Awakening continued into 1906. Calvary Methodist Episcopal Church there continued to be packed, with extra chairs brought in, and numerous conversions recorded.[7] Many city churches were revived. On another Sunday, 4th February 1906, Calvary Church in New York received another large number of accessions, and Janes Methodist Episcopal Church in Brooklyn admitted 250 by letter, confession of faith and probation the same day, of that number the new-made converts being about 200.[8]

The Rev. F. B. Lynch of St. Luke's Church, Philadelphia, reported that the 7th January 1906 was 'the greatest day of my ministry. The meeting was continued during the week with small abatement of religious fervor,' the total number of conversions in that week being 135.[9]

What was true of the East Coast was true of the Middle West also. Under the ministry of W. E. Biederwolf, one of Chapman's associates, afterward a ranking Federal Council evangelist, the city of Elgin, Illinois underwent one of the most remarkable experiences of its history, observers of its church life reported.[10]

Successful evangelism was realized out West.[11] In Utah, the Mormon stronghold, remarkable revival accompanied the evangelistic ministry of W. F. Coburn[12] in Salt Lake City. The earthquake in San Francisco was not without its effects upon Californians, and in particular the ferment in the city of Los Angeles continued, giving rise to a new movement of worldwide proportions, modern Pentecostalism, later to be considered.

The Southern Baptist leaders announced to their whole constituency with rejoicing 'the glorious ingatherings in the home lands,' which not only strengthened the churches at home but dramatically increased their missionary interest and giving. This was true of the other Protestant denominations besides the Southern Baptists, of course.[13]

Throughout the Southern States, the movement went on unabated, in the reviving of congregations and in the awakening of the masses, and in the evangelistic efforts of the former to meet the needs of the latter.

It was noted by qualified observers that there appeared to be four distinct types of the outpouring of the Spirit— as seen in the phenomenal outburst typical of Wales; in the organized evangelism typical of the Torrey-Alexander work; in the united fellowship of the churches witnessed in the city of Schenectady and other places; and in local congregational movements, as demonstrated in Gloversville, New York and in similar examples.[14] Of the four, church historians seem to be aware only of the mass evangelistic campaigns of the famous evangelists, such as Wilbur Chapman, Reuben A. Torrey, W. E. Biederwolf, Rodney Smith, Henry Ostrom, and (of course) Billy Sunday, whose manner of preaching was so sensational that the journalistic historians found him irresistible, writing volumes about his eccentricities while utterly ignoring the movement from which he angled off.

The Southern Baptist Convention met in Chattanooga in 1906, and surveyed the outlook for evangelism since the commencement of the Awakening:[15]

> The spirit of evangelism is abroad in the land. From every part of the country there come the tokens of increased revival fervor among the churches of all denominations of Christians. In many of our cities there has been very distinct and extraordinary evangelistic enthusiasm. More people have been reached by the gospel in our great cities through evangelistic agencies in the last year than ever before. This seems to be specially true of the centers of population where it has hitherto been so hard to reach the masses. Generally speaking, the notable revivals of this year have been of a cooperative character, either different denominations coming together or groups of churches of the same denomination... Great halls, theatres, skating rinks and other large central meeting places have been utilized by evangelists and thousands of non-churchgoers have been reached in this way. The country sections and small towns have likewise shared in the evangelistic sweep.

Southern Baptists were at times critical of simultaneous evangelistic campaigns of the interdenominational-type led by Wilbur Chapman.[16] In advance of these efforts, they often deplored their lack of effectiveness, hence their cooperation was sometimes less than that of the Methodists and others. Then, if the number of the inquirers joining the Baptist churches reflected the lesser enthusiasm of their members, they were quick to point out that they had not received the numbers of additions that the general figures had led them to expect. This has been typical of lukewarm cooperators in other decades and among other denominations.

It could be said that there was a loss of inquirers between campaign enrollment and church membership in city-wide interdenominational campaigns; whereas it was a Southern Baptist practice to take inquirers into membership directly after almost immediate baptism, in which case the loss of the imperfectly converted became 'non-resident members.' Half a century afterwards, the Southern Baptists were the major proponents of the simultaneous evangelistic campaign, but operating without cooperation of other denominations.

In considering the weaknesses of evangelistic campaigns in general, Southern Baptist leaders reaffirmed their faith in the practice of mass evangelism, whether congregational or inter-congregational:[17]

Admit that every pastor should do the work of an evangelist, and, as far as possible, hold his own meetings. Admit that every church should be an evangelistic church, expecting conversions and having them in large numbers. Admit that the normal state of the church is a state of revival. Set the ideal as high as you will; keep the fires burning intensely; and yet you will need evangelism and evangelists. Admit again all the evils and abuses which have been alleged against evangelism. Admit that some evangelists have rare and wonderful mathematical genius which enables them to manipulate and get results which leave the average mind baffled and paralyzed. Admit that occasionally one of them becomes vain and belligerent and bumptious. And yet we maintain that sane evangelism, New Testament evangelism, remains a necessity... the other and spurious kind is a parasite at the roots, not evangelism itself.

This kind of thinking continued to influence the Southern Baptists in the next sixty years, and helped cause their own numbers to pass the ten million mark. That it was not due to the superiority (by denominational assumption) of 'Baptist distinctives,' can be seen in the growth of such bodies in the same period and in other areas as the Nazarenes. It can be seen in the lack of growth of others neglecting evangelism.

Despite the rise of a Landmark secession movement in the territory of the Southern Baptists, sloughing off a number of churches and associations, the major Baptist body grew steadily through the influence of the Awakening:[18]

years	1904	1905	1906	1907
associations	790	809	808	811
churches	20,402	21,802	20,776	21,266
baptisms	103,021	105,905	124,911	129,152
members	1,832,638	1,899,427	1,946,948	2,015,080

Baptists in the other states, from whom stemmed the American Baptist Convention and its secessions, grew also:

members	1,070,969	1,090,176	1,130,958	1,114,053

The number of Negro Baptists was approximately equal to that of the Southern Baptist body in the 1900s.

Reuben A. Torrey had returned to the United States at the end of 1905, hailed as the successor to Moody, whose Bible Institute in Chicago he had directed. In Toronto, he announced that he believed that Revival had already begun in North America, and that he was expecting that the movement would touch not only the great cities, but the smaller towns.[19]

Like Dwight Lyman Moody, Reuben Archer Torrey was short and stocky. The general public had noticed that he preached and talked without the genial wit of Moody, and was lacking in his winsomeness. A veteran Oxford professor commented to the writer that Moody preached love while Torrey preached judgment. Torrey was a man of singular honesty and dedication of purpose, and soon the laymen who had backed Moody were urging him to campaign nationally.

For six years, Torrey engaged in big city-wide campaigns before his 'retiring' to the Bible Institute of Los Angeles—campaigning in Toronto and Ottawa; in Philadelphia, Atlanta, San Francisco, Omaha, Cleveland, Nashville and Chicago.[20]

In Philadelphia, after two months of meetings there were about 3500 inquirers. On the opening day, 12,000 had tried to enter the Armory which seated only 6000.[21] Thousands of people were turned away on the last night. The particularly encouraging feature of the movement was the formation of prayer circles by children as well as adults. Nothing like the 1906 Campaign had been seen since the days of Moody.

Charles Alexander, Torrey's song leader and deviser of the modern song-leading technique in evangelism, parted company with Torrey in 1908 and joined forces with Dr. J. Wilbur Chapman, engaged in simultaneous campaigns.[22]

In 1908, Chapman conducted a campaign in Philadelphia, assisted by a score of evangelists and a score of singers in two-score districts of the city. Four hundred churches of the various denominations cooperated. The meetings lasted six weeks and the attendances aggregated about a million and a half.[23] Seven thousand inquirers, twice as many as reported in either Moody's or Torrey's campaigns, received counsel, and an encouraging number joined the churches.

Chapman tackled Boston in 1909, using thirty evangelists, holding nearly a thousand services in three weeks, with seven thousand inquirers. The chief characteristic of the campaign was the great calm pervading the assemblies. Chapman reached the educated and cultured classes. Local churches reaped a harvest of additions throughout New England.[24]

Of a much more tolerant temper, Chapman won a wider support among ministers than did Torrey. In retrospect, Chapman acknowledged the weaknesses of the simultaneous method. The disappointments, his friends claimed, were always with subordinate meetings, not with the central ones conducted by Chapman and Alexander.[25]

William E. Biederwolf was a graduate of the Princeton Graduate School and Seminary who, like Torrey, studied abroad, at the universities of Berlin and Paris. In 1906, after experience in evangelism with Mills and Chapman, he went out into his own campaigns. He rejoiced in all the opportunities of the Awakening. In 1913, W. E. Biederwolf was appointed secretary of the new Commission on Evangelism established by the Federal Council of Churches.[26] He carried on as an Evangelical in an evangelistic ministry.

Another evangelist rose to fame in the aftermath of the post-Welsh Revival movements.[27] As a baseball player of note, Billy Sunday enjoyed a ready-made popularity. His platform manner—to say the very least—was spectacular. There was much criticism of his thankoffering method of financing his great campaigns.[28] Yet, it cannot be gainsaid that his manly appeal and his straight-forward message won many converts, and affected social habits wholesale.

For ten years, mass evangelism became big business in the United States. While it lost, in some measure, its spirituality, it owed its great opportunity to the spiritual influence of the worldwide awakening of the early 1900s. It is often easy to judge an Awakening by its mass evangelism—and to forget the unpublicized good accomplished in so many other ways. Without doubt, the 1900s were years of blessing, and mass evangelism was only one manifestation.

Evangelism in the United States suffered much after the period of spiritual awakening had passed, chiefly because of the commercialism and sensationalism and irresponsibility shown by freelance evangelists without loyalty to any organization or submission to any discipline.

Billy Sunday succeeded to the popular fame of Finney and Moody, and obviously much good was accomplished in his crusades. But how much his evangelism had become big-business rather than an operation of the Spirit may be judged by his excuse for taking huge offerings, which in ten years amounted to more than $1,000,000, this pathetic utterance being reported: 'What I'm paid for my work makes it only about two dollars a soul, and I get less proportionately for the number I convert than any other living evangelist.'

It was estimated in 1911 that there were more than six hundred active, professional evangelists operating in the United States, most of whom copied Billy Sunday in style and method.[29] Billy Sunday built temporary tabernacles, working with sponsoring committees of the majority of ministers in a city, and responsible laymen. His later imitators found that the device of a tabernacle enabled them to work independently of the local ministers. Their evangelism too often became not only crassly commercial but sadly divisive.

Bishop J. F. Berry voiced the common objections to this tabernacle evangelism: first, the first two weeks of vitriolic attacks upon local ministers and church members; second, the exaltation of the role of the visiting evangelist and lack of recognition of local supporting pastors; third, a 'shake-my-hand' method of dealing with those who inquired after salvation; fourth, an over-emphasis on statistics and their misleading character; fifth, the vulgar display of presentation of gifts to the visiting evangelist; and sixth, the high-pressure methods used to obtain large freewill offerings for the evangelist.[30]

Thirty years later, the writer published his comments upon the situation then prevailing, confirming much of what was said in 1911,[31] and attributing the sad deterioration in the quality of mass evangelism to the same factors. It was not until the rise of Billy Graham that mass evangelism was largely redeemed from its deplorable handicaps.

Christian editors were impressed by the immediacy of the social impact of the Awakening of 1905, saying over and over the same thing: [32]

> We find evidence of a revival of righteousness in the popular and pulpit protest against the 'sharp practice' and 'double-dealing' of insurance managers; the indignation against rate swindling, oppressive corporations, dishonest officials of banks and trust companies; the public wrath against political scoundrels and the successful overthrow of many such; and the elevation to power of fearless, honest, competent men in many states and cities.

It was recognized by those who experienced revival that the movement had not begun as a crusade for righteousness, as such:[33]

> Fancy someone in Wales saying: 'We must have an ethical revival first. We must enter upon a crusade against profanity, obscenity, prize fighting. We must close up the saloons, make kindling wood of the gambling tables, and raid the brothels before we can have a revival.' All these infamies vanish before the Spirit's baptism like bats and owls before the light of day.

The awakening in Schenectady, according to secular New York City journalists, meant 'stronger and better citizens, brighter and happier homes, a cleaner city life, and the strengthening of all the churches and other agencies for good.' No one offered any contradiction.[34]

The leading journal of the Methodist denomination took note of Philadelphia's 'Revival of Civic Righteousness': [35]

> We are in the excitement and enjoyment of a great civic righteousness revival... To a delegation of businessmen at City Hall, June 1, our mayor John Weaver said, 'the hand of the Lord is in it.'

Two weeks later, it was stated that Philadelphia's municipal revolution had taken place at exactly the right time. A week later, it headlined 'The Redemption of Philadelphia,' a happy fact attributed to the Evangelical Awakening.

An editorial in one of the regional journals of Methodism spoke of the general situation in all the denominations: [36]

> Even the secular papers are noticing it. They are speaking of "the vivid, plain and vigorous statements that come weekly from a thousand pulpits," and of "the attitude of all the people toward that style of sharp dealing, long regarded with a kind of pride as essentially characteristic of the American people, an attitude now reflected by the shock that was felt at the disclosures of duplicity in the management of great insurance companies, and by the plain expression of indignation against bossism and political corruption." "These expressions indicate moral progress and a revival of simple faith." They are a thousand times more indicative of genuine revival than any degree of quietness and assurance in the presence of these evils could be. So completely have the principles of righteousness permeated the common thought and feeling that even the long tolerated forms of stock gambling and swindling rate-methods have come in for exposure and sharp censure. The guilty perpetrators of these crimes are mercilessly castigated. They are made to writhe under the lash of public condemnation until many of them are driven out of responsible offices into seclusion and shameful hiding. . .
>
> Preachers are more courageous in their utterances, as if backed by more than mortal energy. It is a relief and satisfaction to the multitudes when the lightnings of public wrath seem to be playing against the workers of iniquity. We believe that the aggregate result will be infinitely beneficial to the cause of God. Men are coming to see that the safety of society and the stability of our free institutions depend upon civic righteousness and social honor, and that wealth obtained dishonestly or by oppressive methods is a crime and a curse. Let the good work go on. Our nation greatly needs the practical subscription to a higher code of morals which the people generally are giving. The vast public trusts will be more secure and profitable hereafter by reason of the present uprising in moral stamina and increased devotion to righteous principle. Truly the teachings of our Christ are beginning to take a fresh hold on the world.

The pastors of congregations felt a new sense of power when their sermons against the social evils of the day produced an immediate effect upon their parishioners, who did not long wait to tackle the abuses.

In Cincinnati, civic reform followed spiritual revival, a new impulse being given by the citizens of the Ohio metropolis, who seemed 'to have profited by the wave of reform that swept over the country,' according to the annual Baptist Congress, representing opinion north and south.[37]

The Methodists, in their leading journal, reviewed 1905 as 'a Great Twelvemonth.'[38]

> Throughout the Republic, there are signs of the revival of the public conscience which, in many states and cities, has broken party lines, rejected machine-made candidates and elected Governors, Senators, Assemblymen, Mayors and County Attorneys of recognized honesty and independence . . . first fruits of a new zeal for the living Christ as the Lord of all human activity . . . social, industrial, commercial and political.

The Presbyterians were quick to acknowledge that a moral and ethical awakening was producing political effect in the wake of the Revival of 1905. Their leader-writers rejoiced that the movement was awakening the moral sense of cities, where for too long a combination of vested interests in the whiskey, gambling and prostitution rackets had thwarted the will of the masses of decent people by outrage at the ballot-boxes. Corrupt regimes were toppling here and there.[39]

The Congregationalists also commended the Awakening. Even Washington Gladden, sometimes called the 'father of the social gospel,' (but better remembered for his choicest of hymns, 'O Master, let me walk with Thee!') conceded that there was evidence of a true religious revival, though not appearing in traditional form. He was satisfied that the general awakening was creating a moral revolution in the life of the people.[40]

It will be remembered that Benjamin Fay Mills had left evangelism and the evangelical fold because of his feeling that they had no social message. He said, in retrospect[41]

> I left my evangelistic work first because I despaired of the possibility of a genuine widespread awakening . . . second because . . . I came to conceive Christ as the Saviour of the social organization rather than of individuals, and third, . . the Bible ceased to be to me the exclusively inspired Word of God.

Mills's 'pilgrim's regress' may be followed through its three stages: loss of spiritual power; adoption of the social gospel; and denial of the authority of the Word and of the Deity of Christ. Many former friends continued to pray for him, even mobilizing intercession publicly, as in Los Angeles, where his old friend Chapman asked the revived multitudes to pray that the beloved Mills would return to the fold. The prayer was answered in due course.

Mills saw the power of God at work again. It was hard for him to deny the Awakening when such as Washington Gladden admitted it. In 1915, in what Chapman called 'an answer to prayer,' but a later historian 'a strange postscript,' Mills reversed himself and re-entered the Presbyterian ministry. The Lord allowed His servant to depart in peace during the year following.

Another life affected by the Awakening of 1905 was that of William Borden, a young millionaire converted in times of revival. He threw himself into the evangelical activity at Yale with abandon. With Charles Campbell and John Magee, Bill Borden founded the Yale Hope Mission, a skid-row project.[42] Borden volunteered for missionary service with the China Inland Mission, and proceeded to Egypt to master Arabic, useful in China's great northwest. There he lost his life, but his challenge lingered on to recruit men and women for China and other missions abroad.

Less dramatic but just as fruitful was the experience of Kenneth Scott Latourette, thrust into the revived Christian groups at Yale in 1905, after seeing the results of the local revival at McMinnville College in Oregon:[43]

> In my final year, I was made Bible study secretary of Dwight Hall . . . That year we had about 1000 undergraduates enrolled in these groups. At the same time, Henry Wright had his freshman class in the life of Christ, with an average attendance of about 100.

> I attempted to know every man in the classes of 1909, 1910, and 1911 . . . From the class of 1909, which I knew throughout its four years, with possibly one exception, came more missionaries than from any other class in the history of Yale College.

Latourette, of course, went to China as a missionary, was invalided home, became a member of the faculty at Reed College in Oregon, then Denison University in Ohio; finally he became one of Yale's most distinguished professors— but not until he had passed through a spell of agnosticism.

13

LATIN AMERICAN QUICKENING

Interdenominational missionary cooperation till 1910 was generally evangelical in its direction. The addition of 'High Church' participants brought about a change.[1] The Edinburgh World Missionary Conference was limited to societies working among non-Christian peoples only, effectively excluding Latin America from the conference agenda.[2]

This decision was not approved by Evangelicals (particularly American or interdenominational) whose spokesman, Dr. Robert E. Speer, led a rump session at Edinburgh which resulted in the formation of the Committee on Cooperation in Latin America, leading to the Panama Congress in 1916.

The encyclopedic historian, Stephen Neill, observed:[3]

> Roman Catholic writers admit that the conversion of many of the aboriginal peoples was superficial in the extreme; and in recent years the shortage of priests has been such that for many of the inhabitants there is extremely little chance of any real instruction in the tenets of the Roman Catholic faith.

If the growth of sturdy Evangelical Churches numbering millions of communicating Christians and the belated recognition of their success by objective Roman Catholic scholars be any test, it could be said that the Holy Spirit 'disregarded' the decisions made regarding Latin America by Catholic Episcopalians. But it could not be said that belligerent Protestant digladiation was the main factor in Evangelical growth throughout the Latin republics. The main factor was evangelism initiated and expanded by phenomenal Revival.

A pioneer Methodist missionary, T. B. Wood, correctly made at the turn of the century a significant prophecy:[4]

> The signs of the times point to the coming of great sweeping revivals. All the work thus far is providentially preparatory to them. And when they once get started among these impulsive peoples, the mighty changes that will follow fast and far throughout this immense, homogeneous territory promise to surpass anything of the kind hitherto known.

101

The abortive attempt of James Thomson and his contemporaries to open up Latin America to the Good News in the 1820s was followed by the more successful entrance through immigration in the 1860s. Growth was very slow. By the turn of the century, optimism arose, and this was accelerated when news arrived of the phenomenal revival in the little principality of Wales, alerting the believers. To this day in Brazil, the great hymn of petition for revival everywhere is 'Vem, visita Tua igreja, O bendito Salvador!' —'Come, visit Thy church, O Saviour Divine!' — and the inevitable tune is the Welsh 'Ebenezer' to which Williams's words 'O, the deep, deep love of Jesus' were sung.[5]

The beginning of the twentieth century found Baptists, Methodists and Presbyterians from the United States engaged in Brazil in aggressive evangelism, supplemented by several smaller interdenomination missions, including the Y.M.C.A. The Presbyterian work, for example, was forty years old. In 1899, L. L. Kinsolving was consecrated as bishop of a Brazilian Episcopal Church and in 1902 he was bold enough to declare that the Roman Catholic Church there had repelled the people by its unchristian terms, its service in an unknown tongue, celibacy of priests, and abuse of the confessional.[6]

About the same time, a Capuchin friar burned 214 Bibles in the presence of 2000 people, provoking a newspaper in Recife to remark that the time had passed for stifling human intelligence by fire.[7] Brazilian Freemasonry supported this protest, and the eager colporteurs continued to distribute the Scriptures throughout the States of the vast country. The Bible Societies were scattering one hundred thousand copies of the Scriptures annually.[8]

So successful was Bible distribution that Evangelical missionaries were often being greeted by spontaneously grown congregations of interested people.[9] Audiences of hundreds met first-time visitors.

Dr. W. G. Bagby, a Southern Baptist pioneer, reported 'a steady and blessed work of grace' at the turn of the century, 'attended by the blessing of the Holy Spirit.' In 1903, the January Week of prayer in Rio de Janeiro drew large gatherings to four evangelical churches in the city, each one overflowing. Open-air meetings were thronged.

Eliezer dos Santos Saraïva, general secretary of the Young People's Societies (C. E.) of Brazil, hence in contact with the pastors of many churches, secured reports of additions to the churches in 1905, 600 in the first three months, 1350 in the first six months; and 3000 were added during the whole year, bringing the total of Evangelical communicants to 25,000.[10]

An influx of untaught inquirers has often lowered the spiritual tone of the body of believers, but in Brazil in 1905 the opposite was true. Instead of a decline, there was 'an apparent eagerness to more faithfully perform each duty.' The Sunday Schools were crowded with eager pupils seeking a knowledge of the Bible; preaching services were character-ized by the same eagerness for God's Word. In spite of the worst financial crisis in the history of the nation to date, money was being poured into the work by Brazilians.

As a result, many churches were not only paying their own pastors' salaries but supporting national evangelists, sent into the country. Teams of young men held evangelistic services in their cities and towns and villages, voluntarily. The Brazilian Young People's Societies played an important role in training the volunteers. Within three short years, 75 C. E. Societies had come into being with 2500 members.

Besides the various operations of evangelism, the more social enterprises of both missions and churches enjoyed financial support, such as the Y.M.C.A. and the Evangelical hospitals and schools. Mackenzie University, chartered in 1891 as a college by the Regents of the State of New York and maintained by the Presbyterians, had graduated its first class in 1900.[11] A Brazilian leader stated:

> You people at Mackenzie do not parade your religion, but you made it felt and stand for it on any suitable occasion, and you are doing the best scientific training that is being done in Brazil today.

Far north, in Pernambuco, a converted Jew, Solomon Ginsburg, had pioneered a work for the Baptists. His reports indicated a rising expectation of unusual blessing,[12] of the imminence of an awakening. His prayers were soon heard.

The 1905 Awakening spread through Brazil much slower than in Wales, four hundred times smaller. For seven years, there was an upsurge. In the State of Bahia, Ginsburg re-ported 'over one thousand souls in one year' in 1911. There the first three months had been used to mobilize prayer and to rally the believers; the second for planning and training; the third to evangelistic services; and the final quarter to baptize and instruct the converts,[13] —850 converts baptized and 150 backsliders restored, besides 500 received into the fellowship after legal marriage.

The first Brazilian Baptist Convention was held in 1907, reporting 5000 members after 25 years' growth. The membership doubled within three years. It doubled again in the next decade. It is fair to say that the Awakening of 1905 added twenty-five years' growth in three years or so.[14]

As a result of a challenge given by a seminary professor in times of revival, Anibal Nora, a young pastor, entered the valley of the Rio Doce, and in ten years from 1908 onwards reported six churches, thirty preaching points and 1371 communicant members.[15] A third of the communicant strength of the Presbyterian Church of Brazil resided there when the present writer preached in the churches and colleges of the valley. This awakening was not untypical.

The Awakening year found the Presbyterians of Brazil suffering from a three-year old division, attributed to dissension over Freemasonry and secular enterprise. Together, at the end of 1905, the two Presbyterian bodies had 14,000 members and were larger than the Baptist, Methodist and Episcopal denominations combined.[16] The Igreja Independente trebled its membership in a quarter century; so also did the larger body, indigenized shortly after the separation.[17]

Indirectly, the Awakenings of the 1905 period had an enormous effect upon the evangelization of Brazil—although the narration belongs to the Pentecostal aftermath of the worldwide Revival. The Pentecostal movement of 1906 in Chicago thrust forth two very different teams of pioneers, one Swedish-American,[18] leading to establishment of the Brazilian Assemblies of God; whereas the other, Italian-American,[19] culminated in the founding of the Christian Congregation. The Pentecostals in Brazil within fifty years numbered more than a million and a half members.

Gunnar Vingren and Daniel Berg arrived in Belém, Para, in 1910 and built up a congregation and a movement throughout Brazil which passed the million mark in membership in the 1960s.[20] Louis Francescon arrived in São Paulo in 1910, and reached out to the multitudes of Italian immigrants pouring into Brazil, establishing a more exclusive Italo-Brazilian Pentecostal fellowship.[21]

The extraordinary awakening in the Republic of Chile during the first decade of the twentieth century was not the first phenomenal outpouring among Evangelical believers. In 1884, in the port-city of Constitucion, the postmaster, Alberto Vidaurre, was converted by study of Scripture. He became an impassioned evangelist whose preaching moved the whole town.[22] By the end of 1885, the infant church there had grown from two members to sixty-four. Chile's mission presbytery investigated the awakening, which was marked by certain charismata; and the commission of inquiry deemed the work an 'outpouring of the Spirit.' There was, however, a general distrust of anything unusual manifested by mission leadership, and the revival did not last long or spread far.

In the 1890s, the German Baptists in Chile enjoyed a time of refreshing in which 'some of the meetings continued all night' and several of their Spanish-speaking younger folk professed conversion.[23]

An American Methodist mission-teacher, W. C. Hoover, sent out by a church in Chicago enjoying perennial revival, began to teach at a school in Iquique at a time when the Methodists were enjoying rapid growth.[24] Vidaurre, who had seceded from the Presbyterians to Methodism, split the church of which Hoover was pastor; the incident enlightened Hoover on national feeling.

In 1902, W. C. Hoover became pastor of the church in Valparaiso. A local revival began among the members, in which (to Hoover's surprise) they raised their voices in simultaneous and audible prayer.[25] About a hundred people joined the church, the whole conference increasing by 44%.

Valparaiso was judged 'one of the wickedest cities on earth.' It was wrecked by an earthquake in 1906, the same year as the San Francisco earthquake.[26] The local clergy blamed it, and also a previous smallpox epidemic, upon the Evangelicals, some of whom, losing their place of worship, were meeting in homes for lay exhortation.

In 1907, Pandita Ramabai's American helper, Minnie Abrams, sent Mrs. Hoover (a classmate in Chicago) some information about the awakening at Mukti in India.[27] The Hoovers and their Chilean associates sought a new outpouring. In the first service in the reconstructed building, almost everyone burst into simultaneous prayer and praise——an occurrence often repeated, to this day.

While Hoover was absent in Temuco, church members seeking blessing prayed and confessed far into the night. On Hoover's return, services of confession and prayer continued until unusual manifestations were evidenced, including tongues, visions, trances, laughter and crying. They were accompanied by the fruit of changed lives. Auto-suggestion and fraud were also recognized as a 'satanic counterfeit.' The movement spread to other congregations.[28]

Hoover had much closer rapport with his own Chilean brethren than with the missionaries who were often more interested in education than in evangelism; his colleagues regarded him as critical,[29] overconfident and 'holier than thou.' In due course, Hoover resigned from the Methodist ministry, but regarded himself as a Methodist until he died. His following organized themselves into a national organization, la Iglesia Metodista Pentecostal.

Attendances at the meetings shot up, 800 in August, 900 in October, and Sunday School also increased.[30] Hoover was charged in court with intoxicating the people with a beverage called 'the blood of the lamb.' The case was dismissed.[31]   In the aftermath of the Revival, there were squabbles and disagreements, misunderstandings and lawsuits. Years later, the Methodists recognized the legitimacy of the movement.

Meanwhile, there was also a measure of reviving in the churches of other denominations.[32] J. H. McLean reported 'a turning to the Lord' in great numbers at the Presbyterian church in Valparaiso, almost one hundred confessing Christ for the first time, 'without the semblance of frenzied emotion.'

Protestantism experienced a phenomenal growth in Chile, Evangelicals becoming as numerous as practising Roman Catholics.[33] Within two generations of the Awakening, communicants exceeded 450,000, of whom 350,000 were indigenous Pentecostals,[34] noted for their honesty and zeal.

A phenomenal revival began in mid-winter of 1905 among the Welsh colonists in Argentinian Patagonia.[35] Evangelical strength was small in the Argentine, but from 1905 onward the Baptists and the Brethren made steady progress, being overtaken later by the Pentecostals. In 1909, a Southern Baptist missionary wrote from Rosario:[36]

> We are having a real revival. A special prayer meeting was followed each day by those attending going to homes and market places. As many as 300 attended each of the evening services. On the closing night, there were 22 professions of faith ... never in Argentina ... have I seen such a manifestation of God's Spirit.

In the other republics, the years of awakening were marked by occasional local revivals, by an influx of new workers from the sending countries, and by steady evangelism. The Evangelical constituency was tiny in tropical America, and even its doubling represented only a few hundred gained.

The first use of the word 'revival' in newly-pioneered Ecuador occurred in 1909,[37] when Harry Compton reported to the Methodists more than a score converted and added to the church, with strong opposition following. As in Venezuela and Peru, Evangelical missionaries and colporteurs were engaged in a struggle for existence, often subjected to beatings, jailings, expulsions and the like. Seven societies entered Colombia in 1907, but the fruit of their travail was long deferred. In Peru, a difficult field for any Evangelical enterprise, a revival began under the ministry of a Peruvian evangelist.[38]

News of the Welsh Revival stirred up united prayer meetings among English-speaking residents of Mexico City, and in 1905 an awakening was reported.[39] A revival began in the Methodist church in 1907, believers moved to tears, night after night bringing converts.[40] Evangelicals then numbered only .004 per cent of the total population.

Evangelicals gained an entrance to Cuba and Puerto Rico at the end of the Spanish-American War, and, as in the Philippines, local awakenings and a heartening response to evangelism were experienced.[41] In the British Caribbean, awakenings began in Jamaica,[42] with great open-air meetings. There were hundreds of conversions in the Jamaica Revival. This Awakening in the West Indies spread from island to island.[43] There was an awakening on Trinidad, and another on Barbados, while the congregations on smaller islands such as Dominica, St. Eustasius and St. Kitts attracted much attention. St. Kitts witnessed Welsh phenomena, 335 being added to the membership of the Methodist church, whose tone was vastly improved by the transformed lives and homes.

Throughout Latin America, the effect of the phenomenal awakenings and regular evangelism was reflected in the growth of the Evangelical churches. In 1903, there were some 1438 missionaries, 6000 national workers and 132,388 communicants in Latin America and the Caribbean; seven years later, there were 2112 missionaries, 6199 national workers, and 369,077 communicants, the latter representing an increase of 180 per cent.[44]

The gains of the revival period proved to be the prelude to a burgeoning Evangelical advance after World War I throughout Latin America, in which the main factors again were the 'sweeping revivals' and biblical evangelism which had been prophesied at the turn of the century.

Of all major sectors of Evangelical Christendom, Latin American Evangelicals most of all have continued and extended the fervent action peculiar to the Welsh Revival.

14

THE AUSTRALASIAN AWAKENING

The genesis of the Australasian Awakening of the early twentieth century was traced back to 1889 when Australian-born John McNeil—an evangelist not to be confused with the Scottish evangelist, John McNeill—with the backing of four Melbourne ministers, started a prayer meeting for revival which continued each Saturday evening for eleven years, till a total of two thousand groups were thus interceding.[1]

In 1891, a remarkable series of meetings was conducted by the Anglican missioner, the Rev. George Grubb, making an impact throughout Australia but particularly stirring the Sydney churchmen; the Church Missionary Society was revived. In 1891 also, the Evangelization Society of Australia was begun, leading to continent-wide operations.

The eager Evangelization Society decided to ask Dwight Lyman Moody to campaign in Australia. In 1899, while in Los Angeles, Moody was presented with a petition signed by 15,831 people,[2] asking him to visit New Zealand and Australia. D. L. Moody died that very year.

The invitation to Australia was not unfruitful. In 1899, a Week of Prayer at Moody Church and Moody Bible Institute was continued as a regular Saturday evening prayer meeting for the reviving of the Church throughout the world. The attendance rose to three hundred nightly. Dr. Reuben Archer Torrey was deeply moved,[3] and decided to go to Australasia.

Even before the arrival of the Torrey party, there were reports of unusually effective evangelistic campaigns in the southern commonwealth, simultaneous campaigns in larger cities, directed by Australian evangelists and by visiting Scots and Americans—among the latter, W. Edgar Geil.

A young Scot, James Lyall, was converted at the age of seventeen under the ministry of John McNeill, who had hired Newsome's Circus in Edinburgh for evangelistic meetings. Lyall sailed for the United States, where he studied at the historic Oberlin College. He served as an evangelist in the States before returning to Britain to assist Henry Grattan Guinness at Harley College in London.[4]

An Edinburgh businessman, Andrew Stewart, enlisted a team of evangelists to visit Australia, and James Lyall joined them. A Presbyterian-sponsored campaign in Queensland brought so much blessing to Brisbane that it became fully interdenominational and was extended three months.[5]

Lyall also assisted another friend, Dr. Harry Guinness, in campaigns in Launceston, Hobart, Adelaide, Melbourne, Sydney, Auckland, Dunedin, and Christchurch. Simultaneous missions based on fifty locations were held in Sydney lasting two weeks and registering about five thousand inquirers. In place after place, James Lyall enjoyed remarkable success, two hundred converts supplying written testimonies in his campaign in New Zealand's capital, Wellington.[6]

Meanwhile in 1902, Torrey and Alexander and their party embarked for the island continent and there enjoyed an unprecedented success in evangelism accompanied by revival, in which twenty thousand inquirers were enrolled.

Greater Melbourne's population then was 500,000. The Melbourne Mission began in the Town Hall,[7] continued as a simultaneous campaign conducted by fifty missioners in fifty suburban districts, and concluded in the vast Exhibition Building, seating 7000. Great crowds attended the meetings, and quite a number of converts were added to the churches.

From the metropolis, the missioners moved to Victorian towns, and thence to Tasmania. In August, they tackled the metropolis of Sydney in New South Wales. Again they enjoyed success in both the attendances and response. Their reputation was established in Australia, and expectation began to rise in New Zealand.

In New Zealand at the turn of the century, an editorial in the leading interdenominational journal declared:[8]

> New Zealand's greatest need at the present time is a great religious awakening when the power of the Holy Ghost shall be poured out upon the Church militant and a determined assault made upon the godless masses.

And an official Methodist report spoke of conditions thus:[9]

> ... our feeble week night services, our decadent fellowship meetings, the absence of so many of our members and officials from the Lord's Table, the difficulty in raising local preachers and the infrequency of conversion from the outside world . . .

A year later, the same denomination stated that 1902 would be memorable on account of the 'gracious spiritual influences accompanying the Torrey-Alexander and other missions.'[10]

The Torrey-Alexander series began in the big Skating Rink in Wellington.[11] Canterbury Hall in Christchurch was filled two hours before the service and five thousand attempted entrance.[12] The southern city of Dunedin witnessed an extraordinary movement of power.[13] Among the many converts was Robert A. Laidlaw, who later became a leading New Zealand businessman and Christian layman.

Torrey and Alexander spent only nine days in Dunedin, and James Lyall followed them up, filling the Garrison Hall nightly with two thousand auditors.[14] Lyall visited the rarely evangelized West Coast of South Island. In all, he conducted twenty-six missions during fourteen months in New Zealand.[15]

The success enjoyed by Andrew Stewart, James Lyall, Hugh Paton, and other Scottish evangelists in New Zealand and Australia in the opening years of the new century showed that the movement of revival was by no means confined to the great campaigns of Torrey and Alexander and their team. Yet few Australians and New Zealanders two generations afterwards ever heard of the Scottish team of evangelists. (A son-in-law of Andrew Stewart, Alfred Coombe, became a leading layman in all sorts of evangelistic and missionary enterprises in Australia between the 1930s and 1960s.)

After his great Campaign in Australia had concluded, Dr Reuben Archer Torrey reporting in London, summarized for interested ministers the four major factors in the success of the great evangelistic work in Australia and New Zealand:[16]

> First came 'the power of believing and united prayer'
> undergirding their enterprise; second, 'the power of
> the inspired Word of God providing the message; third,
> 'the power of the atoning blood of Christ' upholding the
> thousands of inquirers; and finally, though not least,
> 'the power of the Holy Spirit' ensuring great success.

The Torrey-Alexander Campaigns in Australia and New Zealand represented organized evangelism of the churches working collectively, but they were undergirded by a great reviving of believers and the awakening of their friends.

Early in 1905[17] came news of a 'strange revival' in Wales, and a second wave of revival swept New Zealand. The news of Wales stirred up interest in Wanganui, in which overflow meetings were held after church services,[18] the movement being of the spontaneous kind. In Waihi, a mining community, news of Wales provoked similar movement in which churches once half empty were crowded out,[19] repeating 'many of the salient features of the wonderful Welsh Revival.'

Contrary to common opinion in Australia, the communities of the southern commonwealth had experienced phenomenal revival and awakening during the late 1850s and early 1860s, and there were survivors who remembered.

The news of the Welsh Revival created great interest throughout Australia. The campaigns of Torrey and Alexander had been followed up by Australian evangelists, and the members won to the churches were thoroughly instructed.

Australia's leading interdenominational journal carried a 'call to prayer,' written by a Congregational minister in Redfern, New South Wales.[20] Exactly a month later, on 10th March 1905, the Rev. F. Binns's own prayer was answered —reported in the same paper, 'The Revival in Redfern':[21]

> Here and there all over Australia, there is a gracious movement and manifest presence of the Spirit of God. Perhaps nowhere is this more apparent than at Redfern, Sydney. A great spiritual uplift was given to the Congregational Church some time ago through a special mission held by Rev. Loyal L. Wirt, then of Newcastle. The soil had been well prepared for the seed by the pastor of the church, Rev. F. Binns. The work in the church has never ceased since Mr. Wirt's mission...

Not only were the churches of New South Wales alerted. The Queensland Council of Churches issued 'A Clarion Call to Prayer.'[22] The Victorian Council of Churches convened a representative gathering in the Assembly Hall, Collins Street. Interest rose in the churches of Tasmania and in South Australia, while Western Australian congregations stirred. Daily prayer meetings were held in the Assembly Hall in Melbourne and elsewhere, correspondents reporting that the 'pulsations that have stirred Wales are reaching here.' They were spreading throughout the Commonwealth.

Typical of the Australian response was a report supplied by Methodists, which noted that the Rev. T. B. Angwin, M.A., was conducting evangelistic services in Bowden Methodist Church, attended by 'some remarkable evidences of power.' In them was experienced a repetition of Welsh enthusiasm. One service was closed at 9.40 p.m., but not one person left the church, as the people seemed constrained to remain. The power of God was distinctly felt. After some time, the evangelist again closed the meeting, but no one indicated the least desire to leave. 'Manifestations of the Divine Presence and power were marked and felt by all present,' some of whom made a public profession of new-found faith.[23]

A deepening of the spiritual life followed, serving as a preparation for a continent-wide campaign again to come. Australian Christian Endeavour became the vehicle of new spiritual power, from its weekly meetings and annual conventions raising a host of volunteers for service. Australia in its second century was becoming a land of opportunity for the preaching of the Gospel, attracting world-leaders in evangelism with the hope of significant success.

In 1909, Chapman and Alexander toured the Australian and New Zealand cities successfully. They commenced in the great Exhibition Hall in Melbourne, and continued in the largest halls in Sydney, Brisbane, Adelaide and lesser towns. In 1912, Chapman and Alexander returned there, missioning besides in New Zealand cities from Invercargill in the south to Auckland in the north. Wilbur Chapman carried in his party a number of younger men as associate evangelists.[24]

It could be said that, just as those faithful ministers in Melbourne interceded with the Author of Revival for nearly twelve years before seeing their prayers answered, so also twelve years of spiritual revival and successful evangelism harvested with joy their sowing with tears.

In the Islands of the Pacific, to the northeast of Australia and New Zealand, the spiritual tide was rising. The Hawaiian Evangelistic Association, responsible for evangelism and missions there and in Micronesia, reported in 1906: 'There can be no question that throughout the entire field our local churches have taken on new life. This is especially marked among the Hawaiians . . .'[25]

In Hawaii, the churches produced the best record for many a year. In all five groups, among Hawaiians, Portuguese, Chinese, Japanese and union congregations, additions to the memberships were noteworthy, the Chinese leading the rest.

The inhabitants of the other island groups also enjoyed spiritual wellbeing. At the same time, an awakening occurred on the phosphate island, Nauru, in the Marshall Islands. More than one thousand were gathering at services, and 362 professed conversion in a single meeting. In the following year, more than half of the island's 1500 inhabitants were attending regularly, 600 of them being active members.[26]

Missionaries at Edinburgh World Missionary Conference (1910) announced that in every considerable group of islands throughout Oceania, especially in Indonesia, there was no period like the decade just past.[27] This was also true of the newly-opened Philippines, despite war and insurrection.[28]

Bishop James Thoburn of India commenced a Methodist work in Manila, finding it hard to collect an audience of a hundred at first, but reporting 12,000 auditors and more than 6000 members after three years' work—more than the total Methodist membership in South America after sixty years.[29] Meanwhile, the first Presbyterian missionary[30] won Paulino Zamora, a nephew of the Filipino martyr-priest, Jacinto Zamora. Nicolas Zamora, son of Paulino Zamora, became in turn a Methodist minister.

Likewise, the Baptists entering the Bisayas found such an openness that a real awakening followed. Seven thousand Filipinos in a single district in Panay petitioned American Baptists to send a missionary. Many of these were second and third generation followers of the evangelical Padre Juan who preached in the 1860s. C. W. Briggs reported in 1906:[31]

> I have had the great privilege of baptizing more than 1000 disciples, most of whom have been Protestants for three or four years ... The great movement among the peasants in Panay in 1901, is now a greater and more significant reality than it was then.

Before long, the indoctrinated Filipinos were subject to spontaneous revivals which produced a 'spirit of prayer and penitence,' confession and dedication.[32] Thus a circle was completed: revival, evangelism, awakening, instruction and revival.

In the islands of Indonesia, an extraordinary awakening occurred in Borneo. German Rhenish missionaries reported that 'a congregation at Musang has sprung into existence, almost in a moment.'[33] This was followed by news of spiritual awakenings elsewhere in the great island. The same mission reported a 'gracious revival' and a 'wonderful movement' spreading throughout the German territory of New Guinea.[34]

Meanwhile, Batak churches maintained growth, 103,528 having been baptized out of a population of 600,000. This Sumatra Christian community had been born from the 1860 Revival and grew with every movement of the Spirit.[35]

The most striking example of the effect of phenomenal revival in Indonesia occurred off the coast of Sumatra on the island of Nias, among a proto-Malay people. Nias had been evangelized in the 1860s revival period by the same Rhenish missionaries. After thirty-five years, there was a Christian community of 5000. Then came the awakening of 1908 and within seven years 20,000 had been baptized and were being instructed in the faith.[36]

After these seven years, a great spiritual revival began on Nias during 1916, named the 'Tangesa dodo'—'the Great Repentance.' It was indigenous. It began with broken-hearted confession of sin—murder, adultery, petty pilfering, ghastly crime. Some who resisted fell critically ill. In the first stage of conviction and misery, folk were called 'seekers': in the final result of forgiveness and joy, they were called 'finders.' This is the usual pattern of experience.

What began as a revival among Christians extended into an awakening and evangelism, giving way to a 'gerekan peng-kristenan massa' or a folk movement.[37] Native evangelists emerged, and also native prophets. Within five years, the number of Christians doubled and candidates for baptism reached 28,000.[38] The island became two-thirds Christian. Within fifty years of the Awakening, within a century of the entrance of the Mission, the number of Nias Christians exceeded quarter of a million,[39] possibly eighty per cent of the total population of the island.

Growth of the Christian Church in Indonesia was achieved at the expense of animism rather than of Islam. The movement among the Bataks represented a folk movement, but it was accelerated by awakenings in the community wrought by the Spirit of God, revival movements not at all alien to the evangelistic Rhenish Mission.

During the first decade of the twentieth century, a folk movement began among the Toradja people of Sulawesi (Celebes).[40] The turning to the Christian faith seemed to be at first social, but spiritually alert missionaries engaged in both instruction and evangelism, and the movement of tribal groups accelerated till within twenty years the majority had adopted the Christian faith. They continued a Christian folk while resisting the pressures of Islam.

In all the island clusters of the Great East, Evangelical Christianity continued to grow—in the Halmaheras, in the Moluccas and in Timor. Java, Muslim citadel of Indonesia, remained so far unmoved, although its smaller Christian groups enjoyed more growth than experienced in any other Islamic country.

Partly through the teaching and preaching of missionaries and native pastors, partly through folk movements, and partly through phenomenal revivals and awakenings, the number of Evangelical Christians in Indonesia increased from a hundred thousand to three hundred thousand in the decade before 1910, more than all other Protestants in the rest of East Asia.[41]

Here included in Oceania with Australia, New Zealand, and Polynesia, Micronesia, Melanesia, and Indonesia plus the Philippines, the people of Malagasia (inhabiting the big island of Madagascar and its dependencies) are mainly of a Malay-Polynesian origin.

The first wave of revivals in Madagascar began in 1894, with the conversion of Rainisoalambo, a Betsileo former soldier who practised sorcery.[42] Though converted through British missionaries, he resided in Norwegian Lutheran territory. He insisted that his followers should learn to read and write and maintain cleanliness of person and property.[43] Thus began the Disciples of the Lord movement.

By the turn of the century, the Disciples were journeying extensively throughout the great red island, independent of but not antagonistic to the missionaries.[44] Rainisoalambo told his helpers that the missionaries had given up all to preach and teach, but that Madagascar should be fully evangelized by the Malagasy. Their peculiarity was exorcism of demons, on which the missions frowned,[45] although it touched a vital area of native resistance to culture and progress.

The Betsileo country was first evangelized by Welsh workers of the London Mission but was a field of Norwegian Lutherans. Wales had been swept by extraordinary revival, and Norway was being moved likewise, when a remarkable work of Divine power occurred among the Betsileo people, a movement begun by Ravelonjanahary.

Ravelonjanahary was a woman of little education, but was backed by the prayers and advice of a Welsh missionary, Mrs. Rowlands.[46] The second awakening spread from the Betsileo country all over Madagascar, working a deepening of the spiritual life of believers through confession and repentance, with the conversion of unbelievers following. 'There were physical manifestations, like those seen in Wales . . . but there were great searchings of heart and confessions of sin, manifest repentance and many conversions.'[47]

When news of the Welsh Revival had reached the island, missionaries formed a solemn league and covenant to pray for a like outpouring.[48] James Sibree, of the L. M. S., said: 'All these things make us feel that a breath of the same Divine influence which is working so mightily in Wales and elsewhere is also passing over many hearts in Madagascar.'[49]

The Malagasy Awakening[50] continued in force into 1907, with prayer and consecration meetings, spiritual agony and deeply moving confessions.[51] The churches multiplied.

15

SOUTH AFRICAN RESURGENCE

The twentieth century began with war raging in one corner of the globe, South Africa. The Boers showed a determination to fight for independence: and a counter-determination to unite South Africa forcibly became evident in imperial British circles. Efforts made at compromise failed.

The Republics declared war on 11th October 1899, and invaded Natal and the Cape Province with fast-moving Boer commandos, besieging Ladysmith and Kimberley. The first battles were credited to the Boers, the British on defensive. A measure taken by the British Army to break resistance and bring the war to a merciful close brought more bitterness to the out-fought Boers than did the actual fighting in 'the last war of gentlemen,' for many thousands of women and children died in epidemics in relocation camps.

Yet, out of tragedy came lasting good from these concentration camps.[1] Both Afrikaans and English-speaking ministers served heroically the tens of thousands of non-combatants held in these widely scattered refugee camps by force.[2] Thousands of their civilian population attended daily services and made lasting professions of faith.[3]

While the High Veld was being 'pacified,' the captured Afrikaner commandos were still being shipped from South Africa[4] to St. Helena and Bermuda, to Ceylon and India. On Bermuda, there came about a great awakening; and on St. Helena, Ds. A. F. Louw preached to discouraged men, many of his converts meeting in crowded dawn prayer meetings[5]
At Fort Ahmednagar in Maratha India, about a thousand men were detained behind thick walls and barbed wire[6] A group of spiritual men met together daily in prayer, until a great revival ensued. The same was true of other camps in India. In Ceylon, there were five thousand Afrikaner prisoners-of-war at Diatalawa under close guard; the prisoners suffered from boredom and from sickness, a severe typhoid epidemic killing many. The Afrikaner prisoner chaplains held services and helped the distressed. A little prayer group of men grew into thousands, resulting in the conversion of hundreds.[7]

116

Two hundred prisoner-of-war 'volunteers' for missions were trained and equipped for service in a 'remarkable outburst of missionary zeal,' and evangelistic enthusiasm also spread to the congregations of South Africa[8] There arose an interest in spiritual renewal in the country.[9]

Shortly after the cessation of hostilities, the principal of Lovedale Institution (James Stewart) asked significantly:[10]

> What can the Church militant do to heal the sore between two brave peoples, and bring this land within the Kingdom of the King of Kings? A revival of true spiritual religion, reaching Boer and Briton alike, would do more towards raising the standard of national righteousness than can be readily imagined.

Spencer Walton, beloved by Briton, Boer and Bantu in South Africa, commenting on postwar conditions in South Africa, admitted that racial hatred between the two European communities was very bitter and that the country as a whole was in a deplorable condition.[11]

There were two main factors in the spiritual uplift, first the success of a Mission of Peace to South Africa by a British evangelist in 1904,[12] and second, the stirring of extraordinary revival in Afrikaans and English-speaking churches by the news of the Revival in Wales and elsewhere.[13]

Invited to South Africa before the outbreak of war, Gipsy Smith reached Capetown in April of 1904, but his sponsors among English Churches found difficulty in locating a suitable building. The only likely auditorium in Capetown was the Groote Kerk of the Dutch Reformed Church, and that was definitely refused to the committee—such was the state of feeling between Afrikaners and English-speaking folk.

A deserted corrugated-iron building, Fillis's Circus, was seated for three thousand and packed out.[14] More than three thousand inquirers were enrolled in the Capetown Mission of Peace[15] In the concluding Capetown rally, pastors told of the congregations revived, prayer meetings come alive and crowded, and whole families won. The Capetown Mission had attracted vast crowds not hitherto seen in any religious gatherings, yet conversions were reported in continuing church services all around the Cape.

On May 14, Kimberley Town Hall was filled, and on each subsequent night crowded to the doors.[16]

> In Kimberley, the like had never been seen before... At times, the feeling was intense; strong men wept like children... Results far exceeded all expectation ...

British and Dutch mingled together, as they had never
done since the war. There were cases of those who had
been actually fighting against each other on the battle-
field, one pointing the other to the Lamb of God.

Thirteen hundred inquirers were instructed, a third of
them Dutch Reformed, half of them young people.[17] Fullest
cooperation was given by the churches of the Diamond Fields,
and family life was greatly strengthened by the movement.

In Bloemfontein, night after night the Town Hall was packed
in a way unprecedented in the Orange Free State. And again
men predominated in the auditorium and inquiry room.[18]

Johannesburg, which had accumulated in only eighteen
years a population of 160,000, was the venue of the next
Mission of Peace, which was sponsored by the Witwatersrand
Church Council.[19] A big tent had been erected in Krugersdorp
and a special train took the people there. Crowds increased
from 2500. Afrikaner correspondents announced that 2337
inquirers had professed faith, 980 of Dutch Reformed preference, 450 Methodist, 290 Anglican, 240 Presbyterian, 145
Baptist and 101 Congregational, 131 being of other loyalties.[20]

The Town Hall in Durban was crowded out for the Mission
of Peace, 24th July onwards.[21] More than eighteen hundred
attended nightly meetings, sponsored by some forty Durban
churches. But in Pietermaritzburg, Gipsy Smith encountered
'a most bitter opposition from the people in the liquor and
theatrical and gambling professions.'[22]

Campaigns were conducted in Pretoria, East London and
Port Elizabeth with similar results. The aggregate attendances at the Gipsy Smith Mission of Peace in South Africa
exceeded three hundred thousand, and converts and inquirers
15,000 or more.[23] One sponsoring denomination 'endeavoured
faithfully to garner the results of Gipsy Smith's Mission,' and
enjoyed its greatest numerical growth of the decade.[24]

The news of the Welsh Revival electrified the Christian
community, Afrikaner and Britisher. Prayer meetings and
conferences on Revival multiplied in churches. At Whitsun,
1905, Methodists at Wittebergen sponsored 'a week of prayer'
which provoked unusual response, attendance at 4.15 a.m.

A month later, a great revival in the Dutch Reformed
congregation at Villiersdorp occurred.[25] 'Indescribably wonderful' happenings on Sunday 23rd July were reported by
Ds. E. G. Malherbe.[26] About 130 were engaged in a Christelijke
Strever service when an 'outpouring of the Holy Spirit' took
place, with conviction, repentance and prayer for salvation.

Each evening following, the people gathered in meetings of up to three hours' duration, and attendance increased from 350 to 500. Sometimes a score of people prayed at the same time audibly, so great was the individual preoccupation with God.[27] Already more than a hundred outright conversions had occurred, including the roughest and the most reckless of sinners. Some testified openly with power, urging their friends to respond and praying for them by name.[28] Among the residents professing conversion were six young people who had been charged with murder—one of whom, Karl Zimmerman, later became a pioneer missionary to the Tiv in Nigeria.

The whole congregation at Villiersdorp was changed. The revival transformed the Young People's Society, which soon increased from 22 to 62 active workers. Yet quite a number of the converts were fifty years of age or more. The minister reported that the revival was spreading and appealed for help to fellow ministers. Three months later, he observed:[29]

> It is surprising to see how God's Spirit takes control of the gathering without human pressure being used. It is a usual occurrence for several people to pray simultaneously, yet always in good order and earnestness ... arising from a concern for the unconverted.

This revival movement began to influence thirty other Dutch Reformed congregations, chiefly in the Cape Province.

News of the Villiersdorp Revival caused the Christians at Prince Albert to begin meetings for prayer in the various homes until these proved too small, when they adjourned en masse to the schoolhouse.[30] On the Sunday evening, an extraordinary work of the Holy Spirit began among the young people. Children of the parish filled another building also and phenomenal happenings occurred among them, astounding the leaders seeing such amazing workings of the Holy Spirit. Whole households of people professed conversion.

On 7th August, the Young People's Society of Villiersdorp visited the church at Fransch Hoek and told the people of the great spiritual work in their dorp. Hence much prayer was offered for a similar visitation in the Huguenot colony. Within a month, 'the drops began to fall.' Some young people decided to hold a prayer meeting the following day in a private home.[31] To their astonishment, forty-two intercessors arrived, although no announcement had been given. Next day, the meeting for prayer filled the consistory room and, becoming too small, was moved to the old school building and thence to the big church, with as many as six hundred present.

Although the movement had originated among the Young People's Society, older folk were deeply moved, including scores over eighty remembering the revival of 1860. The church was crowded for a thanksgiving meeting on Sunday. Meetings that followed became difficult to close, crowds dismissed from a service re-entering another door. The attraction was not the preaching but an irresistible urge to 'marvel at God's Spirit' at work among the people.

The leaders at Fransch Hoek reported that the awakening changed the lives of older Christians also. 'The cold in soul became warm in heart, wayward children returned to the Father, misunderstandings were set right.' An old Boer rose to say: 'I never could forgive the English. Now I must!'

The records of the period of many Reformed congregations confirmed the scope of the revivals. A visit of enthusiastic Christian young people from Villiersdorp created a stir in Heidelberg, Cape Province, according to a centennial report given by the Dutch Reformed congregation there. Conviction brought about by the sudden death of two younger people accelerated the movement.[32]

Similar extraordinary awakenings were in evidence in the English-speaking congregations. William M. Douglas, appointed as the Methodist connexional evangelist following Gipsy Smith's Mission of Peace, witnessed 'a great uplifting' during August at Somerset East, 'an echo of the Revival in Wales.' Husbands, wives, mothers and daughters, young and old, sought salvation.[33] Times of refreshing were experienced also at the historic town of Graaff-Reinet.[34]

At the Wellington Convention, presided over in late September by Dr. Andrew Murray, the Rev. W.M. Douglas shared ministry with Albert Head of England and participated in extraordinary happenings.[35] A couple of hundred people engaged in prayer from 10 p.m. until 1 a.m. when half those present retired, but the remainder continued with a fresh intensity.[36] Like the 1905 Keswick Convention in England, the Wellington Convention was the largest for several years and was long remembered for its memorable happenings.

The Methodist weekly published a stirring account of a spontaneous revival in Simonstown on Cape Peninsula, where the main instrument was the fiery preaching of the Rev. J. McAllister of the Methodist Church of South Africa.[37] It was marked by an intense conviction of sin. Another 'gracious awakening' during the spring of 1905 (November)[38] occurred at Woodstock following the October movement at Simonstown.

Meantime, the Rev. William M. Douglas was witnessing a 'work of God in Aberdeen' in October in which a profound impression was made on the whole town, bringing Dutch and English closer.[39] And in November, Douglas wrought a remarkable work in Port Elizabeth, where the greatest results were seen among the Christians.[40] At Seymour,[41] there were 'striking and convincing proofs of the genuine and deep work of the Holy Spirit.' This was the beginning of a lifetime of effectiveness for William Douglas.[42]

The Baptist, Congregational and Presbyterian churches shared in the upsurge of revival. The Minutes of Grahamstown District 1906 Methodist Synod assembling in Graaff-Reinet took note of much cause for thankfulness for the good work going on in the various churches of the district. 'The Spirit of prayer is abroad,' it was reported, adding that in missions held, saints were strengthened, sinners saved.[43]

South African Methodists provided a gauge to growth in the Awakening. From an increase of nearly 7% recorded in 1902, possibly due to the presence of many British Methodists in the British Army and Navy, additions dropped to 2% in 1903. In the years of the revival, the increase in membership grew to 8% in 1904, 14% in 1905, and 8% in 1906, thirty percent in three years, thereafter practically no gains until 1910.[44]

Though not directly involved in the Boer War, Rhodesia suffered its sorry impact. European congregations in both Salisbury and Bulawayo were hindered by a lack of interest in spiritual matters, the numbers of communicants in 1900 being deplorably small, while the work among Africans faced 'anxieties, difficulties and disappointments.' In 1901, depression was reported in Salisbury and anxiety in Bulawayo. In 1902, a big incursion of new residents into Salisbury augmented European congregations, but, in Bulawayo, matters were at a standstill, ministers alternating between hope and despair, while work among the Africans showed no worthwhile progress or some little decline.[45]

This state of affairs persisted into 1903 and 1904, with a continued depression among English-speaking Christians and a rising interest among the Africans.[46] In 1905, David Russell conducted evangelistic campaigns in both Salisbury and Bulawayo, the church members being quickened and some outsiders being converted to God. So the movement of 1905 was only a recovery, although a definite awakening followed among Africans, both Shona and Ndebele.[47] African church growth continued steadily.

16

THE AFRICAN AWAKENINGS

The revivals in the concentration camps and prisoner-of-war camps overseas led to a general awakening in the Afrikaans-speaking Christian community, an awakening that soon took missionary form, for a Dutch Reformed missionary magazine jumped from 2000 to 6000 circulation in months![1]

More than two hundred prisoners-of-war volunteered for missionary service, a remarkable outburst of missionary zeal and a cause for wonder in the missionary world.[2] This amazed and delighted the leaders of the Dutch Reformed—— for the number of Dutch Reformed missionaries serving in other parts of Africa had been severely reduced by illness, so that more than a hundred candidates were needed.

At a conference in Stellenbosch on the 16th of October, 1902, it was decided to build a college to prepare the candidates for missionary service, and within four months the Moderator of the Cape Synod, Ds. J. H. Hofmeyr, opened the college in Worcester with Ds. A. F. Louw as principal.[3]

Already in Basutoland, a movement was under way, the Paris missionaries reporting additions of 1178 to bring the total of communicants in 1902 to 12,,676, a rapid growth.[4]

In 1903, there was an awakening among African students studying at Lovedale. In eight days of meetings, attendance averaged 600 or so[5] and 242 inquirers registered decision. In 1904, a most significant General Conference of missionaries operating throughout Southern Africa was convened. From it stemmed a great missionary advance as well as real cooperation between the denominations and societies.[6]

The visit of John R. Mott in 1906 resulted in a drawing together of Anglican, Baptist, Dutch Reformed, Methodist, Moravian, Presbyterian and South Africa General Mission ministers at Lovedale. The conference not only healed the wounds of war but resulted in a great movement of the Spirit, marked at first by an intense stillness in the assembly.[7]

Charles Pamla was a veteran in his seventies at the time and retired to supernumerary status only when he became an octogenarian in 1913. He itinerated again as the Methodist connexional evangelist.[8] At times his congregations exceeded one thousand, and as many as two hundred 'came forward.' There were threescore converts from paganism, and double that number of youngsters professing their faith for the first time, and twelve times as many restorations from backsliding in Bensonvale.[9] Then followed campaigns in Zulu and Xhosa and Sotho towns, and in Aliwal North, Burghersdorp, Colesburg, Kimberley, Winburg, Parys, Kroonstad and Capetown.

In 1911,[10] the South Africa General missionaries reported an extraordinary awakening in Tembuland, in the Transkei, marked by intense conviction of sin, many confessions—including some of murder—and heart-warming restitution. A severe challenge to Christianity was reported in 1914 by the same Mission to the north in Gazaland through a revival of African paganism.[11] A year or so later, in April 1915, there began a quickening among the Christians,[12] a turn of the tide. Three months later, Rees Howells sailed for South Africa. Coming from the 1905 Revival in Wales,[13] he stressed the confession of all known sin and total commitment to God.

On 10th October 1915, an evangelical awakening began in earnest at Rusitu.[14] In the New Year, the missionaries were experiencing a measure of reviving throughout Gazaland. At Rusitu, it was said, 'not a soul comes into a meeting without coming under conviction of sin.' Throughout May and June, the awakening spread across the field, affecting tribesmen in Rhodesia and Mozambique all of 1916.

In 1917, the missionaries happily gathered at Mount Tabor in Natal for a revival conference which produced its own 'showers of blessing'[15] among missionaries and Africans. Rees Howells next visited Lutubeni in Tembuland, in the heart of the Transkei. By 1918, an evangelical awakening was in fullest force among the Tembus, Walter Searle writing of 'another gracious visitation of the Holy Spirit.'[16]

The revival in the Transkei spread to Swaziland in mid-1918. The movement made a deep impression on the people, including royalty—letters written at the time confirming reports given the writer by high-born Swazi Christians who vividly recalled the king humbling himself in church:[17]

> At Ezulwini, the power of God came down on the very first meeting ... the next two days I shall never forget. We were in the church eleven and twelve hours a day dealing with the people ... from 6 or 7 a.m. until midnight. For two days and nights, many could not eat or sleep, either because of conviction of sin or the great joy that flooded their hearts when sins were forgiven.

Jeremia, a former Lovedale student and a henchman of the Swazi King, had been ill for several years, scarcely able to walk. Praying under conviction, he suddenly leaped to his feet and danced for joy, running hither and yon—healed of his infirmity.[18] There were many startling events.

The blessing overflowed to the heathen, eighty repenting in a week as real fear fell upon the people. The same effects were seen at Bethany where, in a few days, 120 made their profession of faith. Meetings at Mbabane had similar effect. Rees Howells and his colleague Medill assured all fellow missionaries that 'in every way, it was like the Welsh Revival.'[19] The missionaries simply said 'the power in the meeting was indescribable.'

The awakening spread in 1919 to Zululand and again Rees Howells became the outstanding evangelist.[20] Awakenings were notable at Mseleni and Makowe, where there were many 'confessing sin, with weeping.'

Before long, by the middle of 1919, 'renewal of life' was reported from Christian communities in Natal, Swaziland, Tongaland, Zululand, Pondoland, and Tembuland.[21]

In the first decade of the twentieth century, the Hottentots and the Hereros revolted against German rule in Southwest Africa, slaughtering the German (but not Boer or British) settlers. The retaliation was severe, the Hereros reduced to a fifth of their numbers. It was not until 1910 that a turning to Christianity occurred among them.[22]

Meantime, the discipling and indoctrination of the tribes of Malawi had been going on apace. The brave but bloodthirsty Ngoni warriors were learning to live in peace with other tribes, also moved by Christian teaching.

The conventions at Loudon increased in power year by year, until 1910, when Rev. Charles Inwood, of the Keswick Convention, visited the country. For months before, the missionaries had roused the expectations of the native Christians until about a hundred prayer meetings were being held. In them, Christians confessed their shortcomings and prayed for the power of God upon the convention. And up to three thousand admission tickets were distributed by the elders, to encourage and control attendance.

The addresses were given in English, translated into Tembuka, with little outward response at first; but a spirit of prayer and confession fell upon the elders. On the Saturday morning, a young man began to sob hysterically and was removed. A period of silent prayer followed the set address.[23]

An elder began to pray, confessing before all the sin of
having cherished a spirit of revenge for an evil done him.
Then another began to pray, and another and another, till
two or three were praying together in a quiet voice, weeping and confessing, each one unconscious of the other.
Suddenly there came the sound of 'a rushing wind.' It was
the thrilling sound of two thousand five hundred people
praying audibly, no man apparently conscious of the other
—I could think of no better image to describe the noise than
the rushing of wind through the trees. We were listening
to the same sound as filled that upper room at Pentecost.
Not noisy or discordant, it filled us with a great awe.

Some began to cry out in uncontrollable agony, so the
missionaries judged that an unwholesome physical excitement would break out unless the meeting were controlled.
Fraser started a hymn but each person for a while 'sang
what was uppermost in his mind and heart in a volume of
tumbling waters' until all at last united in the words of a
psalm of confession. The benediction was pronounced and the
vast congregation dispersed in utter silence to pray.

Better to control the meetings, the womenfolk were asked
to meet in the school quadrangle and the men in the big church.
In both gatherings, 'torrents of prayer' flowed as the whole
audience engaged in simultaneous prayer. On Sunday about
7000 gathered, thousands of heathen having heard of the
astounding events. An evangelistic message was given and
again the overwhelming response. In the afternoon, 1250
communicants partook of break and wine, a eucharist indeed.

In the weeks following, at Chinde's, Ekwendeni, Bandawe
and Livingstonia, Charles Inwood preached at conventions
'with the same mighty and awe-inspiring results,' while the
local missionaries held a series of local conventions.

There were permanent and ethical fruits, for feuds were
healed, debts paid, bitter quarreling gave way to brotherly
kindness, prayer became joyous, candidates volunteered for
Christian service, and the heathen were brought into the
Christian faith. Although the intense fervency of revival died
away, the Malawi Church inherited a memory of [24]

the rapture and power that comes when God reveals
Himself to men, a longing for renewed displays of His
glowing presence, an intense conviction that there is no
power in the world so irresistible as the Holy Spirit.

It was the same in Zambia. Dan Crawford, a Scottish
Brethren missionary, met a man carrying a string with more
than thirty knots—each of them representing a convert won

for Christ. On investigation, his converts were found meeting among the rocks at Lofoi, praising God.[25]

In the eastern provinces, following the Dutch Reformed revivals at the end of the Anglo-Boer War, came a great ingathering into the Reformed Mission, baptized members increasing from 600 to 2029 between 1903 and 1910.[26]

The great breakthrough in missionary work in the Congo, according to Bishop Stephen Neill, came about when African evangelists were sent out in village ministry.[27]

> The system of village evangelists was developed everywhere in Protestant missions; first, and with greatest success, at Luebo among the Baluba . . . The Kasai region is thickly populated. In 1904, Luebo already had forty out-stations, each provided with a literate evangelist. Church membership stood at 3000. . .[28]

The mission station at Luebo was only ten years old, but the population had reached 10,000. By 901, the American Presbyterians were reporting a 'Pentecost on the Upper Congo,' with crowds of six thousand listening to the preaching on Sundays. In the following year, the Mission claimed a total of 854 members, 382 new converts receiving instruction.[29]

On 11th May, 1902, there came a remarkable revival at the Luebo station, with forty additions to church membership. In packed out services,[30] five hundred soon became church members: another nine hundred were receiving instruction. In 1903, a new church was dedicated at Ibanj in the same field, a thousand seats provided. In the thanksgiving offering, fifty thousand cowrie-shells (about $42 in value) were received. Some said that the area had now become evangelized.

By 1906, 9000 were members, 2000 preparing for membership, 6000 in young people's societies, and 20,000 pupils in various schools.[31] That year, 2180 were added to the church, 'a church of spontaneous growth . . . originated in itself and the Holy Spirit.'[32] In 1914, more than a third of all Protestant communicants in Congo (30,000) were Kasai Presbyterians.

In Kifwa, thirteen churches baptized 648 converts in 1906, giving instruction to eighteen hundred more in preparation for baptism.[33] The Congo Balolo Mission, commenced by Grattan Guinness, experienced an abundant harvest at its stations in the Congo, particularly Bonginda.[34] It was stated that 'this African Revival has been remarkable for the spirit of prayer demonstrated, Saturday evening prayer meetings being crowded in preparation for the fruitful Sunday services.' A peculiar feature was the occurrence of prophetic dreams.

In 1906, Alliance missionaries in the Congo commented: 'We need an outpouring of the Holy Spirit to reveal and convict of sin and to quicken, and for this we are praying.'[35] In 1907, a marked revival began at the Alliance mission stations at Kinkonzi and Yema, reported in 1908 as 'fruitful revival.'[36]

After a period in which the work languished, Baptists at Banza Manteke[37] reported an outbreak of conviction of sin, followed by conversions—a Congo resumption of progress.

In 1897, the American Disciples of Christ had sent out a scouting party to the Congo but received little encouragement from Belgian officials. Fraternally, the American Baptists turned over one of their stations to their Campbellite friends and from there the enterprise spread. The wave of revival reached the Disciples' field, 1912 being their 'greatest year,' a revival at Lotumbe being their 'most notable event.'[38]

In 1908, after speaking to tens of thousands of men in his crowded meetings in Britain, C. T. Studd (of cricketing and missionary fame, himself in middle age, heard the call of Africa, and came out to the Congo to found the Heart of Africa Mission, later the Worldwide Evangelization Crusade.[39]

The Christian and Missionary Alliance began its Angola work in 1910,[40] and (by way of Northern Rhodesia) the South Africa General Mission entered the country, supplementing American and British missions established decades before. In Angola, in areas pioneered by Christian Brethren of the Garenganze Mission under F. S. Arnot, an awakening commenced among the tribes. In the north of Angola, the revival among related tribes in the Congo affected Baptist work.

In southern Cameroon, from 1906 onward, the American Presbyterians witnessed a wonderful transformation of the M'bey people, regarded as thieves and cannibals by nearby tribesmen.[41] The Bulus also experienced a great awakening. Likewise in Cameroon, American Presbyterians reported 'most encouraging signs' of spiritual awakening, together with increased zeal in all evangelistic work in 1906.[42] The year following was even better, more than eight hundred men, women, and children having confessed Christ in a single church, where the attendance averaged a thousand.[43] It was announced that practically all those churches having native pastors had come to self-support in the previous two years.

In 1908, church attendance was reported on the increase, Sunday services at Elat attracting sixteen hundred people; at Lolodorf a thousand.[44] In 1909 was reported their 'greatest advance' upon that field, and a 'marvelous growth' in their churches, fed by a 'continuous revival.' Attendance at the July communion was 1200 at Batanga, 1600 at Efulon, 1700 at Lolodorf, and 3500 at Elat.[45] There were 2000 inquirers.

German missionaries reported a revival of interest in Christianity in Tanganyika fields. In Ostafrika, from 1888 to 1906, the fighting was almost continuous between Germans and native tribes,[46] sometimes a hundred tribes in revolt.

Near Mombasa,[47] the Church Missionary Society noted 'evident signs of the working of the Holy Spirit' in Freretown, but later news from the area proved disappointing:[48]

> There had always been a marked difference between the dioceses (Uganda and Mombasa) while they agreed in methods of work and in the type of men which they attracted to their staffs. In Uganda, more attention was paid to the training of African teachers and evangelists and there were fewer, but reasonably well-equipped, mission stations ... while in Kenya less emphasis was placed on the training of indigenous workers, and the European was often found working single-handed in an isolated station.

By late 1905, Christians in Uganda recognized that there was a need of numerical increase as well as spiritual uplift. Attendance had dropped and Christians were falling back into their old ways.[49] A 'cycle of prayer' was arranged for a month throughout the diocese of Uganda. Prayer was offered for the Bishop and clergy and workers, native and European both, various areas receiving attention from intercessors. The New Year of 1906 thus began in marked expectation.

In Uganda, awakening to spiritual life occurred in Toro country, resulting in intense conviction of sin and followed by awakening to missionary responsibility. In the year following, the Toro churches were still crowded out, communicants at Kabarole alone increasing from 1208 to 1376 in five years, the Christian constituency from 2286 to 4118. It was said that the ingathering of new converts caused a lowering of spiritual standards.[50]

Bishop Tucker reported in March, 1906, that[51]

> We are in the midst of the Mengo Mission services, which are being attended by vast crowds—between 3000 and 4000 at a single service. The preparatory work of prayer and visiting has resulted in much blessing and we are earnestly praying that large numbers of backsliders —some of whom we have not seen for years and who are daily attending services—may be restored.

This revival attracted the largest attendance of Baganda until then seen for any purpose, religious or otherwise! Morning meetings exceeded four thousand attending all the week through, and aggregate attendance was more than 50,000. Many were the conversions. Such was the deepening of spiritual life that the impact was felt over East Africa.[52]

Late that year, it was reported that church attendance by non-Christians was up by 33%. So great a change was experienced by inquirers that many postponed baptism as unimportant, later instruction reversing this trend. Local statistics reflected fewer revival results than expected: an epidemic of sleeping sickness was the reason.

In Nigeria, in West Africa, there was a great awakening in the Niger Delta, an extraordinary visitation of the Spirit marked by an agonizing conviction of sin among people whose notions of sin had hitherto been discouragingly feeble.[53]

A people's movement in Nigeria followed the Awakenings of 1905. Within a decade, the number of inquirers under instruction for membership in the Church Missionary Society Niger Mission rose to 20,668, a far cry from less than a thousand at the beginning of the century.

The 1900s were a time of pioneering for two interdenominational missions, the Sudan United Mission and the Sudan Interior Mission, the former[54] founded in 1904 by Karl Kumm and the latter[55] in 1893 by Rowland Bingham.

In Ghana also, there was marked improvement of the spiritual life of the churches, following the worldwide 1905 Awakening. The Wesleyan Methodists multiplied sevenfold in the next quarter of a century. African prophets arose to reach the tribes in the interior.

One among the many, a native prophet unrelated to any mission arose to preach in the hinterland of the Ivory Coast and Gold Coast. William Wadé Harris, a native of Liberia, influenced by some Anglican missionaries, came to Christian faith and felt a call of God to preach. Without foreign support or sanction, he began to itinerate with a message of the One True God, the observance of the Lord's Day, the destruction of all symbols of idolatry, and the renunciation of adultery. He won thousands of followers, as did others who copied him in method and message.[56]

Unlike the nativist Bantu prophets of South Africa, Harris urged his disciples to seek instruction from the missionaries, the Methodists gaining thereby a constituency which increased to more than a hundred thousand.

The Methodist Episcopal work in Liberia enjoyed a time of awakening. At Grand Cess, 200 people gathered for 5 a.m. prayer meetings, 700 for class meetings and 1200 for the preaching services on Sunday, continuing into 1909.[57]

Awakenings in Liberia continued into the next decade. A young woman dreamed that God had commanded her to put away ju-jus and seek God. The result of her obedience was the turning of many to righteousness, a Kru preacher taking over the care of the new church. Another awakening occurred in Kru territory after the believers had sought deliverance from a fearful drought. About forty young people professed conversion, and the enthusiasm spread to the nearby towns. Men and women would rise from sleep at midnight and hurry several miles along the beach for prayer. No building could accommodate the crowds attending the preaching.[58]

In North Africa, shadowed by Islam, 'the glory of the impossible' occurred also—for in 1903,[59] an awakening in the mission-sponsored college at Assiut in Egypt provoked fifty students freely to offer themselves for missionary service. By 1906 in Egypt, there were signs of an evangelical awakening, for a town of about twenty thousand in Upper Egypt (Nachaileh) became the scene of an 'amazing work' which thronged the assemblies of the Christians, emptied the resorts of vice, and converted thieves, robbers and drunkards, with 'at least one convert in every household.'[60]

In Algeria, the French evangelist from Paris, Reuben Saillens, addressed an audience of 1200 in Algiers on the subject of Revival in Wales, that meeting on 27th November 1905 being the precursor of lasting blessing. And in 1906, Saillens reported 'the most encouraging time ever known in Algiers.' A local theatre was crowded nightly by two thousand and many were the converts counselled in French.[61]

Throughout Africa, Christianity advanced in the first decade of the twentieth century. There were many factors in that growth, but the main factor was the phenomenon of evangelical revival appearing among African congregations. The missionary expert, David Barrett, has stated: [62]

> The fact is that, since around 1910, Africa has been the only one of the world's six continents in which the entire Christian community has expanded uniformly at a rate over twice that of the population increase.

No wonder that it was reported in 1910[63] at the Edinburgh Missionary Conference that 'by far the greatest progress of Christianity in Africa has been achieved in the past decade.'

17

REVIVAL, EASTERN INDIA

Five years before the end of the nineteenth century, a rising tide of spiritual expectation was noted in India. Books on the ministry of the Holy Spirit circulated, and the need of a pentecostal outpouring upon India was acknowledged. In Bombay, the first Saturday of each month was set aside for prayer for Bombay and for India. In other cities, there was similar concern—from Mussoorie in the north to the Nilgiris in the south, Christians met to pray for a spiritual filling.[1]

In 1897, the leaders of the Student Volunteers suggested 'a Day of Prayer for the Awakening of India,' which was observed in December in many parts. In August 1898, the Reverend R. J. Ward of Madras urged that another Day of Prayer be set apart;[2] it soon became an annual happening. So Bishop James Thoburn declared at century's end:[3]

> The next great movement of the kind will find India prepared for it throughout all its extended borders, and the results will be such as have thus far never been seen in the mission fields of the world.

It may be asked, why were such awakenings not experienced until the beginning of the twentieth century when evangelization had begun so much earlier? A possible clue to the answer may be found in a statement made by the Reverend W. T. A. Barber, of the Wesleyan Missionary Society, at the Ecumenical Missionary Conference in New York in 1900:[4]

> Now as far as my knowledge goes, ordinarily the Holy Spirit does not move on heathen populations (at any rate in Eastern lands) in this wondrous way. He does mightily save men in every heathen land, but revival in the sense we have learned to associate the term with the labours of such men as Moody does not occur among unprepared Chinese or Hindus. The remarkable thing is that such revivals do occur amidst the generations that have been leavened by the influence of Christian schools. When a year or two ago the Reverend Thomas Cook, one of our most successful English evangelists, made a special campaign in Ceylon, he found that many were brought to conversion, but, with scarcely an exception, every convert had been educated in mission High Schools.

There seems a certain 'coming of age' in Revival. The Awakenings of 1905 in Asia were indigenous, and the period was marked by a rising of Asian ministers and laymen to fuller responsibility.

R. J. Ward was one of those used to prepare India for the outpouring of blessing. He was an Englishman who had been in the ministry for all of twenty-seven years when he experienced a vital change at the Keswick Convention of 1891. In 1902, he joined with others in instituting a general prayer circle among missionaries of all denominations committed to pray for an outpouring of the Holy Spirit, reaching to a membership of more than 800 in India in a few years.[5]

At the same time that R. J. Ward was moved to a life of prayer in Britain before proceeding to India, an American student, John Hyde, had a similar experience and sailed for India in 1892.[6] Until the end of the century, John Hyde thus engaged in prayer more and more, until it became his consuming passion. As Ward was used in the South, Hyde was used in the North, forming a prayer fellowship also.[7]

At the turn of the century, a company of missionaries met together at a southern hill station, Kodaikanal, and decided that the time had come to pray defintely for a mighty awakening in the Indian Church.[8] They issued a prayer circular, and sent it to Britain, America and Australia to mobilize intercession for India.

That the Awakenings that followed in India were not unrelated and isolated movements was recognized, for a long-term missionary in India wrote at the time:[9]

> It will be difficult to dissociate our experiences from the great spiritual movements throughout the world. Ours seem to form only a small part of a wave that at present is encircling the globe.

The recognized antecedents of the 1905 Revival in India were first, united prayer overseas for Indian missions; second, a revival of Bible study in many missions in India; and third, the faith and obedience and self-sacrifice of many Indian Christians, particularly those in praying bands.

Pandita Ramabai became burdened for India's need of a revival. In 1903, she became interested in the movement of prayer in Australia which preceded the Torrey-Alexander campaigns there. In 1904, she learned of the Revival in Wales. Hence Pandita Ramabai commenced special prayer circles at the beginning of 1905, and hundreds of her helpers and friends attended the sessions at Mukti.[10]

The famine which distressed India in the year before the Revival redoubled the prayers of the Christians all over the country,[11] as also did the great epidemics that followed in its train of misery.

There was immediate contact also between Wales and Assam, for there were many Welsh missionaries serving up in the hills of Assam.[12] A Welshman, the Reverend John Roberts of Cherrapunjee, was on furlough in Wales in 1904.

Early in 1903, a church at Mawphlang in the Khasi Hills of central Assam announced Monday evening prayer meetings to seek an outpouring of the Holy Spirit throughout Khasia and all the world. In 1904, these prayer meetings became more fervent in spirit as, by the end of the year, the news from Wales created an immediate, heart-felt hunger.[13]

The annual General Assembly of the Khasia Presbyterian Church was held at Cherrapunjee in 1905, and it proved to be a remarkable one indeed. The delegates returned to their villages with increased faith and an intensified longing.

On the first Sunday in March, at Mawphlang, when their Bible lesson dealt with the baptism of the Holy Spirit, an unusual manifestation of feeling filled the congregation with prayer and weeping and praise.

A presbytery meeting at Pariong broke the pattern of its usual procedure. When the chairman invited one or two by name to lead in prayer, others also stood up to lead the congregation in intercession. It became impossible to close the usual service the following Sunday, simultaneous prayer and praise and weeping, and even fainting, affecting the congregation. These manifestations accompanied the extension of the awakening into other parts, and continued for eighteen months or so.[14]

The Khasi tribes people being head-hunters, with human sacrifice persisting in obscure cults, it is therefore interesting to note how the impact of the Welsh Revival affected the Christian community drawn from such people.

The intense conviction of sin which began in March gave way in June to a wave of rejoicing. In a united presbytery meeting of fifteen hundred folk, the singing overwhelmed the preaching, many of the awakened people dancing for joy, their arms outstretched, their faces radiant. Missionaries were astounded to see principal men and leading elders jump for joy. At first some missionaries disapproved, changing their minds as the revival transformed the Christians and won hundreds of non-Christians to the fellowship.[15]

There were setbacks in some quarters when 'spurious signs and prophecies' appeared, but the Khasi Christians quickly learned to distinguish between the true and false, noting the way of life of those deceived by alien impulses.

To the west of the Khasi Hills are the Garos who inhabit the hills where the Brahmaputra emerges into Bengal, an American Baptist field. By 1907, the Garos had a total of twenty-one churches with 5694 members, of whom 499 had been added by baptism.[16] Two years later, it was reported that work among the Garos was being maintained with more than ordinary aggressiveness.[17]

In 1906, tidings of awakenings were received from the Nowgong, Golaghat, Sibsagor and North Lakhimpur fields in Assam.[18] The Baptists stated that the Holy Spirit had of late 'moved in remarkable ways' along the Brahmaputra valley.

Nowgong was the first of these river stations to be reached by the revival influences which had so profoundly influenced the Khasi and nearby hills.[19] December 2nd, 1906, had been set aside as a Day of Prayer for India.[20] The Sunday morning worship went as usual, but in the 2 p.m. meeting of young men, followed by the women's meeting, all of the young people continued praying. Some broke out into bitter crying. Then followed confessions of sin, while groans and cries and earnest prayers arose. This continued until eight p.m. No one seemed to think of going out to prepare their rice for the evening meal. 'Showers of blessing are still coming,' the missionaries reported in 1907.[21]

At Nowgong, all the churches joined more or less heartily in a special 'concert of prayer' for a great advance in the kingdom of Christ as well as the salvation of the lost multitude, especially in the district and province. It continued for several months and was marked by a degree of spiritual enthusiasm that was refreshing, revival spreading from the valley towns to the hills.[22]

From North Lakhimpur, the awakening began to spread into the tribal areas north of the river Brahmaputra, the missionaries reporting in 1907:[23]

> The past nine months have seen a marvelous change in the condition of our churches. The growth in Christian knowledge, the giving up of old sins and of hidden heathen practices, a reaching out after the life and love of God, and a sense of responsibility for the conversion of the heathen, have characterized almost every church in the North Lakhimpur area.

The Awakening spread to south of the river. The revival was first manifested while a Bible class was in session in Golaghat at a conference which was attended by delegates from the churches. On Saturday night, the whole congregation broke down weeping and were in great agony because of their sins; both young and old cried for mercy. On Sunday, the meetings began as early as 6 a.m. and continued until nearly midnight, with only short intervals for meals.[24]

From Golaghat and Sibsagor, the Awakening spread south and southwest into the Naga Hills. The movement among the Naga Tribes proved less spectacular than that among the Khasis. The year 1905 'had been one of reaping as well as one of steady sowing of the seed.' Results had appeared in unexpected places and places where long years of work prepared the way. Thus the Naga Christian body grew.[25]

> We have not had an emotional revival, but the number of baptisms has been three times the average for the last five years and there has been in some directions a marked spiritual uplift... The association meeting this year was the most widely representative Christian gathering ever held in the Naga Hills.

Evangelists reported a great change in the attitude of the Angami Nagas toward the Gospel.[26] They claimed that people, listening well, were inquiring about Christ as never before.

In the year 1907, a large ingathering was reported from the Imphur field among the Nagas. The year was one of unusually large increase, and was one of more than ordinary success, for one hundred and three were baptized in a single out-station.[27] Evangelism among the Nagas went steadily forward, large additions to the churches being reported, as well as hundreds of converts who begged to be baptized.[28]

Christian influence in the Hills had become so great that in 1906 the Deputy Commissioner declared liberty of conscience for all Nagas, which act represented a deathblow to paganism among the Naga tribes.[29]

The news of the Khasi Hills Awakening was received among the Mizos (Lushai Hills tribes) far to the south, and stirred great interest in the Christian community,[30] Baptist down south and Presbyterian up north, both of Welsh origin.

Early in 1906, it was decided to send some young people to attend the Khasi Assembly held at Mairang. The party of ten set out—Chawngo, Khuma, Thanga, Pawngi, Thangkungi, Vanchunga, Siniboni from North Lushai (Presbyterian); and Thangkunga, Parima, Zathanga from South Lushai (Baptist).

They walked the whole distance through mountain jungle, taking two weeks. The ministry was all given in Khasi, of which they understood not one word. But they wondered at what they saw and sensed a strange power in it all. They made their way back to Lushai feeling sadly depressed. At Chatlang, two miles from Aijal, they paused to offer prayer and felt their hearts filled with a strange joy. (The revival was regarded by some as beginning here.) But the joy died away. At Aijal, prayer meetings were held every night for a week, but 'nothing happened.'

On 9th April 1906 (Monday), the three southerners decided that it was time for them to move on, for they still had four or five days' walking ahead. In a short farewell meeting, they were singing 'God be with you till we meet again!' when 'the Spirit was outpoured upon them' in a remarkable manner. Others from nearby houses joined them, and they continued in prayer and praise, with the phenomena of revival seen for the first time in Lushai. It spread to all parts, creating extraordinary interest.[31]

The Reverend D. E. Jones prophesied at one of these prayer meetings in Aijal that revival would break out in a very large village named Phullen, several days' journey from Aijal. So a teacher originating from Phullen set out, it being expected that he would initiate a movement; but upon his arrival four days later, he found that revival had begun at the time of the prophecy being made.[32]

As a result of the Awakening, membership in the Church increased, and hundreds gave their names as inquirers, but during the revival there was not the tremendous increase that occurred in Khasia. The chief characteristic was conviction of sin among believers and adherents.

Unlike the sweeping success of the Khasi work, one of the immediate results of the revival was an intense persecution of the Christians which broke out in the autumn. The growing churches in Phullen and surroundings suffered intensely. Christians were evicted at midnight from their villages and driven into the jungle. The chief and his henchmen made life miserable for believers in many villages. It was a sad time, but worse was to come. The 1907 persecution was followed by an 'anti-revival,' a resurgence of blatant heathenism that mimicked the revival in form, heathen lyrics being sung with great abandon and young people of both sexes dancing in ecstasy, followed by great feasts. It spread like wildfire, with demonstrations in every village.[33]

The Christian Church suffered a serious set-back in the anti-Revival, the leaders despairing. Paganism ran rampant in the Lushai Hills until, in 1911-12, the flowering of the bamboo brought a horde of rats. Although stores of rice had been laid up in anticipation, the rats appeared almost over-night and devoured the stores of food and the grain in the fields. The havoc was terrible. People subsisted upon roots in the hills, and the refugees poured onto the plains, while multitudes died of starvation. Missionaries cared for the orphans. In Wales, collections were made, and Christians in Lushai shared their food ungrudgingly with hungry pagan people. The distress and the charity brought an end to the pagan revival among the Mizos.[34]

Revival was rekindled in 1913, breaking out with great power at presbytery meetings in 1913, when the first Mizo was ordained to the pastorate. In 1919, an even greater Revival broke out simultaneously in three separated places, spread-ing with speed even to Tipperah and Manipur States. Four thousand were converted, more than the total number of current communicants.[35] Hymn-singing accompanied by the drum swept the land in a wave of rejoicing.

One effect of these Revivals, within a generation, was to make head-hunters into a predominantly Christian people, inhabiting India's most Christian and most evangelical area, in zeal far surpassing the early evangelized fields, as well as the places which claimed a thousand years or more of a traditional Christianity.

*   *   *   *

Half a century after the Assam Awakening among the Hill Tribes, the Nagas (twenty tribes) numbered 420,230,[36] the Khasi and Jaintia tribes, 389,969,[37] and Mizos of the Lushai Hills 224,180.[38]

The overall percentage of literacy in Assam province in 1961 was 27.36%, but typical Hill Tribe literacy was 44%— the figure for the Lushai Hills—and 86% among the Christian folk there. The total number of Christians in the Tribal Areas of Assam was 567,049 (highest per cent in India), and liter-ates among them were 474,189. In the Tribal Areas of Assam, many primary schools had been run by the churches, and these churches in Khasia, Jaintia and Lushai as well as in Nagaland were, by the mid-twentieth century, completely indigenous and self-propagating.[39] The Hill Tribes set forth, in indisputable evidence, the power of the Gospel to trans-form a primitive people.

The rapid Christianizing of the Hill Tribes encouraged interest in self-government. Tribes people encountering the communities upon the plains of Assam discovered that their standards of education and ethics were far inferior. Thus the Hill peoples began to think of themselves as a people apart—no longer apart because of head-hunting, but because of the success of a cultural and religious revolution.

How to satisfy this obvious desire for local autonomy while integrating the tiny populations into the secular society of the sub-continent of India became a problem for Indian statesmanship in the Government of the Republic of India, which wisely granted the project high priority.

*   *   *   *

It was in 1906 that revival was felt in many parts of Bengal.[40] In Calcutta, the Reverend D. H. Lee gathered his family, teachers and workers for a day of fasting and prayer on 9th February. Five days later, the house was 'full of prayer,' many praying audibly and some sobbing aloud. A number were 'brightly converted.' After much prayer, a number of Bengali young men formed an evangelistic band and toured the villages, the first being Janjara, a village on an island where converts were won among the islanders— the nucleus of a growing church.[41]

In October 1906, a group of sixty missionaries met at Darjeeling to hear the account given by a C.M.S. missionary, the Reverend E. T. Butler, of the awakening in the Nuddea district of Bengal. He prefaced his report by saying that he and his wife were matter-of-fact people engaged in a teaching ministry. Thus, when Revival came, it took everyone by surprise. The Anglicans also burst into simultaneous praying and confession of sin. Lives were transformed and earnestness replaced carelessness, while a number of people were converted. Butler spoke guardedly of the manifestations, but told of individuals entering a state of trance and of a meeting in which he saw pentecostal 'tongues of fire'— an interesting observation by an Anglican teacher.[42]

At Darjeeling, a Bengal Prayer Union was formed. Its members carried the revival longing far and wide in the language-area and many were the reports of local awakenings. These movements among the Bengalis were not to be compared with the Hill Tribes awakenings. Yet Bishop Robinson testified that he had seen more wonders in the Awakening in Bengal than in all his previous lifetime of service in India, and he wrote as a veteran.

18

SOUTH INDIA AWAKENINGS

The first movement of revival in Andhradesa occurred in the Akidu district in 1905, almost a year before the 1906 Awakening.[1] In September 1905, an evangelist (S. E. Morrow) went to Peddukapavaram where his ministry produced deep conviction of sin, followed by confessions.[2] At Siddapuram, villagers were so fearful that they could not sleep at nights until they had confessed openly to receive the forgiveness of God. The revival affected Atmakur in October. But in the greater part of Andhradesa, there was still no outbreak:[3]

> The number of members excluded or dropped seems to have been larger than usual. But this is often a good sign . . . the cutting off of dead wood will result in a healthier growth. It is a temporary separation which results in true repentance, reformation and restoration. One of the most encouraging things in the year's work was the unparalleled sale of Scriptures.

Ten months passed from the initial outbreak in the Akidu area. A missionary, E. S. Bowden of the Godavery Delta Mission, reported revival in Chettipet.[4] It began simultaneously at Akidu and Yellamanchili on Sunday 11th August 1906:

> The meetings last from five to ten hours and some even longer. Yet no one gets tired and the people are loth to leave even at the end of such sessions. There is no order of service, no leader, no sermon in any meeting except the divine order of the Spirit as He leads. Be it noted that there has been absolutely no human instrument in this wonderful visitation: we missionaries have taken no part in it except to pray, not even that in public at first.[5]

The very day the revival began, Dr. Brown, Secretary of the Canadian Baptist Mission Board, and Messrs LaFlamme and Craig were praying, burdened to tears, in an upper room in Toronto for an awakening in that area of Telugu country.[6]

One evening in 1906, at Chambers Hall in Nellore, it was agreed that the Telugu church should be asked to pray every evening until the blessing of revival came.[7] This continued for ten days until, one evening, 'the Spirit came' with power:

> There was a rumbling noise like distant thunder, and a simultaneous, agonizing cry went up from the whole congregation. Some were sobbing, some crying out, and all were confessing their sins and beseeching God for mercy. This continued far into the night.

The strange phenomena of revival were manifested in the movement which swept the churches of Nellore district.

A missionary had sent to Ongole some Telugu leaflets describing the great awakening in Wales.[8] Later, when the High School students were holding a Sunday English service, it became evident that a strange influence was pervading the place, each one present feeling that the Spirit of God was there. Eleven of the High School boys arose during this meeting and requested special prayers—later one of them, Professor J. Ramanjulu, recalled it to the writer.

Prayer meetings grew larger, lasted longer. Then came the usual April quarterly meetings for all the field workers and elders, for which the church had laid out a customary selection of lectures, papers and discussions. Dr. Boggs of Ramapatnam preached on Sunday morning and his sermon was heard with an unusual intensity of interest. The next morning early, the Lord's Supper was observed, followed by a season of prayer. Up to this time, the proceedings had been largely in the conventional order. The Rev. J. A. Baker, Dr. John Clough's successor, reported:[9]

> Suddenly without warning the usual stoical mindedness of our Indian assembly was broken as by an earthquake. Everyone present was shaken. One of the most quiet and retiring of our workers arose, striking his breast, and cried in Telugu in a loud voice 'Perishudatma!' (Holy Spirit!) 'Perishudatma!' Many others followed. For the first time at Ongole, the Holy Spirit of God was glimpsed in the act of convicting His people of sin.

Ordinarily, the workers returned to their own villages after the four weeks for which they received allowances; but this time they stayed on at their own expense for nearly two weeks more, holding meetings day and night. Before they left for their homes, many confessions had been made, old quarrels had been settled, and wrongs put right. The various schools of Ongole began to hold meetings of their own, often far into the night. The bed time hour was extended; their chapel was constantly in use by praying bands of students. Children in the boarding schools began saving rationed grain to share with unfortunates.[10]

After reaching their homes, the field workers spread the spirit of the meetings throughout many of the villages. During the hot months of April and May, while all the missionaries were away in the hills, revivals were constantly in progress over the field. In July came another conference. A missionary who had been in the midst of the revival in Wales, told quietly in Telugu the simple story of God's dealings with the people of his native land. There followed silent prayer. All heads were bowed and there was an intense stillness. Then, in a flash, the spirit of confession broke forth and swept through the assembly. A thousand Indian Christians were in the church, the volume of their prayers tremendous. Pagan people from nearby places came running to see what was the trouble, but no one heeded them.[11]

The Canadians reported frightening things.[12] A teacher was so convicted that he jumped up and ran from the church but fell upon his face a few yards from the door. He was brought to full confession and cleansing and soon began to pray and witness. At another village, he contracted cholera and died. His brother cursed God, crying: 'God, how dare you take my brother away.' Something snapped in his mind, and he became as a raving maniac. It was days before his reason and his faith returned. Elsewhere there was joy:[13]

> The Spirit came like a flood and we had three glorious weeks, which to experience is worth a lifetime. Our meetings were comparatively quiet with an occasional outburst of joyous laughing and clapping when some victory was gained. One woman went into a trance-like state and seemed to give messages directly from God.

A comparison of the annual statistics published by the Canadian Mission showed that the work was effective mainly among nominal Christians. The ingathering came later, the 1904 membership being 5924 and adherents 8276; the 1914 membership being 9,482 and adherents 13,909.[14]

Reports of the American Baptist Mission highlighted the Awakening: 58,898 communicants in 1904 had decreased to 54,649 in 1905, a loss of 4091; but the 54,327 communicants in 1906 increased to 56,001 in 1907, and to 56,525 in 1908.[15]

In the nearby American Lutheran missionfield at Guntur, baptized membership had risen in the decade 1890-1900 from 13,566 to 18,964; but in the revival decade it rose from 18,964 to 40,198; and in the Godavery district, baptized membership rose from 11,938 at the beginning of 1905 to 16,953 in 1910. Yet Lutheran records of the revival are scarce.[16]

The historians of Lutheranism in Andhradesa make no mention of the 1906 Awakening among Telugu churches, for whatever reason.[17] However, in Dolbeer's chapter titled 'the Upsurge: Reaping the Harvest,'[18] it is stressed that a large class of catechists was given Bible training at the time by Hermannsburg missionaries,[19] while in the Guntur Mission the staff of native workers, which had increased by 43 in the last decade of the old century, grew from 418 to 723 in revival times, a 600% acceleration.[20]

In the various local reports, one may uncover evidence of the impact of the Revival upon the Lutheran missions. Citing a fourfold increase of membership at Chirala,[21] it is noted that the Rev. E. C. Harris (appointed there in 1904) saw the local work develop 'very rapidly.' Rajahmundry reported 'steady growth' in the same period, as did other districts with but few exceptions.[22] These are evidences of an Awakening.

It was noteworthy that caste people displayed an interest in the Christian faith during the time of Revival, between 400 and 500 being baptized in the Guntur locality alone.[23]

The number of village congregations grew by about 25%, as reported by Lutheran missionaries, adding to the evidence for the conclusion that Lutheran work was just as strongly influenced by the movement which so powerfully affected the Baptists, even if the latter seemed more eager to report the phenomenal awakening to their home constituency.

There was a similar ingathering in Anglican fields in Andhradesa, taking on the proportions of a mass movement in some areas;[24] the Church Missionary Society grew steadily.

To the east of Hyderabad, in a neglected corner of the Nizam's Dominions, in Dornakal district, a folk movement occurred in the decade of the Andhra Awakening. It was guided by Vedanayakam Samuel Azariah, the first Indian Bishop.[25] In 1902, Azariah had accompanied Sherwood Eddy to Jaffna in Ceylon and was impressed. In February of 1903, he helped form the Indian Missionary Society of Tirunelveli.

The Anglicans of the Indian Missionary Society took over the field of the Dornakal Telugus, and within a decade, Azariah was consecrated a bishop. Baptizing three thousand a year for thirty years, Bishop Azariah followed methods developed in the earlier Tinnevelly Revival, as soon as possible appointing village workers and teachers as catechists, and then ordaining to the priesthood those who were qualified. Thus the results of the Revival in Andhra were conserved.

South of Andhra, Christians in Tamilnad were moved by
the Revival. Many in Madras had been praying for outpouring
of the Holy Spirit, for the Madras Missionary Conference
had issued a call to prayer and reported revival begun.[26]

At the close of 1905, the Rev. H. D. Goldsmith (serving
the Madras Divinity School of the Church Missionary Society)
reported Anglicans praying for the outpouring of the Spirit.
Zion Church of the Anglican Southern Tamil Pastorate in
Madras had been awaking to a real revival under its devout
Indian pastor, and its fervency communicated itself to the
Anglican Divinity School.   The Indian pastor commented:[27]

> I am passing through a new spiritual experience. I can
> not explain it in words. I dread the very idea of telling
> anyone about the great and wonderful things that God the
> Holy Spirit is commencing to do through 'the Revival.'

Night and morning meetings were held in the Sathyanathan
Memorial Hall. In the Northern Pastorate of the C. M. S.,
there were meetings attended by the same extraordinary
blessing as seen in other parts of Madras.[28]

Poles apart from Anglicans were the Christian Brethren.
Brethren missionaries were holding an annual conference
in Coimbatore in June, 1905, and visitors from the various
parts of India as well as members of the local assemblies,
Indians, Eurasians and Europeans, took part.

At the customary Sunday morning 'breaking of bread,'
the Holy Spirit came upon two or three 'in mighty power,
causing them to sob and cry out in pain for the sins of the
Church.' A season of confession and humiliation followed.
Wrongs were righted, questionable things judged and abandoned, and estranged brethren reunited.[29]

This went on until four o'clock in the afternoon, when
adjournment for the Sunday School and evening meeting became necessary. At the close of the evening meeting, many
sinners were converted. The believers again gathered and
confessions of the day continued till all had humbled themselves and were consciously right with God. Then, at three
in the morning, the long delayed service of Holy Communion
was completed by disciples rejoicing in forgiveness.[30]

Soon all the missionaries and visitors returned to their
stations, but the Revival continued in the local assemblies
at Coimbatore and nearby. Handley Bird, who had worked
twelve years in the area, wrote to his friends: 'God has come
to Coimbatore and we are like them that dream. Our mouth
literally is filled with laughter, our tongue with singing.'[31]

Various Congregationalists were moved and the London Missionary Society at Nagercoil experienced a quickening wave, the Rev. George Parker announcing that 'It is evident to all that the young men who were the terror and disgrace of the village are at any rate striving after holy living. There is also a renewed interest in Bible study.' [32]

The Danish Lutheran Mission at Tirukoilur reported a movement of the Spirit in their midst.[33] And at Chitoor, in North Arcot, among the staid Reformed people, there was a great awakening in October of 1906, the leader being Dr. Scudder. There was 'a great breaking down under conviction of sin,' with the usual accompaniments of manifestations of the Spirit.[34]

The result was a time of witnessing by life and word; more joy in the study of the Word and in prayer; keener sense of sin; more love for brethren; and greater sense of responsibility for the salvation of friends and townsfolk. This was said about Chitoor. It applied to countless places.

A Wesleyan Methodist missionary, the Rev. C. H. Monahan, also reported from Chitoor:

> Some weeks before I went, the Holy Spirit had fallen on the people. What struck me was the fact that men who before were all too ready to spend the time in talk, seemed now to be possessed with the one desire to spend all the time of the meeting in the study of the Word of God and prayer.

Amy Carmichael, in common with other folk in Tamilnad, had been praying with her helpers for a visitation of the Holy Spirit to all of India ever since the Welsh Revival and its overflow upon the Khasi Hills. Thus she wrote: [35]

> On October 22nd, to quote one of the little girls, Jesus came to Dohnavur. He was there before, but on that day He came in so vivid a fashion that we cannot wonder that it struck the child as a new Coming.

It was at the close of the morning service that the break came. Amy Carmichael, the one who was speaking, was obliged to stop, overwhelmed by sudden realization of the inner force of things. It was impossible even to pray. One of the older lads in the boys' school began to try to pray, but he broke down, then another, then all together, the older lads chiefly at first. Soon many among the younger ones began to cry bitterly and pray for forgiveness. It spread to the women. Amy Carmichael found it hard to recall all the details of that eventful day:

> It was so startling and so aweful—I can use no other
> word—that details escaped me. Soon the whole upper
> half of the church was on its face on the floor, crying
> to God, each boy and girl, man and woman, oblivious
> of all others. The sound was like the sound of waves
> or strong wind in the trees.

.   .   .   .

Amy Carmichael continued her narrative thus:

> For the next fortnight, life was apportioned for us much
> as it was for the apostles when they gave themselves
> continually to prayer and to the ministry of the Word.
> Everything else had to stand aside. At first the move-
> ment was almost entirely among convert boys, school-
> boys, our own children and workers, and some younger
> members of the congregation. But as the older ones
> were caught in the current, more or less, at first it was
> impossible to gauge its real depth.

What were the results? Looking back after nearly seven
months of testing, they had enough of true results to make
them sing with all their hearts. Almost all of the children
were truly 'out and out' converted. Most of the workers too
were thoroughly revived. The bungalow servants were greatly
blessed and backsliders restored. Many of the schoolboys
were converted and very few, if any, of the convert boys were
unchanged. In the village, there were several notable conversions and the true Christians were quickened to walk in
newness of life. Anglican parishes around were moved.

The appetite for blessing was quickened also, for Amy
Carmichael wrote: 'For all this we do praise God . . . We
have seen just enough to make us very hungry to see more.'

Christian communities in both highlands and lowlands of
Mysore received a stirring through the Indian Awakening of
1905.[36] There were local revivals from the Kolar goldfields
in the southeast to Belgaum in the northwest. The Kanarese
churches of all denominations shared in the movement, and
rural areas as well as city circuits felt the impact.

The missionaries and national Christians with amazement
and expectation heard of the strange movings of the Spirit,
first in faraway Assam and then in other parts of Dravidian
India.[37] It was not long before their prayers were answered.
The answers came in the same way experienced in other
parts of India, in conviction of sinners and confession of sin,
followed by conversions. On the west coast of India, 'wonderful scenes' were witnessed, and extraordinary confessions
of sin among the congregations were followed by outright
conversions of outsiders.

The English Wesleyan missionaries reported details of revival in their various Indian fields in 1906, there being marked results in their Kanarese churches, particularly in Bangalore and Tumkur circuits, a typical awakening.[38]

The characteristics of the Awakening were a 'quickened sensitiveness to sin, a keener experience of godly sorrow for it, instant continuance in prayer, a clear grasp of forgiveness and acceptance.' One missionary gave way to misgivings at a station, saying 'emotionalism overflowed its banks.'[39]

Walker of Tinnevelly conducted a successful mission in the great cantonment city Bangalore,[40] congregations of all denominations reaping the benefit of his sane evangelism. And the German Lutherans of the Basel Mission around Mangalore reaped a harvest following an awakening in 1906 on the coast of Kannara. In the opening years of the twentieth century, their enterprises and churches were Indianized.[41]

Among American Methodists, who had just taken over the Belgaum operations of the London Missionary Society, arose a spirit of expectancy. Church members were higher caste. The pioneer J. H. Garden declared in 1902[42] that an awakening would bring thousands of outcastes into the Christian Faith.

The awakening in Belgaum started through a revival in a girls' orphanage and spread to the local churches.[43] There were limits of outreach, so far as the higher castes were concerned, but at their door were thousands of interested outcastes. Within a few years, low caste people in Belgaum and Bailhongal circuits were entering the Church.[44]

Ready for innovation, the American Methodists 'clinched their contacts' with the groups of interested low-caste folk from 1905 onwards, the resultant growth being regarded as a great triumph of the Gospel. Four thousand in 1905 had become forty thousand by 1925. The whole of the Methodist fields of the South India Conference gained in the movement.

As early as 1904, an increase of baptisms heralded the beginning of a group movement into the Methodist fellowship at Shorapur, and a Home Missionary Society was begun in the Raichur area in 1905, and within five years low caste people were being discipled by the growing Church.

In 1905, the Church Missionary Society noted a 'great spiritual thirst in Kerala.'[45] It was stated that 'God was about to breathe into the dry bones new life and power.' The effect of the general awakening in Kerala in 1905 was immediately felt in the Mar Thoma and Anglican and all other evangelical communities in Kerala.[46]

It is recognized that Walker's ministry built up an expectancy of revival in Kerala after 1900.[47] A convert of the Wardsworth and David Awakening, Punchamannil Mammen by name, received a call from God during the prayer times of 1904. In his meetings in Kizhakkenmuthoor, Tiruvalla and Venmoney, there was much conviction of sin and weeping and repenting and confessing. The people flocked in from other towns, and the evangelist extended work to Alleppey, Niranam and Kattunilam. In Venmoney, the people skipped for joy, which caused some questioning.[48]

In the year following, Punchamannil Mammen preached in Tiruvalla, Kottayam, Kunnamkulam, Mepral, Kottarakara, and Chengannoor, visiting Malayalam-speaking churches in Madras also, with much encouragement.

The 1905 awakening in Kunnamkulam in Kerala was typical of the movement among Malayalis. Kunnamkulam was a large town of 8000, all of them Syrian Christians.[49] The revival began with prayer that soon brought conviction of sin. There were demonstrated in a very practical manner genuine repentance, open confession, immediate restitution, unity and love. The outcome of the movement was seen in the ending of all personal animosities, the settling of social quarrels, and the mediation of congregational disputes, even former enemies uniting in the 'praying-and-preaching bands' that evangelized the nearby villages.

The 1905 Awakening in Kerala was marked by simultaneous audible prayer, which was alien to both the Anglican and Mar Thoma liturgical traditions. Some Anglican missionaries criticized the informality of the movement, but they readily admitted its power and the sincerity of its prophets.[50] Even at Maramon Convention, seventeen thousand people broke into simultaneous audible prayer.[51]

Effects reported in the 1905 Revival were deep repentance, joy in the Spirit, and a desire to spread the Good News to the unconverted. In some places, Christians and Hindus were taken up with visions of holy doves and sacred fire, but the Hindu converts were found standing true after fifty years.[52]

The Mar Thoma Sunday School Samajam was founded in 1905 and in sixty years grew from fifty to 800 Sunday Schools, with 5000 teachers and 60,000 pupils. From a community total of 37,713 in the 1901 census, the Mar Thoma Church increased to 74,866 in 1911, an almost 100% gain, its 135 congregations served by more than eighty clergy. In the second decade, it increased 50%.[53]

19

REVIVAL, WESTERN INDIA

Ramabai, daughter of a Brahman scholar who believed that a girl could be educated, influenced by Anglo-Catholic folk in Poona, was baptized as a young widow in England in the year 1883.[1] She became an outstanding educationalist.

Ramabai also became a dedicated Christian, regarded as a saint. Paraphrasing Hindu lyrics, she could have said:[2]

> Christ have I sought;
> The price He asked I paid:
> Some cried 'Too great!'
> While others jeered 'Twas small!'
> I paid in full,
> Weighed to the utmost grain,
> My love, my life,
> My self, my soul, my all.

Pandita Ramabai returned to India with a great concern for the lot of young and neglected widows who were forbidden by Hindu custom to marry again. Famine led her to extend her care to orphans, and soon she had a remarkable work in Maharashtra near Poona at Mukti, 'place of deliverance.'

Besides teaching the orphans and training the widows, Ramabai paid occasional visits to the Western countries. On her way home from the United States in 1898, Ramabai attended the Keswick Convention in England and requested four thousand people there to pray for the evangelization of India. She sent her daughter to Australia to enlist prayer not only for the widows but all the people of the country.[3]

As noted, Pandita Ramabai developed an interest in not only evangelism, but the revival of the Church at large.[4] In late 1904,[5] she learned of the Welsh Revival and rejoiced in an expectation of a similar movement in India in due time. Narayan Vaman Tilak, ordained in 1904, was at Mukti in Kedgaon with Ramabai in early 1905.[6] Pandita Ramabai had commenced special prayer circles at the beginning of 1905, and hundreds of helpers and friends attended these sessions at which incessant prayer was offered for the reviving soon of the work of God in India.[7]

Not only the workers but the students there participated. At 3.30 a.m. on June 29, a senior girl had an extraordinary spiritual experience.[8] On June 30, Ramabai was expounding the eighth chapter of John in a quiet way when her hearers began to pray aloud, more and more engaging in it, until the volume of simultaneous prayer brought the lesson to a close.

Girls were stricken by conviction of sin, and the school became a vast inquiry room for the penitents. Conviction was followed by confession. Noteworthy were all the emotional accompaniments, the physical phenomena, the sensation of burning, simultaneous prayer, and speaking with tongues, and (later) women praying with loud crying, though always Ramabai conducted herself quietly.

What must have been the thoughts of this well-educated Indian lady of highest caste, influenced in her Christian ideas of propriety by Anglo-Catholics when the phenomena of an evangelical awakening burst upon her spiritual family? Said Ramabai, in her prayer letter two years later: 'I looked upon these features with much concern for some time, but did not try to interfere with God's work in any way.'[9]

But another reference by her own pen showed that Pandita Ramabai tried to lay down some rules for the work of the Lord at the beginning of the Revival:[10]

> But I soon found that I stopped the work of the Holy Spirit by interfering with it. I wanted to be proper and conduct meetings in our old civilized ways. But God would have none of it. He laid His hand upon me, put me low in the dust, and told me that I had better take my proper place, that of a worm. He said, 'My thoughts are not your thoughts, neither are your ways My ways.' I humbled myself under this severe rebuke and took my hand off the work. The Holy Spirit has full liberty.

The awakening went its way utterly unhindered. There consequently resulted the conversion of hundreds of young women. Dr. Nicol MacNicol, Ramabai's more scholarly biographer, wrote in retrospect: 'Those whose religion in 1907 seemed too emotional to endure long, twenty years later were bearing their witness steadfastly.'[11]

The awakening at Mukti was revolutionary in its scope. The results, reported Pandita Ramabai, were 'most satisfactory.' Lives were changed, rebel wills were subdued, undisciplined natures were brought under a higher control, with purity instead of grossness; uprightness and fidelity for falsehood and deceit; gladness instead of gloom.[12]

An older girl who 'had sinned against the light' and was hardened in heart came under the hand of God and was truly converted. No indication of illness had been noticed, for she was doing her usual work and attending school.[13] On July 5, she was being instructed in Bible when she was taken suddenly ill and died within an hour. Doctors and nurses gave her every attention. She remained conscious to the last and told the nurse on duty that the Lord standing by was calling her to Himself.

The veteran world-evangelist, G. H. Lang of the Christian Brethren, wrote about his visit to Mukti, and commented on something quite alien to Brethren practice:[14]

> It was a new experience to hear a thousand women and girls praying aloud at one time. The sound rose and fell like the roar of the sea or the wind in a forest. But what to a Westerner might seem like mere confusion did not so strike me, for I had before heard in Egypt a whole school of boys similarly. The mind of each was on his own recitation undisturbed by the noise around. Similarly, each woman and girl was oblivious of the rest and, when each finished praying, she arose quietly from the ground and left the hall.

Lang asked 'What is the force of Acts iv, 24?' When the disciples lifted up their voice with one accord, does it mean that the whole company was suddenly moved by the One Spirit to say unitedly the same words? 'The New Testament was not written as a description of modern conferences,' commented he. The present writer has heard the same sort of simultaneous praying among European people in Latin America and the Soviet Union.

At first, Ramabai refused to permit even true friends to publish an account of the Mukti movement. She was convicted of refusing to give the glory to God so she permitted accounts to be sent to Christian newspapers in Bombay and in other Indian cities.[15]

Then she took a band of revived workers to Poona, forty miles away, planning a series of prayer meetings to reach the Indian Church. In these meetings, there was no break, but in the meetings held in schools and orphanages there came an awakening similar to that at Mukti.[16] It was noticed that the waifs of the famine being cared for on principles of faith were the first to receive blessing. An orphanage at nearby Dhond was so moved, and another in faraway Allahabad in the plain of the Ganges.[17]

The Free Methodist Mission at Yeotmal in the eastern parts of Maratha country closed its schools in order to intercede for Revival. In the last week of August 1905, on Saturday night, 'the power of the Spirit came like lightning,' it was said by the missionaries.[18]

The Methodist churches in Bombay city next received a visitation of the revival spirit,[19] followed by other churches and schools of other denominations.

The Friends' Mission in Hoshangabad held four days of meetings to intercede for blessing. The visitation came as a 'rushing mighty wind,' and within moments hundreds were praying publicly and simultaneously.[20] Miss Evans, a deaf missionary, commented: 'Being deaf, I rarely hear a prayer, but in the rush of sound I could plainly hear those around me and how direct and different each prayer was.' Confession of sin and restitution followed that first outpouring.

The annual Mela of the Friends' Mission in January of 1906 proved to be an extraordinary time of blessing, the revival at Hoshangabad having stirred other congregations.

At Khudawandpur, the news of the awakening in Poona stirred the Boys' Orphanage, a blind lad being the first converted.[21] Some there were who scoffed at the manifestations, whereupon a missionary who had prayed all night delivered a message in Marathi from Isaiah xxviii, 'Therefore hear the word of the Lord, you scoffers. . .' Such a conviction fell upon the hearers that an agony of soul continued for five or six days. The missionaries were moved to humble themselves before their Indian brethren. The awakening moved nearby orphanages in Bhaisdehi and Chikalda.[22]

In November 1905, a band of girls from Mukti arrived at Ratnigiri, on the Maharashtra coast.[23] They began by praying for the Ratnigiri people, and soon their voices were joined by a general outbreak of prayer in the room.[24] On December 3rd, a day of prayer for India, the local people used the time to put their affairs right with God. Next day, a Biblewoman in agony of spirit confessed the sin of having robbed the Lord. Confession of sin went on all the succeeding week. It ended in songs of deliverance and dancing for joy; and a determined outreach to the unbelievers around followed.[25]

The Mukti bands continued to visit towns and villages in Maratha country, reporting the same extraordinary praying, conviction of sin, and confession, restitution, reconciliation and restoration, with aggressive evangelism and with many conversions of unbelievers.[26]

In April 1906, a call came from the Church Missionary Society at Aurangabad for a praying band from Mukti to visit the congregation. Fifty preachers had gathered from eleven churches. The awakening began among the young men of the Normal School. The preachers objected to the simultaneous audible prayer and to confession of sin in public, and to the ministry of women. Summer heat had reached 109 degrees in the shade, and yet the meetings went on, overcoming the handicaps, physical and spiritual.[27]

A girl on vacation at Aurangabad returned to the C.M.S. School in Bombay, where an extraordinary movement ensued. Not only were the girls revived and restored and converted to God, but phenomena followed. One Christian girl had been accused of stealing. The girls in assembly were faced with the matter. No one would admit the theft. They went to prayer and independently two girls reported to their teacher that they had been 'shown' in prayer the guilty one, who first denied but then confessed her guilt.[28]

Revival was felt in the Gujerati fields in 1906.[29] At the Dholka Orphanage of the Christian and Missionary Alliance there were cries of penitence at the Sunday prayer meeting. Missionaries were amazed to find orphan boys leading spontaneous prayer meetings, even at midnight. Protracted meetings followed, days and nights, with repentance, confessions, and restitution. Sixty rupees of conscience money were restored, as well as stolen articles from blankets to pins. The head carpenter returned ten stolen rupees. Not one of the 300 boys and youths was untouched and a wave of evangelism surged from the place to villages roundabout, continuing for months.[30]

It is suprising to note that at Dholka, among the Alliance missionaries and people, glossalalia occurred in the wake of the 1906 Revival. A report in the Christian and Missionary Alliance journal commented that 'nearly all' missionary and many Indian workers had spoken in tongues, with some interpreting.[31] This occurred at least one full year after the general movement. There was both approval and disapproval of glossolalic phenomena in the Alliance constituency at home in the United States at that time.

Speaking in tongues was by no means general during the Indian Awakening of 1905. Instances[32] are recorded rarely, as at Mukti, where young women in Pandita Ramabai's charge had so spoken. Pentecostal missionaries arrived far later, after the development of Pentecostalism in Britain.

20

NORTH INDIA AWAKENINGS

There is a great contrast between South India, which is predominantly Dravidian in race and speech, and the North, which is Aryan. As a friend of the present writer pointed out to Mr. Nehru's cabinet, the South has had the advantage of a longer British connection, a higher standard of education and a greater number of Christians. It is not surprising that (apart from the non-Aryan tribal areas of Assam) the 1905 Awakening in India affected the South more than the North. Yet what happened in North India was extraordinary.

The Punjab—the 'Land of the Five Rivers'—in the early twentieth century, before the secession, was wholly in India. In 1905, with its mixed population of Muslims, Sikhs and Hindus, it became another 'storm centre' of the Awakening.[1]

John Hyde, an American student volunteer, from the time of his arrival in India in 1892 had more and more devoted himself to intercessory prayer. Praying Hyde, as he was called, with a group of friends, spent days and nights in prayer for an awakening throughout India.

Their prayers were answered in a series of outpourings of the Spirit in the north-west of India, beginning in 1904 in Sialkot.[2] A decided spiritual upheaval occurred in a girls' school directed by Mary Campbell, resulting in confession of sins and repentance toward God.[3] The revival spirit next touched a theological seminary, but missed a boys' school where the director was afraid of the dynamic movement. A new principal, Dr. W. B. Anderson, then called for united prayer meetings.[4] Missionaries and nationals were stirred and the results were seen in a deepening of spiritual life of the Christians of the area, followed by a widening outreach of evangelism among non-Christians.[5]

A Convention for the Deepening of Christian Life was held at Sialkot in the first year of revival. Pengwern Jones, of the Welsh Khasi Hills Mission, in August addressed this convention.[6] Time came to close the meeting, but instead the whole congregation fell before God. Confessions of sin 'often shocked the hearers but later were found hard to remember.'

153

Through the influence of the Sialkot Convention, a local awakening began at Ludhiana.[7] The greatest work was done in the boys' school, a typical outcome of the movement in other parts of North India.

The Sialkot Convention of 1906 increased in size and power.[8] Instead of 300, there were 1300 present, besides seventy missionaries. By day and night, intercession was a continuing feature. It was noticed that those who had come to mock or to criticize were those who were convicted and, in agonies of spirit, were humbled to the ground.

The issue of public confession of private sin was raised and after much prayer it was agreed that confession should be made to God and to any brother wronged, and only publicly if the Spirit of God clearly commanded the individual, never because of pressure from others.[9]

These Sialkot Conventions continued year by year, with a fresh outpouring each year that was felt in widening circles throughout India.[10] Hyde remained a praying force behind the scenes; in 1911 he returned home, dying of cancer in 1912. His prayer life influenced many outside India.

A student in one of the American Presbyterian Mission schools was a young Sikh named Sundar Singh.[11] On 18th December 1904, Sundar Singh had a vision of Jesus Christ, so was converted. He became a Christian Sadhu evangelizing in India and Tibet, into which he disappeared without trace a quarter of a century later. Sadhu Sundar Singh was one of the most unusual of evangelical mystics, exercising a wide ministry in Europe and America.

Revival began at a Church of Scotland camp at Kathala in the Punjab. The good influence of the Sialkot Convention brought the movement among the Young Men's Christian Association campers in several places.[12]

The Church Missionary Society reported a 'widespread spirit of prayer in the Punjab' in 1905[13] and in the following year began a folk movement with 1500 inquirers at Narowal and nearby villages.[14]

An awakening began at Jammu in Kashmir, where liquor drinking and quarreling had disgraced the local church. As confession swept the congregation, ending the troubles of the time and refreshing the workers, the church prospered.

At Dehra Dun, influence of the Sialkot revival brought about an awakening.[15] There was a similar movement begun at Landour by Indian young men whose vital experience disarmed the opposition of the critics.[16]

As far north as Almora, in the foothills of the Himalayas, there were scenes of revival. An awakening occurred at Pilibhit, in the shadow of the ranges, where the experienced American evangelists, Mr. and Mrs. Salisbury, were holding meetings for the Industrial Evangelistic Mission.[17]

After usual evangelism, the movement began with the lads in training; then among the workers came confession of sin; then conviction among hearers, followed by confession, restitution and return of stolen property. The lads went in bands to the farmers nearby, whose fields or orchards they had robbed and asked forgiveness, which was granted often with tears. The news spread around the villages, and the people began to ask what it all meant, leading to fruitful evangelism of non-Christians.

The Salisburys communicated the revival to the Mussoorie branch of their Mission, with the same results beginning among the young men in training there.[18]

The Church Missionary Society congregation at Meerut experienced an awakening in October of 1905.[19] There had been much prayer for two years. The first sign of coming blessing came when a couple of members prayed for an infilling of the Holy Spirit. Then the Anglican missionary dealt with a couple of penitents and their wives. This was followed by 'heart-searching' prayer meetings where confessions of sin and failure were freely made, often with tears and generally with broken voice. In ten days there were fifteen cases of conversion, unusual in North India churches where the response had been so limited and infrequent.

There were no unusual manifestations but the depth and reality of the Spirit's working was acknowledged by all who were concerned; quarrels were made up and peace passing all understanding prevailed in the congregations.[20]

There was an awakening at the Reid Christian College at Lucknow at the beginning of 1906 and Walker of Tinnevelly's preaching mission there brought blessing to Anglicans and Methodists and other believers.[21]

At Moradabad, in February of 1906, revival appeared in a Methodist School for young women and girls. The largest assembly room was opened for evening prayers. On 8th March, there was an outpouring of the Spirit, but Principal Means was absent and the school janitor insisted on turning the girls out of the hall at 9 p.m. They continued upon the verandahs, and the movement went on in great power and with fruitful results.[22]

A same sort of movement was felt in Bareilly where the spirit of prayer began among young people, as before. It was reported that while the girls in one school were engaged in praying for the boys in another community, some of the lads were converted in their dormitories.

The Methodist Bishop Warne claimed that two hundred young folk set themselves apart in a covenant to enter the Christian ministry, knowing well that it was not a lucrative prospect compared to others for which their education qualified them in life. The Bareilly Theological Seminary received an influx almost at once.

Everything seemed to have gone wrong at the Methodist Church in Allahabad,[23] Hindi workers becoming desperate. The prayers of several of the multiplying praying bands were enlisted. The situation seemed beyond remedy.

The revival movement began quite suddenly in a mid-week prayer meeting, with a deep sense of conviction of sin upon all who were present. It seemed impossible to close the meeting, so the Indian pastor announced special meetings that continued for many weeks, with 'conviction, confession, restitution, an earnest effort to put wrong things right, then the consciousness of pardon and unspeakable joy.' The result was that the church was completely transformed; old troubles were settled; enemies were reconciled; evangelism was extended; and the workers went out to preach. Not long after, a District Conference succeeded in spreading revival throughout congregations and mission stations near and far in north-central India.[24]

Quite a new atmosphere was reported in Agra after Walker of Tinnevelly's meetings in 1906. The ten days of ministry left an indelible mark.[25] The Anglican evangelist toured the cities of the north in 1906, 5500 miles all told, reporting a 'floodtide of blessing.'[26] In the aftermath of revival, Thomas Walker wrote: 'Special missions are being called for everywhere. Both the missionary body and the Indian Church are feeling as never before the need of power from on high.'[27]

American Presbyterians reported a great ingathering throughout their fields in North India, which stretched from the borders of Afghanistan to Allahabad. Christian strength in Fatehgarh, Etah, Manipuri and Etawah had grown to 15,000 in 1907, of whom 1,000 had been baptized in the previous four years.[28] For example, Fatehgarh in 1904 had a fellowship of 1200 Christians, but a short five years later there were 6000 enrolled—a 400% increase.

Of the folk movements in the Punjab, it was reported that the Christian constituency, which had doubled between 1891 and 1901 to 37,695, had in the revival decade more than quadrupled to a total of 163,994.[29]

In 1912, an international review of missions reported that the Christian constituency of India had increased by 69.9% as compared with 16.3% among Muslims and 4.6% among Hindus.[30] Thus in one decade, Christians grew sixteen times as fast as the Hindu majority.[31] The Awakening of 1905 was undoubtedly the major factor.

As in the South, the Awakening manifested itself as a 'catharsis of the Church' throughout North India. The impact was one on believers. Following the Revival, regular evangelism and folk movements added multitudes to the Christian community in the North.

The Alliance missionaries noted that after the period of intense prayer and agonizing conviction, the joy of release, dynamic in itself, brought action:[32]

> The revival had given a new body of native evangelists and most of our native preachers have experienced a baptism of the Holy Ghost which has completely transformed their spirit and work.

It is significant that numbers of Indian evangelists and workers doubled 1900-1905, and doubled again 1905-1910. A few years only the actual Awakening lasted, but it was noted that the need of such a revival remained uppermost in mind among those who looked for the redemption of India.[33]

Before the end of the first decade of the twentieth century, Walker of Tinnevelly commented:[34]

> India is in an interesting transition stage; but, spiritually speaking, there seems to be a reaction at present from the promise of the widespread revival that seemed so imminent a few years ago.

Transition? The missionaries noticed that, in the 1905 Revival, independence of the national Church was stressed, for, in the aftermath of revival, new men were ready for new work in new fields, men who had formerly been agents and employees of the Missions now were carrying revival and evangelism to the villages with a possibility of extension of self-government, self-support, and self-propagation,[35] this within the framework of a self-governing country. It is no coincidence that the first all-India Evangelical Awakening occurred at the same time as the Russo-Japanese War in which Asian nationalism received a powerful impetus.

21

THE CHINESE QUICKENING

In the last decade of the nineteenth century, the Empire of China suffered humiliation after humiliation at the hands of foreign powers.[1] The rising anti-foreign feeling became directed against missionaries as well as other foreigners.

In 1900 came the Boxer movement. It cannot be described as a Rebellion, seeing that it was encouraged by the Imperial Government of China. On the last day of 1899, the Boxers killed a British missionary.[2] The Empress gave an order to execute all foreigners. A blood bath ensued, in which one hundred or more missionaries were done to death along with thousands of their Chinese Christian converts.[3]

The Western Powers intervened with strong military forces and captured Peking. The old order was doomed. The Chinese Christians had acquitted themselves bravely in their hour of martyrdom and persecution, so much curiosity and interest was aroused in the hearts of acquaintances. An itinerating bishop reported that all the churches were crowded to capacity,[4] with increased opportunities of preaching.

The twentieth century Awakening in China, it seems, occurred in three phases: there was a prayer movement between 1900 and 1905; there was a widespread awakening in 1906 and 1907; and there was extraordinary revival throughout 1908 and 1909, continuing until the Revolution in 1911.

In the spring of 1900, a revival of great power swept the North China College and a nearby church at Tungchow. It proved to be a baptism for future suffering. The meetings progressed from times of confession to times of consecration, awakened joy continuing for three weeks or more. Regular work in the College was stopped while students toured the surrounding countryside with an impact that was felt in Peking, Paoting and Tientsin. In the Boxer Uprising, forty of these young men were done to death.[5]

In early 1900, an awakening occurred in the Anglo-Chinese College in Foochow, described by the Reverend Llewellyn Lloyd of the C.M.S. as without parallel in China.[6] A high proportion of the students (about 70) professed conversion.

Manchuria[7] was already being moved by revival in 1903. The awakening 'spread simultaneously through almost every district, humbling, gladdening, and establishing churches, remote and near.'

Early in 1903 in the far South, there was a great ingathering at Canton, 747 being added to the little churches upon examination in the faith.[8] In 1903, the Fukien Prayer Union was formed to enlist both missionaries and nationals to pray for the manifestation of the Spirit's power.[9] The effects were seen at the next August Convention at Kuliang, where unusual blessing ensued.[10] The churches in the districts around Amoy were also moved by a spirit of revival in 1905. It was the same in the West, and missionary writers were commenting upon the 'general spirit of prayer in Central China.'[11]

Throughout 1904 the movement continued. In many places there were results in changed lives. The missionaries and nationals alike were 'praying that China might experience a similarly gracious visitation of the Holy Spirit as has recently been seen in Wales.'[12] The answer came in 1906,[13] when[14]

> China also ... had its revivals this year, especially in the north. It is significant that here and in Shanghai and Canton, the initiative has been so often and so largely Chinese. These revivals have been marked by a wholly unusual conviction of sin and by great anxiety for the conversion of friends and neighbours ...
>
> Five denominations in Nanking united in holding the meetings under the leadership of a Chinese evangelist who had left a lucrative government position to take up this work.

Again the reports showed that the awakening was north, south, east and west. In four years prior to 1906, Chinese communicants jumped from a total of 113,900 to 178,000, an increase of approximately 57%.[15]

A 'gracious movement of the Spirit' in Chihli Province brought a widespread conviction of sin, a spirit of prayer and an eagerness to witness for Christ in the churches.[17] It was most marked at Tsangchow where the London Mission had been stirred by news of the Welsh Revival. Students responded most eagerly to the ministry.

Prayer meetings at sunrise in Tsingtao in 1906 attracted six hundred praying people, one lasting from 6.30 a.m. until the afternoon. Soon the Shantung believers experienced an awakening 'resembling the day of Pentecost,' marked by confessions, apologies, and reconciliations occurring in the prayer meetings that went on long after midnight.[18]

At the Union College in Weihsien in Shantung, 196 students out of 200 publicly professed faith. Near Tsingtao, the people of a place distressed by open quarrels were greatly convicted by the Spirit of God, falling on their faces and crying to God for mercy. In another place, dawn prayer meetings began the movement, and in another a prayer meeting lasting nearly six hours resulted in abandoning of law suits in the fellowship.[19] Other communities in northern provinces saw a similar demonstration of spiritual catharsis.

On the east coast of China, revivals occurred. The redoubtable Fredrik Franson, of the Scandinavian Alliance Mission,[20] visited Foochow in the autumn of 1904 and stirred college students.[21] Through the ministry of a Chinese evangelist, the work spread through all the churches of Foochow district. There was similar revival in Soochow. A spiritual awakening began in 1906 in churches in the city of Yanchow in Kiangsu, north of the Yangtse River.[22] The spirit of revival affected churches in Shanghai and upriver also.

In 1907, an evangelical awakening occurred in Japanese colleges among Chinese students,[23] who were streaming to Japan to learn Western ideas and techniques after the Russo-Japanese War. Among them was Chiang Kai-shek. Of the work, a China expert, Arthur Smith, declared that there was an opportunity of 'doing more for China today in one year in Tokyo' than all the missionaries had done in China in a century. A new church was formed to accommodate the 250 Chinese students who had professed conversion.

In the South, an awakening began at Macao in the Portuguese enclave in Kwangtung and others occurred in Wuchow and Hokow in Kiangsi.[24] As Alliance missionaries assessed the Awakening, they noted an intense conviction of believers, a work of cleansing and of spiritual anointing, followed by evidence of demonic attack against believers; they stressed the preponderating results in the salvation of souls.

In the far southwest of China, in the provinces of Kweichow and Yunnan, there was a different manifestation of the power of God in a widespread folk movement among Miao aboriginals in 1906.[25] Protestant work had begun among the Miao in 1895. The second missionary and the first convert were murdered, and persecution raged for years.

In 1902, twenty Miao were baptized at Anshun. The tribes became intrigued. Increasing numbers 'turned to God from idols,' abandoning drunkenness and immorality.[26] A chapel was built at Kopu. Huge congregations gathered, from 2000 to

3000, and as many as 500 came forward as candidates.[27] So great was the work of examining and baptizing Miao candidates that the time and strength of the missionaries was taxed to the utmost. From the Miao converts went forth evangelists to win their own countrymen. One of the most hopeful signs of the movement was 'the wonderful way the converts told others of the Saviour.'[28]

Lengthy itinerations were made by workers. The awakening took the form of a folk movement, spreading by 'let-me-tell-my-kinfolk' methods.[29] It spread across the border into Yunnan, whose Miao were soon seeking out the missionary. And yet there were evidences of pentecostal power, as there were early morning prayer meetings in which simultaneous prayer occurred. The Miao were very musical, and took to singing songs in great choirs with fervent enthusiasm.

In 1908, a third wave of revival swept Chinese churches, north, south, east, west—every province. The most unusual movement undoubtedly was that which began in the north in the Manchurian provinces bordering Korea.

From the 1887 awakenings in the colleges of Canada, there issued a remarkable missionary,[30] Jonathan Goforth, who proceeded to China with the Canadian Presbyterians. Jonathan Goforth had been deeply moved by news of the Welsh Revival of 1904.[31] A few years later, he heard of the 1907 Korean Revival, and immediately visited the nearby kingdom to observe for himself. There he was impressed first-hand with the boundless possibilities of Revival.

Goforth himself became the prophet and the evangelist of the movement that followed. A sweeping Manchurian Revival began in 1908, and demonstrated its power at Changte.[32] The meetings were often marked by public confession of sins and extremes of emotional conduct.[33] Yet it was conceded by critics that permanent moral and spiritual transformations resulted. Some of the converts relapsed, observers claiming that the most lasting results stemmed from the least demonstrative manifestations of conviction. Presbyterians alone reported about 13,000 baptisms in five years of awakening, not counting the multiplied thousands in China proper.[34]

When the movement began in Manchuria, there was opposition from missionaries and nationals. However, an elder was convicted of misuse of church funds and his confession brought others, including the pastor, to their knees. Simultaneous prayer broke out, followed by confession and restitution. Sometimes half a dozen people would commence praying, and on occasion more than seven hundred people prayed together, without any sense of confusion.[35] Rosalind Goforth was impressed by great silences: [36]

> Again and again during these days when dozens were praying at once and when everyone seemed to be weeping, there came a wonderful sense of quiet. For at such times no one spoke or prayed or cried aloud. The presence of God never seemed more real.

Goforth explained that he never asked anyone to confess publicly. He simply told his hearers: 'You people have an opportunity to pray.' There followed in Mukden confession of sins. An elder confessed that he had thrice tried to poison his wife: an awful conviction of sin was manifested: all around people were crying and confessing 'but the noise was so great that it was impossible to hear a word of it.'

Manchuria had been moved by the first and second waves of revival, and now the movement of 1908 in Manchuria sent the third wave over all of China. The effects were the most striking of all, in thrust and phenomena.

Goforth helped spread the revival in China's provinces outside Manchuria.[37] He reported that in two years he had conducted thirty 'missions' in six provinces, seeing God's power manifest in greater or lesser degree, the sense of God's presence being 'overwhelming ... unbearable.'

In Peiping, the university students had decided that the revival was a work of man and not of God. 'When he comes among us and tries to work on our emotions,' they said before Goforth's arrival, 'we won't shed any tears nor confess any sins.' Upon leaving, Jonathan Goforth said: 'Continue the meetings. There is something hindering.' A week after he arrived in London, a letter reached him, saying: 'The meetings went on until Thursday after you left, and then God broke down all those students. We never witnessed such a scene of judgment.'

Qualified observers noted that the 'remarkable movement' that had spread through the churches of Manchuria was passing into Shansi and Honan.[38] A deep and coercive conviction of sin was one of the chief features of the 'wonderful revival.'

The movement traversed Hopeh, Shansi and Shensi to faraway Kansu, Honan and Shantung—in the north; Kiangsu, Anhwei and Chekiang—in the east; Hupeh, Szechwan and Kweichow—in the west; and Fukien, Kiangsi, Hunan, Kwangtung, Kwangsi and Yunnan in the south. Congregations in all of China were affected by the Awakening.

Jonathan Goforth, often the initiator of the work, was preaching three times a day.[39] But Chinese Christians were active in every place. The Revival caused the emergence of Chinese evangelists of great power, including Wang Chang-tai, Ting Li-mei and Drs. Y. S. Lee and S. S. Yao, the last named receiving his call through having 'read of Evan Roberts.'

There was a moving of the Spirit in the faraway Kansu province to the northwest, breaking out at Minchow, served by the Alliance.[40] In Szechwan, evangelist Wang, missionary Arthur Lutley and others participated in a movement which Bishop W. W. Cassels described as 'a terrible time, like the Judgment Day.' It was followed by a harvest.[41]

A godly missionary, F. S. Joyce, reported a stirring awakening at Siangcheng in Honan in 1909.[42] At Taiyuanfu in Shansi, the American Board, Baptist Missionary Society and China Inland Mission shared in the blessing in October 1908.

In 1909, an extraordinary movement stirred the city of of Kiating in West China.[43] Some people left the city in fear of the power of the Spirit. Others stayed away from meetings in fear of the inward compulsion to confess.

In each place the results were the same, the intense conviction of sin, the open confessions: idolatry, theft, murder, adultery, gambling, opium smoking, disobedience to parents and hatred of employers, quarrelsomeness, lying, cheating, and the like were confessed for forgiveness.[44]

Confession, public confession of sin, marked itself as a special feature of the whole movement. Of positive effects, a British missionary gave a summary after a time of study:

> We know now that Chinese are emotionally susceptible in matters of religion: we know now that 'instantaneous conversion' may be seen in China as in Chicago or London. We know that the longing for the fullness of the Spirit, with accompanying willingness to sacrifice all for its attainment, may be felt in Shensi as in Keswick.[45]

Nanking, southern capital, experienced a great awakening in 1909.[46] Attendances in the meetings averaged 1500. Confession of sins were made by professing Christians of all ranks—pastors, elders, deacons, evangelists, and Bible women, church members and inquirers of both sexes; while adultery, gambling, fraud, hatred, division, misappropriation of funds, idolatry and the like were renounced, even petty school quarrels between children being settled.

The Christian and Missionary Alliance noted that 1908 was 'a year of glorious revival' in South China, following the movements reported there.[47] The China Inland Mission reported that, in all, its stations and outstations had increased from 394 to 1001 in the decade 1900-1910, chapels from 387 to 995, communicants from 8557 to 23,000.[48] Hudson Taylor's Mission reported 2720 baptisms in 1907, and twenty thousand regular communicants.

Into the year 1911 the Revival seethed. Prayer meetings in Honan Province drew great crowds to pray together as 'a mighty wave of prayer'[49] seemed to sweep over the place. In central China at Hankow, 60,000 people heard the Word in six days' preaching sponsored by an Evangelistic Association of concerned Chinese Christians.[50]

It was declared at the Edinburgh Conference that the ethical and social changes and transformations were a work of God.[51] The Revival in China in these years proved to be the beginning of an indigenous spirit in the Chinese churches. In spite of opposition, a way was being prepared for the coming of greater awakenings among the Chinese Christians, who had come of age at last.

One of the most significant local awakenings was the Hinghwa Pentecost, in which a young man named John Sung was converted, afterward to become an American Ph.D. and then one of China's greatest evangelists of all time, a link between the Awakenings of the first decade and the third decade of the twentieth century.[52]

Another link personality was Leland Wang, a Chinese naval officer who was converted in 1918, encouraged by an English missionary, Miss Barber, a friend of Jessie Penn-Lewis of Wales. Wang entered the ministry in 1921, and was caught up in the 1925 revival movement in Shanghai. Like his younger brethren, Andrew Gih and John Sung, he exercised a ministry far afield.

The Revolution of 1911, although directed by a professed Christian, Dr Sun Yat-sen, marked the beginning of a reaction against Christianity. The popularity of the Church decreased as the strength of nationalism developed. The churches also became less evangelistic as education took the place of a vigorous evangelism, until more than half the missionary force was engaged in teaching.[53]

Fortunately, another evangelical awakening occurred before China's second revolution, beginning in the latter half of the 1920s and continuing throughout the 1930s. This wide movement was even more indigenous in its personnel than the awakening of the 1900s.

22

THE KOREAN PENTECOST

The awakenings of the 1900s in Korea were indigenous, of missionary derivation and part of a worldwide movement.

The Reverend R. A. Hardie (a Canadian Colleges medical missionary) arrived in 1890 in Korea. He became associated with Southern Methodists in their mission in 1898,[1] at a time when a noticeable turning to Christian profession occurred.

In August 1903, a group of seven missionaries engaged in a week of study and prayer at Wonsan, including Hardie who had for years been yearning to see Koreans convicted of sin and led to repentance and faith evidencing the fruits thereof, but up to that time in his work 'had not seen any examples of plain, unmistakable, and lasting conversion.'[2]

It thus appeared that accessions between 1895 and 1903 included numbers of people entering the Church as interested disciples rather than regenerate members, as later on.

In view of the great need, Dr. Hardie confessed his faults before the missionary body and before the Korean church, leading to confessions of failure by other Christians.[3] Soon after, in October of 1903, the missionary advocate, Fredrik Franson, arrived in Korea.[4] Hardie at once began to prepare for Franson's ministry. When he arrived, a week of meetings was held in which the confession of sins continued to be an outstanding feature of the meetings, yet without abuse. During this awakening, many confessed the theft of goods but offered restitution to the Lord and not to church members (at their request), thus providing the funds for employing a full-time colporteur in the district.[5]

The results of this earliest movement were seen in the transformation of the lives of church members, whose morality was lifted to a high plane of sincerity and purity never before attained. Their brotherhood in this common religious experience led to immediate acceleration of growth in church membership.[6] There were other benefits gained, for in this first wave of revival, Franson taught Hardie and his friends the value of prevailing prayer, for he would cry 'O Father, Thou canst do it; Thou wilt do it; Thou shalt do it.'[7]

The Wonsan Conference was repeated in 1904. In 1905, the armies of Japan defeated Russia and gained control of Korea as spoils of war. A national indignation affected the Christians, and many looked to the churches to provide an organized resistance. Many missionary and church leaders preached forbearance and forgiveness, hence the angrier agitators tried to undermine their work.[8]

The second wave of revival swept Korea in 1905-1906. Spiritual awakenings began in North Korea in 1905. There were remarkable meetings in the city of Pyongyang, both Central and South Gate churches crowded out, seven hundred converts enrolled in two weeks.[9] It was then described as a spreading fire, a continuing religious awakening, the hundreds of conversions not being due to any sudden impulse. More conversions than in any previous year were reported from all over Korea.

In 1906, Dr. Howard Agnew Johnston brought news of the awakenings in Wales and in India.[10] Half the missionaries in Korea were Presbyterian, from the United States, Australia and Canada, deeply moved by the accounts of revival among the Welsh Presbyterians and on their Asian mission fields.

In South Korea, the awakening that began at Mokpo early in 1906 grew steadily until not one square foot in the local building remained unoccupied by the packed congregation, the church being enlarged to double its size.[11] Men stood six deep eagerly waiting their turn to testify of sins forgiven, differences reconciled, and power received.[12]

Dr. S. A. Moffett reported from Pyongyang in 1906:[13] 'We are having another great movement this year, not only in the north but also in the south.' At the New Year, four thousand attended evangelistic services in Pyongyang out of 20,000 population. In North Pyongyang Province, 6507 adherents increased to 11,943, an 83% increase.[14]

In the capital, Seoul, various denominations in 1906 united in the work for the first time and a thousand converts were enrolled.[15] John R. Mott addressed 6000 men in a three-and-a-half hour meeting, 200 inquirers awaiting instruction.[16]

George Heber Jones,[17] a devout Methodist, had worked in Chemulpo without a convert for his travail, but in 1906 he was preaching to as many as 900 in a service, and there were ten thousand Christians in the area. On the island of Kangwha, he reported a turning to Christ with hundreds of converts in the autumn of 1906, and twenty-seven churches catered for the 2500 Christians.[18]

All these were the fruit of the second wave. The coming of the third wave of Revival was imminent. It commenced in North Korea.[19] During August of 1906, various missionaries had met at Pyongyang for a week of prayer and of Bible study, led by Dr. R. A. Hardie, the Canadian who had already experienced personal reviving.[20] All of them shared a deep concern for the need of the country in its time of humiliation. They studied the First Epistle of John, which afterwards became their text-book in revival work. Refreshed themselves, they planned intensive Bible study for the Korean churches. They gave themselves so much to their task that, during the wintertime, social and recreational affairs lost all of their appeal for them.[21]

It was customary for representatives of area churches to come from far and wide at the New Year[22] for Bible study. In spite of tensions, a strange new spirit entered the meeting of fifteen hundred men. So many men wanted to pray that the leader told the whole audience: 'If you want to pray like that, all pray.' The effect was beyond description—not confusion, but a vast harmony of sound and spirit, like the noise of the surf in an ocean of prayer.[23] As the prayer continued, an intense conviction of sin settled on the meeting, giving way to bitter weeping over their misdeeds.

As Lord William Cecil told a London newspaper, an elder arose and confessed a grudge against a missionary colleague and asked for forgiveness.[24] The missionary stood to pray but reached only the address to Deity: 'Apa-ge!' 'Father!' when, with a rush, a power from without seemed to take hold of the meeting. The Europeans described its manifestations as terrifying. Nearly everyone present was seized with the most poignant sense of mental anguish; before each one, his sins seemed to be rising in condemnation of his life. Some were springing to their feet, and pleading for an opportunity to relieve their consciences by making their abasement known; and others were silent, but rent with agony, clenching their fists and striking their heads against the ground in the struggle to resist the Power that was forcing them painfully and agonizingly to confess their misdeeds.[25]

From eight in the evening until two in the morning, it went on, until the missionaries—horror-struck at some of the sins confessed, frightened by the presence of a Power which could work such wonders, reduced to tears by sympathy with the mental agony of their Korean disciples whom they loved so dearly—stopped the meeting.[26]

Some went home to sleep, but many of the Koreans spent the night awake, some in prayer, others in terrible spiritual conflict. Next day, the missionaries hoped that the storm was over and that the comforting teaching of the Holy Word would bind up the wounds of yesternight, but again the same anguish, the same confession—and so it went on for days.

In meetings following, conviction of sin and reconciliation of enemies continued. The heathen Koreans were astounded and a powerful impulse of evangelism was felt. Not only was there deep confession, but much restitution.[27] The movement achieved lasting results. After fifteen years in Pyongyang, one church had a thousand members and the others shared as many, while between 1700 and 2000 attended the Wednesday prayer meetings regularly.[28]

Nine-tenths of the students in Union Christian College in Pyongyang professed conversion in February 1907.[29] A large number of the converts became evangelists with a zeal for the Cross, carrying the fires of revival not only to the city, and nearby country churches, but also as far as Chemulpo and Kongju.[30] The revival did for the characters of some what two years of training could not have done.

The delegates to the Winter Bible Class went back to their homes and carried the revival to their various churches. Everywhere phenomena were the same. There was deep conviction of sin, followed by confession and restitution, a notable feature of all gatherings being the audible prayer en masse —a mode of intercession entirely new.[31]

An elder struggled with his conviction night after night, but received no peace. He gradually lost interest and was removed from office. The confession of a woman exposed his immorality. He sank lower and lower, became a brothel owner, and commercialized his interest in vice.[32]

After the severe judgment, benefit followed. Practically every evangelical church in all of Korea received blessing. Missionaries claimed that the effects were uniformly wholesome, save where believers resisted the Spirit or deceived the brethren. The work could not be gainsaid.[33]

In five years of rapid growth, 1906-1910, the net gain for all the churches of Korea was 79,221, which was more than the total of members in Japan after half a century of Protestant effort, or twice the number of the Protestants in China in the first eighty years of mission work. By 1912, there were approximately 300,000 Korean church members in a total population of twelve millions.[34]

The Student Volunteer Movement in 1910 cited evidences of 'the present day work of the Holy Spirit in Korea,' noting (first) the unity and the cooperation which prevailed among Christians; (second) the remarkable numerical growth of the Churches; (third) the wonderful religious awakening of 1907 which affected 50,000 converts; (fourth) the noteworthy interest in the Word of God; (fifth) the dedication of national Christians to service, including generous giving; and (sixth) the wonderful prayer life of the Korean Church.[35]

Regarding quality of results, Bishop C. M. Harris of the Methodist Church averred that general effects following the movement were wholly good.[36] The whole church was raised to a higher spiritual level. There had been an almost entire absence of fanaticism because of previous careful instruction in the Bible. There were found greater congregations searching out the Word of God. Drunkards, gamblers, adulterers, murderers, thieves, self-righteous Confucianists and others had been made into new men in Christ, he said.[37]

There was a curious evaluation of the Korean Revival given by Prof. George T. Ladd of Yale University, a strange amalgm of his enthusiasm for all things Japanese, distaste for all things Korean, acceptance of Freudian values and rejection of Christian views.[38] He was the guest in Korea of Prince Ito, Japanese Governor-General, and he had been received by the Emperor Meiji, who granted him the highest orders of chivalry ever given to a foreigner.[39]

Prof. Ladd visited a missionary family in Pyongyang in April 1907, after the excitement of the meetings had died down and the churches were occupied in regular worship. His information was received second-hand—missionaries' accounts interpreted from the official government position, and his conclusions were governed by his attitudes:[40]

> The 'Great Revival' of 1906-07, which added so much to the encouragement of the missionaries and to the number of their converts, can best be understood in its most characteristic features when viewed in the light of what has been said about the nature of the Koreans themselves

Prof. Ladd assumed that the confessions of the Korean penitents under the compulsion of the Revival were more a proof of the corruption of the Korean character than of the power of Truth. The incidents of extreme agitation he set as the norm instead of the unusual. He deemed the attitude of the missionaries too indulgent of the Koreans, and not sufficiently generous towards the Japanese.

It could be said that the majority of the missionaries were inclined to regard Japanese rule as one way of bringing Korea into the twentieth century; nevertheless, they were profoundly sympathetic with the sufferings of their Korean friends during the worst times of national suppression.

The American Academy published a review of Ladd's book in its official organ, and the reviewer observed: [41]

> Too much of this book is a narrative of personal experiences of no interest to the general reader, and at times it must be doubted whether the close connection of the writer with the Japanese authorities may not account for his not seeing many things that have been only too evident to most observers. The general attitude in all the chapters is decidedly pro-Japanese.

Following the great Awakening of the year 1907, it became the normal and accepted practice to hold an evangelistic campaign in each church or circuit at least once a year. The greater part of the responsibility fell upon the Koreans, many of whom developed unusual ability in this line of operation, so indigenous evangelism increased. [42]

The Korean Presbyterian Church was set up in the post-Revival period, a Board of Foreign Missions organized also. Intense efforts were made to evangelize not only the people of Korea but also the Koreans living in Russian Siberia and Chinese Manchuria and overseas. [43]

Illiterate adults as they became Christian were required to learn to read Korean in a simple phonetic alphabet for admission to membership. [44] A further inducement arose when Christians in the country, close-cropped rather than top-knotted, were challenged by Korean patriots to prove that they were Korean Christians rather than Japanese collaborators by reciting the Scriptures! These factors accomplished an almost 100% actual literacy among the Christians in a short space of time. Christians took the lead in Korean life.

An intensive, country-wide effort to win new believers was put forth by all churches in 1909-1910. It began with a small group of missionaries in Songdo, in July of 1909. The American Methodists in 1900 had mounted a campaign to win a million souls in the United States by an organized crusade, but without much success. One of the Methodist missionaries toured the circuit churches, asking the newly revived people to pray for 50,000 converts in that district during the coming year. The Mission Board decided on 200,000 for Christ as a worthy target for the Methodists. In October 1909, the General Council of Evangelical Missions met in Seoul and decided upon a million converts. So far it was a missionary scheme, full of genuine zeal, but marked with the characteristics of its origin in American promotion. The Council had thus adopted Finney's principle that 'Revival is nothing more than the right use of the appropriate means.' The world evangelists, Chapman and Alexander, arrived the first day to launch the great crusade.[45] All that human zeal could do was done, and all was set to win the million, as decided by the praying committee.

It proved to be very different to the Awakening of 1907. The Rev. James E. Adams made a report of the evangelistic campaign held in Taegu during the Million Souls Movement which followed the decline of the Revival proper. Every night the church building was well-filled by a thousand or so, and between 400 and 500 professed conversion and gave their names and addresses. Only one tenth of the inquirers were successfully reached and not all of them were added to the local church or any other congregation.[46]

Statistically, the outcome was cruelly disappointing. Instead of the 200,000 converts, the Southern Methodists won 2,122. Instead of the 1,000,000 converts, the whole Council together won 15,805—for other times, a goodly accession. Clark described the Million Souls Movement as a worked-up campaign with too little antecedent preparation.[47] That it was a worked-up campaign seems certain, but not to say that there was no prayer, no powerful preaching, no preparation. It seemed just that the Holy Spirit would not surrender His prerogatives for a Pentecost to anyone. In the next decade occurred nine lean years. It was obvious that the Revival was over, the Awakening ended.

The Korean Revival of 1903-1908 had its full effect upon church growth in Korea. From 1895 onwards, there was a significant ingathering in both Methodist and Presbyterian fields of a folk who were to become the subjects of reviving. In 1903, not only were some congregations revived but an acceleration of church growth occurred—seen clearly in any graph.[43] This continued steadily through the second phase of revival in 1905-1906, then sharply accelerated again in 1907 as a result of the third phase of revival, which continued till the programmed Million Souls Movement, after which growth of the Christian community declined and that of communicants decelerated for a few years. In some areas and in certain periods, the movement into the churches resembled a folk movement.

Sixty years afterward, the Korean Revival was still recognized as the spiritual birth of the Korean Church. At the Berlin Congress on Evangelism, one of the most stirring addresses reverted to the Revival.[49] It is a mistake however to speak only of the Revival of 1907, in view of the ingathering of 1895, the limited revival of 1903, the more general revivals of 1905, and then the explosive awakening of 1907. And it seems necessary to separate the evangelistic campaign of 1910-1911 (which neither revived the Church nor yet produced significant church growth) from the three-fold Awakening which followed the seven years of providential ingathering between 1895 and 1902.

It is significant that the evangelists raised up by the early twentieth century awakenings became outstanding leaders in Korean Christianity. A prime example may be found in Keil Shun-ju, a leader in the Revival in Pyongyang, famed afterwards as an evangelist and a Korean patriot, his name a household word in church and state. Evangelists and ardent pastors espoused the cause of self-determination.

At the Edinburgh Conference of 1910,[50] it was declared: 'the Korean Revival . . . has been a genuine Pentecost,' for Korean church membership quadrupled in a decade,[51] and it continued to rise, giving to the one per cent Christians in the population an influence far beyond their numbers. Within thirty years, Protestants in Korea numbered three hundred thousand. This nation moved by revival rapidly became the most evangelized part of the Orient.

William N. Blair has speculated upon what might have happened in Korea had the Christian Church yielded to the temptation of resisting the Japanese by carnal rather than by spiritual methods.[52] The country wanted a leader and the Christian Church was the most influential single organization in Korea. The Koreans would have flocked behind the banner of the Cross, and some Constantine might have arisen to use such a banner. But the result would have been a worldly Church, not a spiritual one.

Instead, the Korean Church retained its zeal for God while maintaining its loyalty to country. The Korean Church became self-supporting in a way unknown in the Orient.[53] The Korean church members became enthusiastic in witnessing and generous in giving. More than thirty years went by with Japanese military power in control of their country, but their faith never dimmed. In Korea, a persecuted Church provided the spiritual backbone for a nation.

23

TAIKYO DENDO IN JAPAN

In early 1900, a call went out for a General Conference of Protestant missionaries in Japan, the first since the historic year of awakening in 1883, when, following an extended week of prayer, an extraordinary work of revival and evangelism spread throughout Japan, a seven year period of rapid growth when church membership rose from 5,000 to 30,000 and the springtime of the Church was acclaimed.[1]

This period of rapid growth had been followed by one of retarded growth, the last decade of the nineteenth century, in which the Evangelicals increased by only six thousand to a total of thirty-seven thousand.[2] There were at least two reasons for this—a political reaction against westernization and a spiritual sabotage of evangelical theology.[3]

There came a recovery at the beginning of the twentieth century, leading to great conferences of prayer in Tokyo in October 1900. A spirit of ardent prayer fell on the Churches. With the summoning of the General Conference went a call to prayer that 'the Spirit of the Lord prepare the way for a meeting of Pentecostal power.' The Japanese Evangelical Alliance met in the spring of 1900, and proposed a united evangelistic campaign.[4] The Missionary Conference agreed both to mobilizing prayer and to organizing evangelism. So the early months of 1901 were spent in meetings to revive the spiritual life of the believers.[5]

The 1900 movement of prayer was followed by a united evangelistic campaign in May-June of 1901. It was under-girded by faithful prayer and armed by scriptural preaching. Called Taikyo Dendo, literally 'Aggressive Evangelism,' it was translated 'Forward Movement' in English.[6] Tokyo was divided into five districts, and more than fifty churches, sixty pastors and a dozen missionaries participated, aided by twenty seven bands of witnessing lay people, 360 persons in all, marching through the streets singing and engaging in a house-to-house visitation. Three hundred thousand tracts were distributed, along with half a million handbills describing the meetings and giving directions.

Prayer meetings were held in the afternoons, as many as eight hundred intercessors gathering at one time. In the evenings were held the public evangelistic meetings in which a simple Gospel message was preached. Cards were handed out to inquirers, and the contacts were followed up by pastors and people. Professed converts were enrolled in catechetical classes for two years.

It was reported that 11,626 had attended local prayer meetings to intercede for blessing, while 84,247 had attended the preaching of the Gospel in Tokyo, of whom 5,307 made a profession of faith.[7]

By mid-1901,[8] missionaries in Japan did not hesitate to describe the movement as 'Pentecost in Japan.' Anglican, Baptist, Methodist, Presbyterian and other denominations cooperated very freely in Tokyo.[9] In the Kyobashi district alone more than a thousand people 'repented of their sins,' and turned to God.

Japanese took the initiative in the preaching of the Good News of Jesus Christ, the workers participating being of the best classes, including members of the Imperial Diet. Usually meetings were held in churches, but there were many street rallies, and in all of them excellent order prevailed, without a trace of fanaticism.

The greatest benefits were reaped by little suburban churches, which received more eager inquirers than they could handle. Some pastors came to the committee to say: 'We have enough, so please don't help us any more. Our houses will not hold the people.'

In little over five weeks, five thousand were enrolled, and during 1901, there were 15,000 inquirers in all Japan, besides countless thousands who were influenced in ideals. The Taikyo Dendo spread from Tokyo to Yokohama, Sendai, Matsuyama, Nagasaki, Osaka, and other cities as the prayer meetings multiplied and preaching increased. In Yokohama, for example, in June 1901, a great spiritual awakening began, with two thousand inquirers instructed. Other cities saw the same results.[10] It was a time of great challenge to the workers, and of overwhelming joy to the intercessors.

Indeed they were overwhelmed, for no less than 17,939 converts were added in a short time to their churches. The Protestant forces, which had numbered less than 40,000, added a full 25,000 in twelve months, according to reliable missionary opinion.[11] None could say that a great spiritual awakening ill-suited the Japanese.

In the far north of Japan, Christians in Sapporo reported sixty-five inquirers, of whom sixteen were baptized shortly afterward. The attendances at the churches quadrupled and a new Y.M.C.A. was built as a result. It was said that before the Taikyo Dendo, a union meeting of the three Sapporo churches attracted two people—while during and after there was extraordinary attendance at the union prayer meeting in the city.[12]

Taikyo Dendo was extended beyond a year.[13] It continued operative until the outbreak of war between Russia and Japan in 1904, and even a great war did not noticeably slow down its drive. Another awakening followed the news of the Welsh Revival, the news reaching Japan during the war fever.

In 1906, the Taikyo Dendo was still making great progress. Evangelist Taniguchi and Pastor Kaneko held united meetings in Shinshu, 200 inquirers being registered, and like work was performed in other districts by other agents.[14] In October, a stirring revival was reported at Takasaki, and one in November at Maebashi in Joshu Province. This continued into 1907, when a similar work was reported in Miyazaki.[15]

Most of the preaching of the Good News during Taikyo Dendo was accomplished by Japanese.[16] A graduate of Moody Bible Institute, one Seimatsu Kimura, appeared as a full-time evangelist—an unconventional preacher who conducted his mass meetings in vigorous style, a thousand inquirers enrolled in his two-week series of tent meetings in Tokyo. Another dynamic graduate of Moody Bible Institute was Juji Nakada, who stressed a Wesleyan view of holiness.[17]

Serious controversy arose between two men of outstanding native abilities.[18] Masahisa Uemura rose to challenge Danjo Ebina, a liberal Congregational pastor, to debate essential doctrines. As a result, the Japanese Evangelical Alliance excluded Ebina—who was reconciled again in 1906.

Y.M.C.A. workers rendered selfless service to Japanese soldiers during the war, and an unprecedented gift of ten thousand yen was made to this work by the Emperor.[19] After the war, missionaries worked among discharged soldiers, one in Tokyo corresponding with a hundred inquirers.

Following the war, a famine hit northeastern Japan in 1905 and 1906. Christians moved quickly to help.[20] Okayama Christian Orphanage, founded by Juji Ishi, took 1200 children of impoverished parents, a similar number being helped in Sendai. Hundreds of Japanese impressed by such selfless service were received into the faith.

During and after the Taikyo Dendo, outstanding American and British churchmen visited Japan and preached in the mass evangelistic meetings arranged by the Japanese local churches. Among them were John R. Mott, William Booth, Reuben Torrey and Wilbur Chapman. In October of 1901, fifteen hundred young men (a thousand students) were won to Christ in John R. Mott's meetings.[21] Subsequently, Japanese Student Volunteer teams conducted an effective evangelistic 'drive.' General Booth held only nine services in a 1907 Japanese series, but 969 inquirers were helped.[22]

To the influence of the Welsh Revival upon missionaries was added the direct influence of the Korean Revival on the Japanese. Not only evangelism, but local quickenings of the churches continued. In 1907, there were local awakenings throughout Japan, including one at Hiroshima among soldiers in camp.[23] One of the most striking evidences of the great work of the Holy Spirit was witnessed in Hokkaido, the northerly island of Japan.[24] A 'wonderful revival' was reported having started in January 1907 in the Tokachi Prison and swept through that institution until nearly every prisoner, as well as officer and guard, had made public confession of faith in Jesus Christ. From there, it was carried to other parts of the island, accompanied by many remarkable healings of bodily sickness.

By 1909, there were approximately 600 organized churches in Japan,[25] a quarter of which were self-supporting. The membership exceeded 70,000, served by 500 ordained and 600 unordained men, and 200 Bible women. A hundred thousand pupils were taught in a thousand Sunday Schools. There were 4000 students in boarding schools, 8000 in day schools, 400 in theological colleges and 250 in women's Bible schools, plus a leavening of secular higher education.

Much of this progress was attributable to Taikyo Dendo, in which the Christians were never more united, and to an awakening renewed by news from Wales and Korea. A local missionary authority assessed the movement thus:

1. Christianity again secured the attention of the Japanese population. 2. Many people were brought into personal relationship with Jesus Christ. 3. New life and courage were injected into the Church in Japan. 4. It was an ecumenical movement in the best sense of that word. 5. Christians were made aware that the Gospel alone is the power of God to salvation. 6. The movement proved that when the Church is revived, the money for its work is available locally.[26]

Taikyo Dendo was more than a well-planned evangelistic campaign.[27] It was a movement of a spontaneous nature— prayer, followed by mass evangelism well-presented by the whole Church. The Edinburgh Missionary Conference noted that 'in Japan, notwithstanding many difficulties and discouragements, the past ten years have without doubt been the most fruitful in spiritual results ever known in the field.' [27]

The number of Evangelical Christians in Japan in 1900 doubled to become seventy-five thousand in 1910. Their influence was out of all proportion to their numbers, tenfold in Parliament, threefold among army officers, and an overwhelming proportion in social welfare work,[28] in which the Salvation Army entering Japan had performed notable service during the Russo-Japanese War.

It is significant that Taikyo Dendo anticipated a Latin American movement of fifty years later, Evangelism-in-Depth, in emphasizing the role of every Christian in witness rather than that of an evangelist and his team; in preparing all believers as soul-winners instead of training an elite group to counsel inquirers; in multiplying the number of active evangelists rather than multiplying the number of hearers for the evangelist; in urging 'go and preach' instead of 'come and hear'; and in mobilizing the Church instead of doing the work for its members. This was true also of a wider campaign held 1914-1917.[29]

One outcome of the period of revival in Japan was the founding of the Oriental Missionary Society and the growth of the Japanese Holiness Church.[30] Charles Cowman and his wife came to Japan in 1901, and worked with Juji Nakada. Tetsusaburo Sasao, a talented evangelist and teacher, one of the men trained by Barclay Buxton of the Japan Evangelistic Band, joined forces with them.

Japanese Christians were numerically weak, but an ardent spirit of nationalism moved them. In 1879, Masahisa Uemura had been ordained in Presbyterian fellowship. He was convinced that the evangelization of Japan should be done by an indigenous body of believers.[31] Uemura founded a theological seminary in Tokyo in 1904, a spiritual expression of rising nationalism. Secular nationalism was being expressed also. Reaction was already setting in, for in 1911, the Government declared that school children must participate in the national Shinto shrine worship. Some refused the explanation that only the veneration of ancestors was involved; many did not, and a problem rose to vex their conscience.

24

THE PENTECOSTAL AFTERMATH

On the worldwide Pentecostal movement, there is (happily for the historian) a growing literature, from academically exact to emotionally vague. Its relationship to the worldwide general Awakening which preceded it is almost entirely unknown or ignored. This is partly due to the fact that most people, whether Pentecostal practitioners within the movement or non-Pentecostal historians outside it, seem to be unaware of the extent of the general awakening of the 1900s.

In Bloch-Hoell's thoroughly documented study of the rise of Pentecostalism in Norway, in its Norwegian original,[1] is found a brief mention of the Lunde Revival of 1905. Also, in Hollenweger's detailed treatise on Pentecostalism, written in German,[2] there is a generous treatment of Evan Roberts. There is a mention of Pandita Ramabai's school in India in a much earlier Danish study, and references to the Welsh Revival in a Swedish volume.[3] But in none of these does there seem to be any awareness on the part of the authors of the worldwide extent of the 1905 Awakening, nor any mention of the relationship between the general awakening in the United States and the subsequent Pentecostal movement therein.

It is the definite conclusion of the present writer that the Pentecostal movement possessed the same relationship to the general awakening of the early twentieth century that the Baptist movement held to the general awakening of the seventeenth century, and that the Wesleyan movement bore to the general awakening of the eighteenth century.

In other words, just as only a minority of those reached in the Puritan movement of the seventeenth century became Baptists, and only a minority of those reached in the Pietist-Methodist awakenings during the eighteenth century became Wesleyans, so only a minority of those reached in the revival of the early twentieth century became Pentecostalists.

The rise of the Pentecostal denominations was as much an aftermath to the awakenings of the early twentieth century as the rise of the Baptist and Methodist denominations was to the precedent awakenings of the seventeenth and the eighteenth.

178

Before 1900, there were sporadic occurrences of glossolalia (speaking in tongues) in Tennessee, followed by some
fanaticism.   Before 1905, glossolalia occurred in Topeka,
Kansas and Houston, Texas, where enthusiasts often naively
thought that they had received a xenolalic manifestation, that
they were speaking in Chinese or some other foreign tongue.
(The character of their leader, Charles Parham, was sullied
by charges of unbecoming conduct made by Pentecostalists)

Among informed students, however, it is usual to trace the
beginnings of the modern Pentecostal movement to a little
meeting in Azusa Street in Los Angeles in April 1906.[4] The
same year, there were glossolalic outbreaks in Chicago,
Toronto and elsewhere, traceable to Los Angeles.[5]

On 8th April 1905, Dr. F. B. Meyer addressed a rapt
congregation in Los Angeles on the Welsh Revival. In May,
a local revival broke out in a Methodist church in Pasadena,
with two hundred professed conversions in two weeks. In
June, an unusual awakening began in the First Baptist Church
of Los Angeles.[6]

In September 1904, First Baptist Church of Los Angeles
had sent its pastor, Joseph Smale, to the Holy Land for rest
and recuperation after illness. On his way home, he visited
Wales in the throes of Revival.[7] Upon his return, he addressed
a packed church on 'This is that which was spoken of by the
prophet Joel . . .' There was an immediate response as 'the
Holy Spirit fell on the people,' and two hundred penitents
pressed to the front. Sobbing and inarticulate prayer preceded
confessions of sin.   Conversions followed, it being noted that
both white and black responded.   The meetings continued for
fifteen weeks, and the crowded gatherings attracted folk from
far and wide, besides church members.

'Holy Spirit freedom' was resented by some regular
Baptists, hence the pastor and some of his people moved to
Burbank Hall downtown to begin 'the First New Testament
Church.'   In February of 1906, several members of this
short-lived fellowship pledged themselves to pray for some
kind of Pentecost, according to Frank Bartleman.[8]

Meanwhile a Negro preacher, W. J. Seymour from Texas,
was invited to Los Angeles,[9] where a growing number of the
people had enjoyed a charismatic experience. He shared his
message with a group meeting in Bonnie Brae Street, and
his wife spoke at Burbank Hall, closer to town. The press
became so great and the action so vigorous that the Bonnie
Brae building collapsed—floors, walls and roof.[10]

The enthusiasts found an abandoned Methodist hall on Azusa Street, and there began a protracted meeting lasting through sessions day and night for three years.

The San Francisco earthquake occurred on 18th April 1906, sending tremors of fear southwards.[11] The crowds increased at Azusa Street. Neither regular churchpeople nor the press of Los Angles viewed their 'goings-on' with great approval.[12] The meetings were inter-racial and were led by Seymour. Speaking in tongues had become a main feature of the gatherings, and a number of sick folk were healed. But, for whatever reason, this little meeting became the focus of interest to seekers throughout the United States and Canada, and Pentecostalism spread even to Europe indirectly from Azusa Street.

W. H. Durham carried the message to Chicago and A. H. Argue to Toronto.[13] Others carried the enthusiasm to the northwest and the southeast. Mixed commendation and caution were offered by W. T. MacArthur to the constituency of the Christian and Missionary Alliance.[14]

A Cornishman, Thomas Ball Barratt, whose parents had settled in Norway, began preaching there in the 1880s and was ordained a Methodist minister in the 1890s. In 1902, Barratt founded the Oslo City Mission and two years later began editing its weekly organ.[15]

Barratt became enthusiastically interested in the Welsh Revival, which appealed to his Celtic soul.[16] He filled his columns with reports of the Revival, corresponded with Evan Roberts, and became a warm supporter of the ministry of his friend, Albert Lunde, in the Norwegian Revival.[17] Barratt started a noonday prayer meeting, telling Evan Roberts of his continuing burden for 'a revival unlike all other revivals' in Norway and the world.

T. B. Barratt crossed the Atlantic to raise funds for his City Mission, but his trip was an utter failure financially, so dismally discouraging that he often went without food. In the autumn of 1906, he was staying in the mission house of the Christian and Missionary Alliance in New York, there seeking the Divine will and a closer fellowship with God. Barrat was feeling poorly in body and poorly in spirit, but he had learned of the developments in faraway Los Angeles. After fasting and prayer, he underwent an ecstatic experience on October 7, which he afterwards called his 'crisis' of commitment. Although he did not speak in tongues, he thought of this experience as a Pentecostal baptism.[18]

The friends in Azusa Street urged him further to seek the gift of tongues. On November 15, in another meeting in which he experienced 'glory,' Barratt spoke with tongues and 'sang in the Spirit.'[19] It is worth noting that, as a young man, he had studied music under Edvard Grieg; and he later published touching hymns, one of which the writer has heard sung with deeply moving lyrics and music, all over Norway.[20]

Barratt returned to Oslo, full of his charismatic message, and before the end of the year had enlisted a following. The new movement soon became front-page news in Norway. The Baptists were interested in the message, and ever since have discreetly shown sympathy with the work. The Methodists opposed the manifestations, and declined in strength after 1907. Many Lutherans became attached to the Pentecostal movement. Speaking in tongues occurred even in the huge Calmyersgate Mission Hall.[21] Albert Lunde did not support the new movement, nor did he declare against it.[22]

The Norwegian Pentecostal movement spread from city to town to village all over Norway.[23] But unlike the Revival of 1905, it was controversial—even though it still was inter-denominational in form. In 1910, the emerging Pentecostal groups took denominational form, and ultimately adopted believers' baptism from their Pentecostal-Baptist friends. They became the largest Free Church in Norway, passing in numbers the Baptists, Methodists and other groups.

In 1907, Barratt visited Denmark, filling the great Concert Palace in Copenhagen in June.[24] The Danish actress, Anna Larsen, at the height of her fame, left the stage to work in the Danish Pentecostal movement.[25] These Danish assemblies were never as strong as those in Norway.

Lewi Pethrus, a Baptist minister active in the Revival of 1905 in Sweden, heard of Barratt's experience and sought the same for himself after a visit to Oslo.[26] He became the leading Swedish Pentecostalist.[27] Barratt himself visited Sweden: in Stockholm one Methodist and two Baptist churches opened their doors.[28] Other Norwegians carried the message to many Swedish towns and cities.

In 1909, Barratt visited Baptist churches in Orebro, provoking confessions, conversions and opposition. Baptists in Sweden were divided over the issue. A new congregation, Filadelfia, was formed in Stockholm, excluded in 1913, and to this tiny assembly Lewi Pethrus was called. Its membership rose from 70 to 7000, while its sister-churches multiplied in number, passing the 700 mark.[29]

Pentecostalism was introduced to Finland in 1907-1908, A. A. Herrmans and J. A. Lindkvist being preachers having a charismatic experience.[30] These new Pentecostalists in 1911 welcomed Barratt to Finland. His ministry won over a noted Free Church editor, Pietari Brofeldt.[31] Soon a Norwegian ex-Salvationist, G. O. Smidt, took over the leadership of the Pentecostal work in Finland.

It was from Oslo that the Pentecostal message spread to the British Isles, with occasional help from Americans who had been influenced by the California movement.

In 1906, a Sunderland Anglican clergyman, the Reverend Alexander A. Boddy (who was active in the 1905 Awakening in County Durham) shared with his prayer meeting group the news of the manifestations in Los Angeles.

Early in 1907, Boddy crossed the North Sea to Oslo to see Barratt's work for himself, and, in September of the same year, Barratt visited Sunderland to preach in All Saints' Parish Church. Evensong was followed by a prayer meeting that continued until four in the morning, and so the Pentecostal movement began in the British Isles.[32]

It was among a minority of 'the children of the Revival' in Wales that Pentecostalism appeared.[33] An American missionary who had shared in the Los Angeles beginnings visited Wales in 1907. At Waunllwyd, near Ebbw Vale, an outbreak of glossolalia occurred in late 1907, in the study of the Reverend T. M. Jeffreys. George Jeffreys and Stephen Jeffreys became outstanding British Pentecostal evangelists.

A strong Pentecostal assembly was formed at Tonypandy. The work spread throughout South Wales, though not without 'regrettable scenes of extravagance.' Tonypandy became the annual venue of growing Pentecostal conventions, as did also Sunderland in Durham. One of the converts of the ministry of Seth Joshua, Donald Gee, embraced the new teaching.

Kilsyth, twelve miles from Glasgow, proved to be a focus of revival interest in the eighteenth and nineteenth centuries. In 1908, Pentecostal phenomena were reported there.[34] The movement spread throughout Scotland, though in smaller groups than those of other Free Church congregations.

Inquirers from Belfast carried the message from Sunderland and Kilsyth to Ireland.[35] It was not until 1915 that the Irish work blossomed with the coming of George Jeffreys and his associates, the Elim Pentecostal denomination being founded in Ulster and spread all over Britain by George Jeffreys, who conducted evangelistic and healing rallies.

Pentecostalism in Britain organized three associations: the Assemblies of God, in which Donald Gee was a leader; the Elim Pentecostal Alliance, founded by George Jeffreys; and the Apostolic Church, differing from usual Pentecostal practice in recognizing the offices of apostle and prophet.

By 1908, the Pentecostal influence had reached Australia and New Zealand, but it did not make great numerical gains. Late that same year, the phenomena appeared also in South Africa. There a South African connexion, the Apostolic Faith Mission, rapidly took shape and attracted a surprising number of Afrikaans-speaking people to its ranks. David du Plessis emerged from this fellowship to a significant place of leadership in a worldwide charismatic movement fifty years later.[36]

Revival had stirred the fellowship groups in Germany in early 1905. Many adherents of the Gemeinschaftsbewegung became interested in the Pentecostal phenomena.[37] A State Church pastor, Jonathan Paul (already noted), had visited Oslo in 1907,[38] and later that year two Norwegian ladies joined forces with Heinrich Dallmeyer in Kassel, where a resulting movement was designated as 'Die psychische Epidemie in Hessen-Kassel' or more simply, the Kassel movement, which in the face of great opposition to its extremes, dwindled.[39] In 1909, the leaders of the Gemeinschaftsbewegung issued the Berlin Declaration against the work.[40] But in October 1909, Barratt visited Mühlheim in the Ruhr,[41] where Pentecostal assemblies under Jonathan Paul were engaging in wholesome ministry and ardent evangelism.[42]

Pentecostalism caught on slowly in Switzerland, for the lack of competent Swiss leadership. Barratt visited Zurich and other cities. In the Netherlands, glossolalia appeared in Amsterdam in late 1907, a link being established with the British conventions. The movement generated little influence, and this was the case in France also for many years.[43]

The Pentecostal ministry began in Estonia in 1908, in Latvia about the same time; it entered Russia through St. Petersburg and Odessa, and grew to 350 Assemblies of God before the 1929 persecutions distressed all of the Russian Evangelical believers.[44]

In India, spontaneous and unsought 'glossolalia' occurred during the Revival of 1905 at Mukti[45] and a few other stations. There were manifestations in China about that time, for in 1908 the Alliance reported recurrence of revival in Wuchow in South China, where a spontaneous outburst of 'tongues' began in the schools.[46]

That year, A. G. Garr proceeded from Azusa Street to South China, where he reported that a couple of hundred Chinese and foreign workers had spoken in tongues.[47] In North China, in 1909, a Presbyterian deacon from Shantung journeyed to Shanghai to seek the 'baptism of the Spirit.' Within forty years, the (Pentecostal) True Jesus Church had grown to a hundred thousand members.[48]

Surprisingly, neither the Taikyo Dendo in Japan nor the Pentecost in Korea was followed by a Pentecostal movement. That the major denominations there supported the Revival is a suggested reason, but this applied to other countries.

Cecil Polhill-Turner (of the Cambridge Seven) sought a charismatic experience in Los Angeles.[49] He retained his place on the Council of the China Inland Mission until he died. In 1909, a Pentecostal Missionary Union was formed, with Cecil Polhill-Turner as president, and a couple of missionaries sailed that year for India, next year a larger party going to China. Before long, a notable work was begun in the Congo under William Burton and James Salter of Preston.

Meanwhile, in the land of its birth, Pentecostalism had spread very widely.[50] Between 10,000 and 15,000 people were reckoned Pentecostal in 1906. Twenty years later,[51] they had increased tenfold; by mid-century, the various denominations of Pentecostal origin claimed more than a million.[52] By far, the largest body was the Assemblies of God, based upon Springfield, Missouri. Another rapidly growing denomination rose from the exotic ministry of Aimee Semple McPherson in Los Angeles, the Foursquare Gospel Church. Both these denominations gained community goodwill, this in spite of bitter opposition, general prejudice, internal weakness, or occasional scandals.

The disrepute into which Pentecostalism fell can be better understood if the records of its extremists be studied. A. J. Tomlinson, later dismissed from oversight of the Church of God, provided an example. In an entry in his journal in 1909, he recorded the following:[53]

> Yesterday was a wonderful day in the camp. . . I was seized with two or three spells of weeping, and finally fell on my back under the overwhelming power of God. After screaming for a while ... I became a little more quiet. Someone said I was prostrated there for two hours . . . The meeting that followed during the day is indescribable. Men, women and children screaming, shouting, praying, leaping, dancing and falling prostrate under God's overwhelming power . . .

There was worldwide opposition to the new manifestations and the most violent attacks came from some of the most evangelical leaders and teachers among Protestants.[54] In 'Pentecost,' no John Wesley had risen to guide by wisdom or recommend by acknowledged scholarship. There were extremes and extravagances that the later Pentecostal leaders deplored. There was a tendency among unconvinced denominationalists to talk of counterfeits and satanic motivation. As the opposition increased, Pentecostals began to withdraw membership from other denominations and form Pentecostal congregations. These displayed a remarkable variety, both in form and affiliation.

As Pentecostalism drew its adherents from Anglican, Baptist, Lutheran, Methodist and Presbyterian fellowships, it borrowed various forms of church government and polity, giving birth to denominations trivially divided from one another in a variety of ways.[55]

Unlike parasitic movements, Pentecostalism developed both home and foreign missionary activity, right from the beginning. As early as 1907, missionaries were proceeding to far off mission fields from American Pentecostal assemblies—sometimes, they naively considered their 'tongues' xenolalic (actual foreign languages),[56] learning by hard experience that 'the gift' was for 'edifying' rather than for evangelism. Yet in spite of this, the Pentecostal missionary enterprise became worldwide, in some places outstripping the older societies and denominations.

Certain simple conclusions are unavoidable. Between the worldwide Awakening of the 1900s and the Pentecostal revival that followed, there were obvious differences: the general Awakening was not glossolalic, though it was charismatic in other ways, whereas Pentecostalism laid its stress on two spiritual gifts, tongues and healing, and even formalized their operation; and there were obvious similarities: for both took their rise from among the common people; both began as a straightforward interdenominational movement; both stressed an unplanned ministry of the Spirit; both were emotionally demonstrative, and both also suffered from a tendency to occasional emotionalism, the exploitation of the feelings to achieve certain reactions.

Now that the story of the worldwide awakening has been told, it will be difficult henceforth for historians to account for the Pentecostal movement worldwide without relating it to the general awakening of the early twentieth century.

25

RENT HEAVENS—RAVAGED EARTH

Prof. Paul Ramsey, in introducing Gabriel Vahanian's treatise upon the absurd 'Death of God' debate, asserted: '... every revival of Christianity in the past three hundred years has revived less of it, and each was less and less an enduring revival.'[1]

It is not easy to imagine what criteria were used on which to base such a remarkable opinion. If Christendom were meant by Christianity, it is easy to scan the scope of a given revival and to gauge the number of people influenced thereby. The Puritan Revival influenced fewer people in a smaller territory than were influenced by the Revival of Whitefield and Wesley's days in the British Isles and American Colonies.

Again, if the number of converts is the test, it is certain that the number of converts added to Methodist churches alone in seven fruitful years in the Revival of 1858-59 far exceeded the total won in Wesley's lifetime, without calculating numbers added to membership of other Churches.[2]

Again, the 1858-59 Revival moved the United States and United Kingdom, affected Scandinavia and other parts of Europe as well as the churches of South Africa, Australasia and parts of India. It was as worldwide as Evangelicalism. But this present treatise has shown that the extent of the Awakening of 1900-1910 far exceeded that of the 1858-1859 Revival. The numbers converted certainly matched those of the mid-nineteenth century in Britain and United States —not to mention unprecedented ingatherings overseas.

It would be wearisome to extend the argument further, to show that the growth of the Church in Brazil or Indonesia exceeds anything experienced three hundred years ago. True, Christianity is in decline in certain countries, but it is not because of Evangelical Revival, rather the lack of it.

If Christian faith were meant by Christianity, it can be stated boldly that successive Evangelical Awakenings are each more radically proto-New Testament in emphasis— the Reformers were more evangelical than the Lollards, the Puritans were more evangelical than the Reformers,

186

and the Revivalists of the eighteenth century were more zealous for soulwinning than the Puritans, while those of the nineteenth were much more enterprising than forerunners in the eighteenth; and ecumenists have conceded that twentieth century Pentecostalists outdo older denominations in zeal.[3]

Sir William Robertson Nicoll, famous religious editor of the period of awakenings under survey,[4] declared:[5]

> It is by revivals of religion that the Church of God makes its most visible advance. When all things seem becalmed, when no breath stirs the air, when the sea is like lead and the sky is low and gray, when all worship seems to have ended but the worship of matter, then it is that the Spirit of God is poured upon the Church, then it is that the Christianity of the apostles and martyrs, not that of the philosophers and liberals, keeps rising—as Vinet says—from the catacombs of oblivion, and appears young and fresh in the midst of the obsolete things of yesterday and the day before.

The worldwide Awakening of the early twentieth century came at the end of fifty years of evangelical advance, following the outpouring of the Spirit far and wide in 1858-59 and the sixties. Thus it did not represent a recovery from a long night of despair caused by rampant infidelity, as was the case in the days of Wesley. It seemed, rather, a blaze of evening glory at the end of 'the Great Century.'

Why did it occur at the time it did? The ways of God are past finding out. One can only surmise. A subtler form of infidelity had arisen, a compromise between Christianity and humanism. A more sophisticated interpretation of human conduct was in vogue, inspired by Freud who spoke of God as an Illusion.[6]

The prescient widsom of its Author may also account for the sudden spread of the Revival of 1900-1910. Within ten years, the awful slaughter of World War I had begun, and a way of life passed into the twilight of history.

Arnold Toynbee, reminiscing, recalled the trauma of the time, when half his classmates perished in battle. Oneself was a child when the news of the Battle of the Somme threw every family in his native city into mourning for the finest of their fathers and sons and brothers killed in action.[7]

The Awakening was a kind of harvest before the devastation of Christendom. It was Sir Edward Grey who lamented in 1914 that the lights of civilization were going out one by one, not to be lit again in his lifetime. The upheavals of war unloosed the times of revolution on mankind. A biographer of Wilbur Chapman observed:[8]

> As we look back over these extraordinary religious
> awakenings which ... so quickened the churches and
> so effectively pressed the claims of God upon the
> consciences of multitudes, we cannot escape the con-
> viction that God in gracious providence was reaping a
> spiritual harvest before He permitted the outburst of
> revolutionary forces that have overwhelmed the world,
> impoverished almost every nation, produced economic
> and social chaos, and stained with dishonor the pride of
> Christian civilization. In the history of revivals, it has
> often been noted that such restoral periods are a warn-
> ing of, and synchronize with, impending judgment. The
> harvest is gathered before the field is doomed to death.

The early twentieth century Evangelical Awakening was
a worldwide movement. It did not begin with the phenomenal
Welsh Revival of 1904-05. Rather its sources were in the
springs of little prayer meetings which seemed to arise
spontaneously all over the world, combining into the streams
of expectation which became a river of blessing in which the
Welsh Revival became the greatest cataract.

Meetings for prayer for revival in evangelical gatherings
such as Moody Bible Institute and the Keswick Convention
greeted the new century—not surprisingly. What was remarkable was that missionaries and national believers in
obscure places in India, the Far East, Africa and Latin
America seemed moved at the same time to pray for phenomenal revival in their fields and world wide. Most of
them had never seen or heard of phenomenal revival occurring
on missionfields, and few of them had witnessed it at home.
Their experience was limited to reading of past revivals.

The first manifestation of phenomenal revival occurred
simultaneously among Boer prisoners of war in places ten
thousand miles apart, as far away as Bermuda and Ceylon.
The work was marked by extraordinary praying, by faithful
preaching, conviction of sin, confession and repentance with
lasting conversions and hundreds of enlistments for missionary service. The spirit of Revival spread to South Africa in
the throes of economic depression.

Not without significance, an Awakening began in 1900 in
the churches of Japan, which had long suffered from a period
of retarded growth. It started in an unusually effective
movement to prayer, followed by an unusually intensive
effort of evangelism, matched by an awakening of Japanese
urban masses to the claims of Christ, and such an ingathering
that the total membership of the churches almost doubled
within the decade. Why did the Japanese Awakening occur

in 1900? It would have been impossible four years later when Japan became involved in momentous war with Russia.

Significantly also for the evangelistic follow-up of the general Awakening, the Torrey and Alexander team found that unusual praying had prepared the way for the most fruitful evangelistic ministry ever known in New Zealand and Australia, and the unprecedented success of the campaigns launched Torrey and Alexander (and later Chapman and Alexander) on their worldwide evangelistic crusades, conventionally run but accompanied by revival of the churches and awakening of the masses.[9]

Gipsy Smith experienced much the same kind of response in his Mission of Peace in war-weary South Africa, successful evangelism provoking an awakening of the population to Christian faith. At the same time, a rising tide of blessing and prevenient local revivals were reported in some churches as far apart as Korea and Chile.

Meanwhile worldwide prayer meetings were intensifying. Undoubtedly, the farthest-felt happening of the decade was the Welsh Revival, which began as a local revival in early 1904, moved the whole of Wales by the end of the year, produced the mystic figure of Evan Roberts as leader yet filled simultaneously almost every church in the principality.

The Welsh Revival was the farthest-reaching of the movements of the general Awakening, for it affected the whole of the Evangelical cause in India, Korea and China, renewed revival in Japan and South Africa, and sent a wave of awakening over Africa, touching also strategic countries in Latin America and the Islands of the South Seas.

The Welsh Revival emphasized confession of sin and confession of faith. Aided by the natural fervency of the Celtic folk, it so moved Wales that in several districts, the magistrates found themselves without crimes to judge. It resulted in a hundred thousand converts added to the Church —every denomination receiving benefit.

Time and again, the writer has been asked why the Welsh Revival did not last. It did last. The most exciting phase lasted two years. There was an inevitable drifting away of some whose interest was superficial, perhaps one person in forty of the total membership of the Churches. Even critics of the movement conceded that eighty percent of the converts remained in the Churches after five years, which is a higher coefficient of endurance than would be claimed by advocates of any other method of church extension.[10]

But there was a falling away in Wales. Why? It did not occur among the converts of the 1904 Revival, other than the minority noted. Converts of the Revival continued to be the choicest segment of church life, even in the 1930s, when the writer studied the spiritual life of Wales closely. Two disasters overtook Wales.[11] The first World War slaughtered a high proportion of the generation revived, or converted, or only influenced by the Revival, leaving a dearth of men in the churches; the coal mines of Wales were hit in the 1920s by tragic unemployment, which continued into the thirties in the Depression; and the class under military age during the war, infants during the Revival, espoused the gospel of Marxism. The Aneurin Bevans replaced the Keir Hardies in the party.

There was yet another reason. The Welsh Revival took scripture knowledge for granted, and preaching thus deemed superfluous was at a minimum. The Welsh revival constituency was ill-prepared for a new onslaught of anti-evangelicalism which captured a generation of otherwise disillusioned Welshmen. The province of Ulster moved into the place held by the principality of Wales as a land of evangelistic activities.

The story of the Welsh Revival has often been told. Most Christian people, including scholars, have been unaware of the extent of the Awakening which followed in the English-speaking world—in the United Kingdom, the United States, Canada, South Africa, Australia and faraway New Zealand.

Church membership in the United States in seven major Protestant denominations increased by more than two million in five years (870,389 new communicants in 1906) and continued rising.[12] This did not include the gains of the younger denominations of Pentecostal or Holiness dynamic whose rate of increase was considerably greater. In Great Britain, it is difficult to count converts in the Church of England, but, in the years 1903-1906, the other Protestant denominations gained ten percent, or 300,000.[13]

It is likewise difficult to estimate the gains in the Dutch Reformed Church in South Africa, for most converts therein already possessed family affiliation. The Methodist Church increased by thirty percent in the three years of revival.[14] No doubt, the same pattern applied in New Zealand-Australia.

How many Christians today have known that Norway was swept in 1905 by a Revival that was unparalleled for a hundred years for its moral and social effects—as in Wales? The same 1905 awakening moved Denmark, Sweden and Finland, and other European countries with Protestant population.

The writer has visited all the States of India, has addressed more than a million people there, and has lectured in twenty of their theological colleges, and to hundreds of missionaries and national pastors. In all this, he encountered only one who knew of the extent of the Indian Revival of 1905-1906, a retired professor of theology. Yet the Awakening in India moved every province and the Christian population increased by seventy percent, sixteen times as fast as the Hindu.[15] The Protestant rate of increase was almost double that of the Roman Catholic.

In Burma, 1905 'brought ingathering quite surpassing anything known in the history of the mission.' The A.B.M.U. baptized 2000 Karens that year, 200 being the average. In a single church, 1340 Shans were baptized in December, 3113 in all being added in the 'marvelous ingathering.'[16]

The story of the Korean Revival of 1907 has been told and retold. It is less well-known that the Revival came in three waves, 1903, 1905 and 1907—the membership of the Churches quadrupling within a decade, the national Church being created from almost nothing by the movement.[17]

The revival campaigns of Jonathan Goforth in Manchuria have been recorded and published, but the extent of the Awakening in China between the Boxer Uprising and the 1911 Revolution has not been apprehended. China's greatest living evangelist, survivor of the China-wide Awakening of 1927-1939, told the writer that he had not even heard of the Awakening in every province in the 1900s, apart from the post-Boxer revulsion. Yet the number of Protestant communicants doubled in a decade to quarter of a million, twice that figure comprising the total Evangelical community.[18]

In Indonesia,[19] the numbers of Evangelicals, 100,000 in 1903, trebled in the decade of general Awakening to 300,000, and in subsequent movements of phenomenal power, the number of believers on one little island (Nias) surpassed the latter figure, winning two-thirds the population. Protestant membership in Malagasia increased sixty-six percent in the years of Revival, 1905-1915. And pioneering success was achieved in the newly-opened Philippines.

The Awakening had limited effect in the Latin American countries: unusual revival in Brazil, phenomenal awakening in Chile, with Evangelical membership in both countries starting to climb—until in our times it passed the number of practising Roman Catholics; pioneering continued in other republics with sparse results but promise of future harvest.

The Edinburgh World Missionary Conference recognized
that more progress had been made in Africa in the first decade of the twentieth century than experienced hitherto. The
Protestant communicants in the African mission fields increased in 1903-1910 from 300,000 to 500,000, there having
been many awakenings in various parts in those years.[20] But
the full impact of the Welsh Revival was not felt until the
war years, when phenomenal revival occurred among the
Africans. In the next half century, the increase was double
that of the general population.

The extent of the Awakening of the early 1900s is sufficient
to mark it off as a very significant movement, and the phenomena of the Revival do likewise. There is plenty of justi-
fication for a meticulous study on the part of experts qualified
in the field of psychology.

The reader of the reports of the Awakening cannot fail to
notice the picturesque descriptions of the onset of the phenomena—in Wales, it was called 'a hurricane of audible
prayer'; in India, 'there was a noise like distant thunder'; in
Korea, 'the noise of the surf in an ocean of prayer'; in Africa
'suddenly there came the sound of a rushing mighty wind';
and elsewhere one reads of earthquake, flood, storm, fire.
These figures of speech were used to describe no ordinary
event in the assembling of believers.

Nor were those who used them people of over-excitable
temperament. Witnesses included such as Campbell Morgan,
Amy Carmichael, Donald Fraser and Lord William Cecil;
so reliable were the observers reporting that a staid Boston
editor felt obliged to inform his readers that [21]

> the fact that the strange phenomena are contrary to
> our own personal experience should not be an obstacle
> to the credibility of the reports. In all other respects,
> these who tell of the wonderful experiences are reliable
> men and women not easily carried away by enthusiasm
> and excitement.

A report from Dr. David Downie, a veteran of thirty-
three years' service in India, told of the dumb speaking: [22]

> In the village of Covur, a little girl about ten years of
> age ... dumb from birth began attending the meetings
> and soon after was seen to be making efforts to pray.
> At first, it was simply an inarticulate noise, but gradu-
> ally articulate sounds were heard—and now she speaks,
> sings and prays, and we have heard her do all three.
> Her older sister is here in school and testifies that till
> then she had never heard her sister speak a word.

Dr. Downie also told of one of the high school girls who went into a trance and remained in it for three hours. She sat with her head thrown back, her arms folded and her face radiant. She was perfectly oblivious to what was going on all around her, but was heard talking to some unseen person or persons. Sometimes she would laugh and other times shake her head in disapproval.[23] Such trances occurred all over India, and elsewhere in many a country.[24]

The 'Christian-humanist' dismisses such odd phenomena as easily explained by psychology, a notion dismissed by qualified psychologists. At the University of California (Los Angeles), Prof. James C. Coleman once remarked to the writer upon the paucity of published works on psychology of religious experience.[25] In an age when psychologists have been enthusiastically analysing every phase of human existence, it seems odd to think that the last definitive work on religious experience was published in 1902 by the versatile philosopher, William James.[26]

A contemporary expert, Walter Houston Clark, offered a thought-provoking comment:[27]

> It is a paradox that, in view of such evidence, modern psychologists should be so incurious about the dynamics involved and so neglectful of a force in human nature with the influence religion has for both good and evil in human personality and human history.
>
> Since the time of William James, the psychological study of religion has fallen on dull days. In our day, its prestige has gradually begun to revive, but the conventional psychologist still tends to observe it warily as a subject that he is not quite sure belongs in his field.

Both Freud and Jung wrote on religion and in America, leading scholars—Gardner Murphy, Gordon Allport, Hobart Mowrer and Abraham Maslow—contributed studies. There are keen students of evangelical experience, such as Owen Brandon in Canterbury. But one must look in vain for any up-to-date works upon phenomena of the great evangelical awakenings, past or present, for extraordinary happenings well attested have been reported in Timor's 1965 Revival.

The Awakening of the early 1900s was noted for its intense conviction of sin, which seemed to be irresistible. There seems to be no way of attributing such intense conviction to any human technique or device or method or influence of a powerful personality. Evan Roberts was a miner; Albert Lunde was a sailor; and neither possessed extraordinary personal magnetism. In India and Korea, the Awakening presented no outstanding personality; the same was true of other countries: observers of the movement simply attributed the work of conviction to the Spirit of God.

The response to such conviction was another matter. The varied response came from the human subjects of conviction and was prompted by temperament and circumstances. The teaching of Evan Roberts certainly directed the response in Wales. His first point of exhortation stressed the confession of all known sin, to God and to the parties wronged. Doubtless, Evan Roberts had derived his message from the very appropriate verses of Scripture which were the subject of study of the missionaries in Korea also. Confession of sin occurred almost everywhere the Revival was effective. Sometimes it was restrained; other times it was painfully unrestrained.[28] The Korean believers used the word 'vomit' to describe their getting rid of the sickness of the soul. It was not an inappropriate word for the relief they felt in spirit when they renounced their sin.

In Asia, it was all the more remarkable that people would risk 'loss of face' to confess their faults. The Chinese are pathologically sensitive to public opinion, and yet in the 1908 Awakening there were sins confessed that Chinese torture had failed to bring out.[29]

This was less true among the tribes of Africa, where what was shocking to Europeans was of no great seriousness to a tribesman. In India, it had been a matter of common remark that the people, rich and poor, never seemed to have any deep sense or real conviction of sin, doubtless due to Hindu theological values.[30] But happenings of the years 1906-1907 changed all that in the minds of the missionaries, who found themselves the unwilling hearers of shocking confessions. Some missionaries deplored the public nature of some confessions; none regretted the judgment and renunciation of the sins confessed.

The compulsion to confess is a recognized human trait. Psychologists can cite examples of its extraordinary outworkings.[31] Scores of unrelated people confessed to the kidnapping of the Lindbergh baby, for example. Confessions in Communist demonstration trials have illustrated the unreal quality of self-incrimination. The Chinese Communists set out to use the public confession principle known in 'revival' meetings to accomplish their own ends, substituting perjured accusers for the action of the Holy Spirit.

Seriously, psychiatrists have organized group confession for its cathartic value. There was the same value in simultaneous audible confession, and even more so when it was followed up by restitution, reconciliation and restoration on the part of the individual concerned. Confession had its dangers, too. The complusion to confess could be exploited, and the confession could be harmfully provocative.

There had been emotional extravagances noted in the Awakenings on the frontier of the United States in the early nineteenth century, as there were similar manifestations in Wesley's day. Yet the Revival of 1857-1858 in the United States was entirely free of emotional extremes, whereas the Awakening of 1859 in parts of the United Kingdom was marked by unusual conduct which provoked criticism.

In Britain later, there were those who decried the Welsh Revival as 'a wind of emotion.' No doubt the writer himself (extremely unemotional by temperament and training) would have found the atmosphere of those Welsh meetings somewhat volcanic. At the same time, the ideal of the 'stiff-upper-lip' in things spiritual one finds without warrant in Scripture.

Fear of emotion has become a phobia. One has seen more passion displayed in a cybernetics post-graduate seminar on curriculum planning than in congregational meetings where the serious issues of life were under discussion.

There appeared to be two dangers in the area of the emotions. The first was emotionalism, the exploitation of feeling for unworthy objects. The other was lack of control. A friendly critic of the movement in Andhra suggested that proper leadership of the meetings by sympathetic but cautious chairmen would direct the wild forces of despair and of joy into the proper channels.[32]

In the Welsh Revival, there was no artificial utilization of emotion. In this connection, it is significant that Dr. Sargant, in a popular book which unnecessarily disturbed some British Christians, blithely suggested that the Welsh 'hwyl' (a device of Cymric oratory) was used during the Welsh Revival to achieve emotional effect.[33] The records of the Welsh Revival show that not only was the 'hwyl' entirely absent, but even sermons were rarely delivered in the revival meetings!

It was most significant that the Awakening of the 1900s was ecumenical, in the best senses of the word.[34] It was thoroughly interdenominational. The foregoing narratives have provided instances of Anglican, Baptist, Brethren, Congregational, Disciple, Lutheran, Methodist, Presbyterian and Reformed congregations sharing in the Revival. There is a total lack of evidence of any response on the part of Roman Catholic or Greek Orthodox communities, but this is not surprising, for it was so in the days of the Puritans, of Wesley, of Finney, and of Moody. Only in the mid-twentieth century, when their changing attitude to Scripture has accompanied a changing attitude to dissent, have heretofore non-evangelical church bodies been affected by evangelical movements.

In his treatise on the mid-nineteenth century Awakening, the writer was criticized for having so short a chapter on the theology of the Revival.[35] This 'default' must occur again, for there was so little or nothing new in the movement. The first seven points of the doctrinal statement of the Evangelical Alliance of 1846 seemed to state all that the leaders held in consensus. There was also a noticeable preoccupation with the doctrine of the Holy Spirit everywhere manifested. The subsequent Pentecostal movement carried this interest farther, but remained within evangelical boundaries. A preoccupation with the doctrine of the Second Coming arose.

The background of the church life which entertained the Revival was evangelical: an emphasis on preaching rather than the sacraments in public worship; congregational prayer meetings; family worship; personal Bible study and personal prayer; a morality based on the ten commandments, with an emphasis on the social virtues of truthfulness, honesty and sexual purity; all of this taken for granted in the churches in which revival began, though not in the areas outreached.

The writer once heard an American professor of church history declare that no Great Awakening, after 1850, exhibited a social conscience, the implication being that the remarkable Revival of 1858 had achieved no social benefit. At the time this remark was made, the standard work on the 1859 Revival in Britain had not been published, detailing the social effects of that awakening,[36] some of which were exported to the United States, which was in the throes of the War between the States in the aftermath of the 1858 Revival.

There is no telling what might have happened in society had not the First World War absorbed the energies of the nations in the aftermath of the Edwardian Awakening. The time and talent and treasure of the people are pre-empted in any struggle for national existence, and what little is over is devoted to the welfare of the fighting men and the victims of war. This was the case in the American Civil War, and the case in Europe between 1914 and 1918.

Even so, no one could possibly say that the Awakenings of the 1900s in Great Britain or the United States were without social impact. In Britain, there was utter unanimity on the part of observers regarding 'the high ethical character' of the movement. The renewed obedience to the four great social commandments reduced crime, promoted honesty, inculcated truthfulness and produced chastity. Drunkenness and gambling were sharply curtailed. It was the same in the United States, for a wave of morality went over the country, producing a revival of righteousness. Corruption in state and civic government encountered a setback which was attributed by observers in church and state to the Great Awakening. For a dozen years, the country was committed in degree to civic and national integrity, until new forces of corruption triumphed again in the 1920s.

The revived Evangelicals were more concerned with the reform of society than with the overthrow of government. Evangelical Christianity, throughout its heyday of social reform in the nineteenth century, repudiated the use of force outside the law. Persuasion was used to convince the people of the evil of slavery, for example, and force was used by legitimate authority to stamp out the slave trade. Hatred and violence were regarded as hostile to the Gospel.

What was the social effect outside Western Protestantism? On mission fields, the missionaries multiplied their schools and hospitals.[37] In twenty years, pupils in Christian schools in India doubled to 595,725; 90% of all nurses were Christian, mostly trained at mission hospitals. In China, missionaries pioneered secondary and higher education and laid the foundations of the medical service; the beginnings of the African educational systems and medical service were due likewise.

The nineteenth century and the first decade of the twentieth century found Protestants largely united in two great loyalties: the authority of Scripture and the unity of the Body of Christ. Both were generally taken for granted.

In the same period, Protestant forces were engaged in two great enterprises: evangelism and social action. True, those who emphasized the social implications of the Gospel had begun to advocate a 'new evangelism,' one which aimed at 'redeeming' societies rather than individuals. But a majority recognized evangelism's priority without denying their social responsibility.[38]

Just as the western world's populations were divided into two opposing camps which finally pitched into open warfare, so also the Protestant constituencies were being polarized. Modernism rose to dominate denominational leadership, and fundamentalism rose to challenge it.

The modernist was weak in the doctrine of the authority of Scripture but strong on the unity of the Body of Christ. The fundamentalist was strong in the doctrine of the authority of Scripture but weak on the unity of the Body of Christ. The modernist was weak in the primary task of the Church, evangelism, the winning of men to personal faith in Christ, but strong in the social work of the Gospel, even making it the primary message of the Church. The fundamentalist was strong in conventional evangelism, but often weak in social action, more so when proposed by the modernist.

The warfare which broke out between the two parties was bitter in the extreme. It affected almost every denominational fellowship. It set brother against brother in a kind of civil war. The story of that fundamentalist-modernist war does not belong to this treatise. But the question arises, was the 1905 Awakening in any way responsible for its outbreak?

The records fail to show a single instance of partisan controversy along the lines which afterwards divided Protestants. True, a vitriolic attack was mounted on Evan Roberts by Peter Price, but the latter claimed to be evangelical and evangelistic, and his venom was personal. Controversy was already raging when the 1905 Revival began in Scandinavia; anti-Evangelicals [39] tried to ignore the Awakening in Europe. Awakening in North America produced a pause in the building up of tension between the opposing forces. There was no controversy in the Latin American countries, where only an elementary evangelism could make headway. In India, and in the Orient, there was an absence of controversy. It could therefore be said that the Awakening of the 1900s, as in 1858, was non-controversial. Reaction came later.

Similarities between the Revival of 1858-59 and that of the 1900s are easily recognized. Both found their beginnings in prayer meetings, and in both the repentance of the Church was followed by the awakening of multitudes of outsiders. In both awakenings, conviction of sin was evident. In the Revival of the 1900s, confession of sin in open meetings occurred more often, but was spontaneous rather than induced.

It is even more interesting to compare the characteristics of the Awakening of that decade with the prototype of all evangelical revivals in the Acts of the Apostles, a perennial textbook for such movements.

Our Lord told His disciples: 'It is not for you to know the times or seasons which the Father has fixed by His own authority. But you shall receive power when the Holy Spirit has come upon you; and you shall be My witnesses . . . to the end of the earth.' Thus was an outpouring of the Spirit predicted, and soon fulfilled.[40]

Then began extraordinary praying among the disciples in the upper room. Who knows what self-judgment and confession and reconciliation went on? There were occasions for such. But, when they were all together in one place, there suddenly came from heaven a sound like the rush of a mighty wind and it filled all the house.[41] The filling of the Holy Spirit was followed by xenolalic evangelism, not repeated in the times of the Apostles, nor authenticated satisfactorily since.

The Apostle Peter averred that the outpouring fulfilled the prophecy of Joel, which predicted the prophesying of young men and maidens, the seeing of visions and dreams by young and old.[42] He preached the death and resurrection of Jesus Christ.[43] What was the response? The hearers were pierced, stabbed, stung, stunned, smitten — these are the synonyms of a rare verb which Homer used to signify being drummed to earth.[44] It was no ordinary feeling; nor was the response a mild request for advice. It was more likely an uproar of entreaty, the agonizing cry of a multitude.

Those who responded to the Apostle's call for repentance confessed their faith publicly in the apostolic way. About three thousand were added to the church. Then followed apostolic teaching, fellowship, communion and prayers.[45]

What kind of fellowship? Doubtless the words of Scripture were often used liturgically, but it is certain that the koinonia was open.[46] What kind of prayers? There are instances of individual petitions of power and beauty, but there are also suggestions of simultaneous, audible prayer in which the main thrust of petition is recorded, as in the prophet's day.

The Apostles continued to urge their hearers to change and turn to God, which they did by the thousands. And no hostile power seemed for the moment able to hinder them. Persecution followed, but the work of God advanced.

The Awakening of the 1900s began in prayer meetings also, with heart-searching and petition. There were numerous reports of a mighty rushing wind, and innumerable accounts of the outpouring of the Spirit and the infilling of believers. One uncovered no authenticated records of xenolalic (foreign tongues) utterance, and but few of (unknown) glossolalic.[47]

There were extraordinary manifestations of prophesying by young men and maidens, and not a few instances of unusual dreams and visions. The same message of the death and resurrection of Christ was preached, and the same sort of results were evident, hearers stabbed to their hearts and smitten with conviction. And the response was the same, a crying out for help and a turning to God in repentance.

The teaching that followed was scriptural, as was the communion. Fellowship and prayer were open, subject to the moving of the Spirit rather than programmed planning.

During the thrust of the movement, there was no immediate retaliation or reprisal on the part of hostile authorities; the opposition was silent. Believers almost unanimously testified to the sense of the presence of God in the meetings. There is no record of any avowed Evangelical Christian expressing doubt regarding the Divine origin of the great outpouring. Many deplored the excesses of the human response, but none regretted the movement and its ethical impact.

The story of this Revival has not been recorded before. It is rough-hewn, unpolished. Soon the debunkers will sharpen their tools. But there is no need for any Evangelical to apologize for an account of a movement following the pattern of Pentecost in the Acts of the Apostles, a pattern which seems to be alien to so many professed experts who have never witnessed the power of God at work in a community.

During that decade of Revival, Dr. Alexander Whyte, the 'prince of Scottish preachers,' a convert of 1859, declared: 'There is a Divine mystery about Revivals. God's sovereignty is in them. . . I may not live to see it. But the day will come when there will be a great Revival over the whole earth.'[48]

Bessie Porter Head, a recorder of some of the events of the 1905 Awakening, wrote for the Church at large:[49]

> O Breath of Life, come sweeping through us,
>   Revive Thy Church with life and power;
> O Breath of Life, come, cleanse, renew us
>   And fit Thy Church to meet this hour.
>
> O Wind of God, come bend us, break us,
>   Till humbly we confess our need;
> Then in Thy tenderness remake us,
>   Revive, restore, for this we plead.
>
> Revive us, Lord! Is zeal abating
>   While harvest fields are vast and white?
> Revive us, Lord, the world is waiting,
>   Equip Thy Church to spread the light.

Information for this chapter was found in Welsh denominational periodicals of the 1900s, kindly translated by Dr. Eifion Evans, who later published his volume, THE WELSH REVIVAL OF 1904. Other sources were newspapers, including a London weekly, THE CHRISTIAN, supplemented by details from the Diaries of the Rev. Seth Joshua in the Archives of the National Library of Wales at Aberystwyth and from notes of the Rev. Peter Joshua, son of the famous Welshman and now retired in California; with bound reports from Cardiff's WESTERN MAIL in the writer's possession, and some references to the very informative biography by Dr. D. M. Phillips, entitled EVAN ROBERTS, the Welsh Revivalist, as well as published reminiscences of Rhys Bevan Jones, founder of Porth Bible Institute. There are many enthusiastic accounts of beginnings of the 1904 Welsh Revival, from the notes of Mrs. Penn-Lewis to the recollections of G. T. B. Davis of Philadelphia, but few are of scholarly value—one of which, THE WELSH RELIGIOUS REVIVAL, a Retrospect and a Criticism, by Dr. J. Vyrnwy Morgan, is marred by an undisguised bias against Evan Roberts and for his bitterest critic. In 1968, Norman Williams contributed an account of the 1904 Revival to THE GLAMORGAN HISTORIAN, a fair statement of Welsh popular opinion after sixty years; and the Rev. B. P. Jones published THE KING'S CHAMPIONS, describing the careers of five of the greatest men of the 1904 movement. In addition, use was made by the researchist of his recollection of conversations in 1934 with Evan Roberts and other survivors of the Welsh Revival.

1   Y GOLEUAD, 11-iv-05.   2   YR HAUL, 15-iii-05.
3   Y GOLEUAD, 3-i-05, cf. Y TYST, 19-x-1904.
4   see Y GOLEUAD; cf. Y DRYSORFA, November 1902.
5   Y CYFAILL EGLWSIG, December 1902;   cf. MISSIONARY REVIEW OF THE WORLD, 1905, pp. 163ff.
6   M. N. Garrard, MRS. PENN-LEWIS, p. 26.
7   R. B. Jones, RENT HEAVENS, chapter ii.   8   Psalms 50, 5.
9   J. V. Morgan, THE WELSH RELIGIOUS REVIVAL, p. 124.
10 THE CHRISTIAN, London, 7-ix-05.
11 see T. M. Rees, SETH JOSHUA AND FRANK JOSHUA.
12 Seth Joshua's Diaries, Archives, Calvinistic Methodist Church.
13 THE CHRISTIAN, 7-ix-05.
14 Y DRYSORFA, April 1961 to December 1963, gives extracts from John Thicken's notes on the Rev. Joseph Jenkins.
15 THE CHRISTIAN, 7-ix-05.
16 Diaries of Seth Joshua; and interviews with Peter Joshua.
17 Seth Joshua Diaries.   18   personal knowledge.
19 Consolidated reports were issued in booklet form, in Cardiff WESTERN MAIL, iii, 31.   20 WESTERN MAIL, iii, pp. 29ff.
21 Evan Roberts, in WESTERN MAIL, iii, pp. 29-30.
22 see John Thickens, Y DRYSORFA, as cited above.
23 D. M. Phillips, EVAN ROBERTS, pp. 124ff, cf. iii, pp. 29-30.
24 WESTERN MAIL, consolidated reports, iii, p. 31.
25 J. J. Morgan, COFIANT EVAN PHILLIPS, p. 332.
26 D. M. Phillips, EVAN ROBERTS, p. 160 & p. 139.
27 cf. J. J. Morgan & D. M. Phillips, cited.
28 D. M. Phillips, EVAN ROBERTS, p. 224.

1   D. M. Phillips, EVAN ROBERTS, pp. 194ff.
2   G. T. B. Davis, WHEN THE FIRE FELL, p. 79.
3   D. M. Phillips, EVAN ROBERTS, p. 223.
4   SUNDAY COMPANION, quoted in Phillips, p. 198.
5   D. M. Phillips, EVAN ROBERTS, pp. 235-236.
6   see WESTERN MAIL, Cardiff, 10-xi-04.
7   D. M. Phillips, EVAN ROBERTS, pp. 206 & 207.
8   THE LIFE OF FAITH, London, 9-xi-04.
9   M. N. Garrard, MRS. PENN-LEWIS, p. 224.
10 WESTERN MAIL, Cardiff, 10-xi-04.
11 Consolidated reports, WESTERN MAIL, i: 4-5.
12 D. M. Phillips, EVAN ROBERTS, pp. 213-214.
13 WESTERN MAIL, i: 6 (report of 13-xi-04).
14 Report of 9-xi-04, WESTERN MAIL, i: 2.
15 WESTERN MAIL, i: 6 (report of 14-xi-04).
16 The Thickens papers, in Y DRYSORFA, 1963, p. 259.
17 Y DRYSORFA, 1905, pp. 250-252.
18 WESTERN MAIL, i: 6 (report of 13-xi-05).
19 Report of 21-xii-04, WESTERN MAIL, ii: 16.
20 W. N. Williams, O GOPA BRYN NEBO, pp. 61-83.
21 see Seth Joshua's Diaries.
22 W. N. Williams, O GOPA BRYN NEBO, pp. 61-83.
23 E. Keri Evans, FY MHERERINDOD YSBRYDOL, pp. 74ff.
24 Information from Rev. H. J. Galley of Widcombe, Bath.
25 WESTERN MAIL, i: 9 (reports of November 1904 onwards)
26 Report of 13-xii-04, WESTERN MAIL, ii: 6.
27 WESTERN MAIL, ii: 25 (report of 31-xii-04).
28 Report of 25-xii-04, WESTERN MAIL, ii: 19.
29 28, 29 & 30 xii 1904, WESTERN MAIL, ii: 21-24.
30 WESTERN MAIL, ii: 25-26 (consolidated reports)
31 see R. B. Jones, RENT HEAVENS, chapter iii.
32 RHOS HERALD, 26-xi-04, 4-iii-05.
33 CARNARVON AND DENBIGH HERALD, 9-xii-04.
34 'The Religious Revival,' 16-xii-04, in CARNARVON AND
    DENBIGH HERALD.
35 THE CHRISTIAN, 2-iii-05.   36 WESTERN MAIL, vi: 29.
37 Reports, WESTERN MAIL, iii: 17, & YR HERALD CYMRAEG
    10-i-05.   38 YR HERALD CYMRAEG, 24-i-05.
39 J. Penn-Lewis, THE AWAKENING IN WALES, p. 38.
40 H. Owen, BRASLUN O HANES M. C. MON, p. 146.
41 D. M. Phillips, EVAN ROBERTS, p. 305.
42 RECORD OF CHRISTIAN WORK, Chicago, 1905, p. 131.
43 R. B. Jones, RENT HEAVENS, passim.
44 The Rev. J. W. Owen, Rev. Owen M. Owen, Rev. W. Myrddin
    Lewis, Rev. Rees Howells, Mr. Edwin Willie, Mr. T. Lawton
    Loveridge, Mrs. Morgan (Llandaff), and Evan Roberts.
45 RECORD OF CHRISTIAN WORK, 1905, p. 131.
46 The Rev. W. Myrddin Lewis of Birmingham.
47 THE CHRISTIAN, 5-i-05.   48 THE CHRISTIAN, 12-i-05.
49 THE CHRISTIAN, 5-i-05.
50 BAPTIST COMMONWEALTH, Philadelphia, 16-xi-05.
51 The Rev. H. J. Galley of Bath, observer in 1904.

Welsh, British, American and specialized periodicals authenticate this chapter describing the impact of the 1904 Awakening in Wales.

1   J. V. Morgan, THE WELSH RELIGIOUS REVIVAL, pp. 248ff.
2   THE CHRISTIAN, 12-i-05.   3   THE CHRISTIAN, 5-i-05.
4   J. V. Morgan, THE WELSH RELIGIOUS REVIVAL, p. 247.
5   YR HERALD CYMRAEG, 24 & 31 i 05.
6   J. Penn-Lewis, THE AWAKENING IN WALES, p. 23.
7   see R. B. Jones, RENT HEAVENS, chapter v.
8   THE ADVANCE, Chicago, 23-ii-05.
9   THE CHRISTIAN, 13-iv-05.
10   R. B. Jones, RENT HEAVENS, chapter v.
11   THE ADVANCE, Chicago, 9-ii-05.
12   J. V. Morgan, pp. 163ff, cf. WESTERN MAIL, iii: 29.
13   J. V. Morgan, THE WELSH RELIGIOUS REVIVAL, p. 248.
14   BAPTIST COMMONWEALTH, 7-ix-05.
15   WESTERN MAIL, i: 31, consolidated reports.
16   YR EURGRAWN WESLEYAIDD, 1905, January, pp. 25ff; &
     February, pp. 65ff; March, pp. 98ff, etc.
17   THE FRIEND, London, 6-i-05 ff, pp. 7, 175, 211.
18   see CHURCH TIMES (Anglican); and CATHOLIC TIMES
     (Roman Catholic); cited in THE CHRISTIAN, 9 & 16 ii 05.
19   THE RECORD, London, 6-i-05.
20   THE CHRISTIAN, 16-iii-05, cf. RECORD, 10-iii-05.
21   THE CHRISTIAN, 5-i-05.
22   Orr, THE LIGHT OF THE NATIONS, p. 155; cf. following.
23   THE CHRISTIAN, 23-ii-05.
24   BAPTIST COMMONWEALTH, 26-i-05.
25   G. C. Morgan, Sermon in Westminster Chapel, 25-xii-04.
26   MISSIONARY REVIEW OF THE WORLD, 1905, pp. 728ff.
27   Report, 1905, MISSIONARY REVIEW OF THE WORLD, p. 168.
28   J. V. Morgan, THE WELSH RELIGIOUS REVIVAL, pp. 227ff.
29   G. C. Morgan, Sermon in Westminster Chapel, London, cited.
30   THE ADVANCE, Chicago, 2-iii-05.
31   R. B. Jones, RENT HEAVENS: Jessie Penn-Lewis, THE
     AWAKENING IN WALES, passim.
32   CARNARVON & DENBIGH HERALD, 16-xii-04; & WESTERN
     MAIL, 22-xii-04.
33   see Henri Bois, LE REVEIL AU PAYS DE GALLES.
34   CHRISTIAN HERALD, 23-xi-05.
35   Norman Williams, 'Evan Roberts and the 1904-1905 Revival,'
     in THE GLAMORGAN HISTORIAN, 1967, p. 35.
36   Thirty years later, A. J. Russell (editor, SUNDAY EXPRESS)
     told the writer of having called to interview Evan Roberts,
     but having been refused, the maid keeping the chain on the door!
37   Critics made much of a photograph deceitfully posed by a DAILY
     CHRONICLE reporter with a young penitent of the opposite sex,
     and J. Vyrnwy Morgan also made use of the photograph (p. 162).
38   Norman Williams, 'Evan Roberts and the 1904-05 Revival,' p. 33.
39   cf. general reports with Norman Williams, after sixty years.
40   WESTERN MAIL, iii: 22-25 (report of 22-i-05).
41   Reports of 24 & 25 i 05, WESTERN MAIL.

42 WESTERN MAIL, 31-i-05.
43 Issues following February 1905, WESTERN MAIL.
44 CHRISTIAN HERALD, London, 16-ii-05.
45 J.V. Morgan, THE WELSH RELIGIOUS REVIVAL, pp. 141-162.
46 cf. Acts viii, 26-40; xiii, 8-12; etc.
47 WESTERN MAIL, iv: 10, 12, 18, 22, etc.
48 cf. Henri Bois, LE REVEIL AU PAYS DE GALLES.
49 THE CHRISTIAN, 16-ii-05.
50 q. W. Arthur, on 'Eccentricity in Revival,' THE CHRISTIAN, 12-i-05.
51 see W. Ambrose Bebb, in YR ARGYFWNG, 1954, pp. 30ff.
52 VARIETIES OF RELIGIOUS EXPERIENCE, pp. 199, 505-506.
53 THE CHRISTIAN, 23-ii-05, quoting from THE LANCET & THE HOSPITAL, respectively.
54 Shaffer & Shobin, THE PSYCHOLOGY OF ADJUSTMENT, 1956.
55 BRITISH WEEKLY, 19-i-05.
56 THE CHRISTIAN, 23-iii-05.   57 WESTERN MAIL, vi: 27.
58 Norman Williams, 'Evan Roberts & the 1904-05 Revival,' p. 36.
59 IRISH CHRISTIAN ADVOCATE, 6-i-05.
60 D. M. Phillips, EVAN ROBERTS, pp. 404-405.
61 M. N. Garrard, MRS. PENN-LEWIS, pp. 230-231.
62 personal knowledge, well-substantiated.
63 Bishop A. J. Appasamy, WRITE THE VISION, p. 40.
64 see WESTERN MAIL, consolidated reports.
65 THE CHRISTIAN, 26-i-05.
66 THE ADVANCE, 16-ii-05.
67 MISSIONARY REVIEW OF THE WORLD, 1906, p. 457.
68 Seth Joshua, MISSIONARY REVIEW, 1906, p. 82.
69 MISSIONARY REVIEW OF THE WORLD, 1906, p. 457
70 Keri Evans, cited by A. T. Pierson in MISSIONARY REVIEW OF THE WORLD, 1908, p. 60.   71 cf. J.V. Morgan, p. 248.
72 J.V. Morgan, THE WELSH RELIGIOUS REVIVAL, pp. 248ff.
73 METHODIST RECORDER, 19-i-05.
74 BAPTIST TIMES, 10-iii-05.
75 Norman Williams, 'Evan Roberts & the 1904-05 Revival,' p. 36.
76 D. M. Phillips, EVAN ROBERTS, p. 275.
77 G. M. Roberts & S. Evans, CYFROL GOFFA DIWYGIAD 1904-05, p. 73. (Evans, missionary to India, married Roberts's sister)

NOTES on Chapter IV
The Irish and Scottish Awakenings

No published work deals with the Irish or Scottish Awakening of 1905, but references occur in biographies of F. C. Gibson, William Corkey and Joseph Kemp, and in denominational periodicals.

1   THE WITNESS, Belfast, 2-23-i-04.
2   IRISH CHRISTIAN ADVOCATE, 17-iii-05.
3   THE WITNESS, 6, 13, 20 & 27 i 05.
4   THE RECORD, 31-iii-05 ff.   5 THE WITNESS, 24-iii-05.
6   THE CHRISTIAN, 6-iv-05.   7 THE WITNESS, 7-iv-05.
8   IRISH CHRISTIAN ADVOCATE, 17-iii-05.
9   CHRISTIAN HERALD, London, 13-iv-05.
10 IRISH CHRISTIAN ADVOCATE, 10-iii-05.
11 MINUTES, Irish Methodist Conference, Belfast, 1905.

12 THE WITNESS, 28-iv-05 & 13-vi-05.
13 IRISH CHRISTIAN ADVOCATE.   14 cf. THE WITNESS.
15 IRISH CHRISTIAN ADVOCATE, 17-ii; 30-vi; 8-viii-1905.
16 THE CHRISTIAN, 7-ix-05.   17 THE WITNESS, 23-vi-05.
18 BAPTIST TIMES, 27-i-05.
19 IRISH CHRISTIAN ADVOCATE, 10-ii-05.
20 THE RECORD, London, 31-iii-05.
21 IRISH CHRISTIAN ADVOCATE, 20-i-05.
22 THE CHRISTIAN, 23-ii-05   23 H. Stephens Richardson.
24 WAR CRY, London, 4-ii-05   25 THE RECORD, 31-iii-05.
26 Synod Reports, Church of Ireland, THE RECORD, 16-vi-05.
27 CHRISTIAN HERALD, 13-iv-05. 28 THE CHRISTIAN, 6-iv-05.
29 Rupert Gibson, AN ABUNDANT MINISTRY, p. 12.
30 Rupert Gibson, pp. 1-16.   31 1st July 1916, Battle of Somme.
32 METHODIST TIMES, 16-ii-05.
33 CHRISTIAN HERALD, 9-ii-05.
34 SCOTTISH BAPTIST MAGAZINE, 1905, pp. 42 & 61.
35 THE WITNESS, 3-iii-05.
36 MISSIONARY RECORD, United Free Church, May 1905, p. 212.
37 THE WITNESS, 17-ii-05, & MISSIONARY RECORD, p. 112.
38 BRITISH WEEKLY, 30-iii-05 & CHRISTIAN HERALD, ibid.
39 MISSIONARY RECORD, May 1905, p. 213.
40 SCOTTISH BAPTIST MAGAZINE, 1905, p. 86.
41 MISSIONARY RECORD, May 1905, p. 213.
42 see D. MacFarlan, REVIVALS OF THE 18th CENTURY.
43 MISSIONARY RECORD, June 1905, p. 252.
44 SCOTTISH BAPTIST MAGAZINE, pp. 64, 86 & 114.
45 The writer's pastor.   46 SCOTTISH BAPTIST MAGAZINE,
47 CHRISTIAN HERALD, 4-v-05.   pp. 64ff.
48 YR HERALD CYMRAEG, 28-iii-05.
49 MISSIONARY HERALD, March 1905, p. 114.
50 BRITISH WEEKLY, 30-iii-05.   51 CHRISTIAN HERALD,
30-iii-05. 52 SCOTTISH BAPTIST MAGAZINE, 1905, p. 64.
53 CHRISTIAN HERALD, 20-iv-05.
54 MISSIONARY RECORD, May 1905, p. 213.   55 May 1905,
p. 213 & Febr. 1906, p. 62, MISSIONARY RECORD.
56 METHODIST TIMES, 9-ii-05.
57 SCOTTISH BAPTIST MAGAZINE, 1905, p. 87.
58 METHODIST TIMES, 20-iv-05, & SCOTTISH BAPTIST
MAGAZINE, 1905, p. 87. 59 MISSIONARY RECORD, p. 112.
60 W. Kemp, JOSEPH W. KEMP, chapter v, 'Revival.'
61 SCOTTISH BAPTIST MAGAZINE, 1905, pp. 67 & 75.
62 EDINBURGH CITIZEN, 16 June 1905.
63 SCOTTISH BAPTIST MAGAZINE, 1905, p. 66.
64 Report, SCOTTISH BAPTIST MAGAZINE, 1907, p. 46.
65 SCOTTISH BAPTIST MAGAZINE, pp. 66 & 86.
66 CHRISTIAN HERALD, 2-iii-05.
67 SCOTTISH BAPTIST MAGAZINE, 1905, p. 65.
68 THE CHRISTIAN, 15-ii-05.
69 MISSIONARY RECORD, 1905, p. 213.
70 THE CHRISTIAN, 30-xi-05.
71 CHRISTIAN HERALD, 16-iii-05.
72 MISSIONARY RECORD, March 1905, p. 252.
73 Opinion, MISSIONARY RECORD, February 1906, p. 62.
74 G. T. B. Davis, TORREY AND ALEXANDER, passim.

NOTES on Chapter V
The Awakening in England

There is no published work describing the 1905 Awakening in England, the Christian public in general and English scholars in particular seeming to know nothing of it. In 1934 and in 1968, the researchist encountered no one who had spoken of the movement. In consequence, the material for this chapter has been derived from denominational and other periodicals almost exclusively, the footnotes being grouped within geographical areas, there being so many of them. Few if any of the biographers of leaders active in the 1905 Revival seemed aware of the part played therein by their subjects, though periodicals detailed their activities and opinions at the time of the movement. One has met survivors who confirmed details of local stirrings, but not of the vast extent of awakening.

1   J. C. Pollock, THE KESWICK STORY, p. 129.
2   Caradoc Jones, 'The 1904-5 Revival,' EVANGELICAL MAGAZINE OF WALES, October & November 1968.
3   BAPTIST TIMES, 17-i-05.   4 BRITISH WEEKLY, 26-i-05.
5   METHODIST TIMES, 23-ii-05.
6   Reports of 26-i-05 & 2-iii-05, METHODIST TIMES; 18-v-05 in CHRISTIAN HERALD.
7   METHODIST TIMES, 4-v.   8 BRITISH WEEKLY, 23-iii-05.
9   CHRISTIAN HERALD, 23-iii & BRITISH WEEKLY, 16-iii-05.
10 CHRISTIAN HERALD, 23-ii-05 & 14-ix-05.
11 METHODIST TIMES, 26-i-05 & METHODIST RECORDER, 2-ii-05, & METHODIST TIMES, 23-ii-05.
12 WESTERN MAIL, vi: 29; vi: 15-20;   BRITISH WEEKLY, 13-iv-05; & LIVERPOOL DAILY POST, 13-iv-05.
13 IRISH ENDEAVOURER, March 1905, p. 33;   METHODIST TIMES, 23-iii & 20-iv-05; THE CHRISTIAN, 8-iii-05.
14 METHODIST TIMES, 26-iii-05.
15 BRITISH WEEKLY, 9-ii-05.
16 METHODIST TIMES, 6-iv-05 & 2-iii-05.
17 METHODIST TIMES, 13-iv-05 & 20-iv-05.
18 BRITISH WEEKLY, 16-ii-05 & CHRISTIAN HERALD, 16-iii-05 & 6-iv-05.   19 CHRISTIAN HERALD, 31-viii-05.
20 Report of 19-xi-05, CHRISTIAN HERALD.
21 THE WITNESS, 20-i-05.
22 METHODIST TIMES, 26-i-05; cf. RECORDER, 9-ii-05.
23 METHODIST TIMES, 9-iii & 4-v; METHODIST RECORDER, 16-iii-05; CHRISTIAN HERALD, 23-iii-05; THE CHRISTIAN, 8-iii-05.
24 THE WITNESS, 17-iii-05; METHODIST TIMES, 9-ii-05; & METHODIST RECORDER, 27-iv-05.
25 BRITISH WEEKLY, 16-ii-05; METHODIST TIMES, 23-ii-05.
26 THE WITNESS, 20-i-05; METHODIST TIMES, 9-iii-05; cf. THE WITNESS, 21-iv-05; METHODIST RECORDER, 9-ii-05; & CHRISTIAN HERALD, 23-ii-05.
27 METHODIST TIMES, 26-i; METHODIST RECORDER, 19-i; CHRISTIAN HERALD, 23-iii-05; METHODIST TIMES, 16-ii; 18-v-05; METHODIST RECORDER, 26-i-05 & 9-ii-05.
28 BAPTIST TIMES, 27-i-05; & METHODIST TIMES, 9-iii-05; & WAR CRY, 11-ii-05.

29   METHODIST TIMES, 4-v-05.   30   Issue of 19-i-05.
31   CHRISTIAN HERALD, 6-iv-05; THE CHRISTIAN, 23-xi-05.
32   METHODIST TIMES, 18-v-05.
33   METHODIST RECORDER, 16-iii-05.
34   BRITISH WEEKLY, 16-ii-05.
35   CHRISTIAN HERALD, 16-ii-05.
36   METHODIST RECORDER, 23-iii-05.
37   BAPTIST TIMES, 10-ii-05.
38   METHODIST TIMES, 2-ii-05.
39   CHRISTIAN HERALD, 1-vi-05.
40   METHODIST TIMES, 18-v-05.
41   CHRISTIAN HERALD, 26-x-05.
42   METHODIST RECORDER, 26-i-05.
43   METHODIST TIMES, 9-iii-05.
44   THE CHRISTIAN, 19 & 26-i-1905.
45   BAPTIST TIMES, 17-ii-05.
46   METHODIST TIMES, 26-i-05;   THE WITNESS, 24-iii-05;
     CHRISTIAN HERALD, 30-iii-05 & 18-v-05; and WESTERN
     DAILY PRESS, 15-iii-05.
47   METHODIST RECORDER, 9-ii-05;   CHRISTIAN HERALD,
     8-vi-05; & WESTERN DAILY PRESS, 15-iii-05.
48   Report of 22-iii-05, WESTERN DAILY PRESS.
49   D. M. Phillips, EVAN ROBERTS, p. 451.
50   CHRISTIAN HERALD, 16-ii-05.
51   METHODIST TIMES, 2-iii-05.
52   Report of 9-ii-05, METHODIST TIMES.
53   Information received from the Rev. H. J. Galley, 1934.
54   BAPTIST TIMES, 3-ii-05;   BRITISH WEEKLY, 6-iv-05;
     METHODIST TIMES, 2 & 9-iii-05;   CHRISTIAN HERALD,
     23-iii & 8-vi-05; METHODIST TIMES, 18-v-05; METHODIST
     RECORDER, 9-ii-05; & CHRISTIAN HERALD, 16-iii-05.
55   METHODIST TIMES, 2-iii-05; THE CHRISTIAN, 4-i-05   &
     16-ii-05; BRITISH WEEKLY, 23-ii-05;   CHRISTIAN
     HERALD, 27-vii-05; METHODIST RECORDER, 6-iv-05ff; &
     WAR CRY, 14-i-05; & CHRISTIAN HERALD, 16-ii-05.
56   Patricia St. John, HAROLD St. JOHN, pp. 10ff.
57   METHODIST TIMES, 16-ii-05.
58   METHODIST RECORDER, 26-i-05.
59   Report of 30-iii-05, METHODIST RECORDER.
60   F. P. & M. S. Wood, YOUTH ADVANCING, pp. 11ff.
61   METHODIST RECORDER, 23-iii-05.
62   BAPTIST TIMES, 10-ii-05.   63   CHRISTIAN HERALD,
     27-iv-05.   64 CHRISTIAN HERALD, 2-iii-05.
65   CHRISTIAN HERALD, 30-iii-05; 27-vii-05.
66   CHRISTIAN HERALD, 23-iii-05; 16-iii-05.
67   METHODIST TIMES, 4-v-05; & METHODIST RECORDER,
     16-ii-05; METHODIST TIMES, 23-iii-05.
68   METHODIST RECORDER, 16-ii-05.
69   EVANGELICAL ALLIANCE QUARTERLY, 1905, p. 73.
70   BRITISH WEEKLY, 5-i-05.
71   THE WITNESS, 20-i-05; BAPTIST TIMES, 3-ii-05;   &
     THE CHRISTIAN, 2 & 9-ii-05; BAPTIST TIMES, 24-ii-05;
     METHODIST RECORDER, 2-iii-05;   CHRISTIAN HERALD,
     23-ii & 25-v-05; THE WITNESS, 26-v-05; METHODIST
     TIMES, 6-iv-05; & CHRISTIAN HERALD, 6-iv-05.

Apart from published accounts of Torrey-Alexander campaigns
details of this chapter have been compiled from religious journals o
Edwardian times. THE KESWICK STORY, by J. C. Pollock, brings
to light the controversy about the Convention and the Revival, which
does not appear in the treatise by Walter B. Sloan.

1   J. C. Pollock, THE KESWICK STORY, ch. xv; cf. ch. vi in
the account by Walter B. Sloan, THESE SIXTY YEARS.
2   THE CHRISTIAN, 3 & 10-viii-05.   3 Pollock, pp. 123-128
4   Personal knowledge.   5   THE CHRISTIAN, 2-viii-05
6   THE CHRISTIAN, 19-i-05.
7   THE CHRISTIAN, 16-iii-05.
8   John Wood, Evangelization Society, THE CHRISTIAN, 16-iii.
9   A METHODIST TIMES correspondent, q. in THE OUTLOOK
Dunedin, New Zealand, 21-i-05.
10   BRITISH WEEKLY, 2-ii-05.
11   G. T. B. Davis, TORREY AND ALEXANDER (in Britain).
12   F. C. Ottman, J. WILBUR CHAPMAN (British campaigns)
13   IRISH ENDEAVOURER, July 1906, pp. 100ff.
14   BAPTIST TIMES, 13-x-05.
15   WESLEYAN METHODIST MAGAZINE, 1906, p. 469.
16   WESTERN RECORDER, Louisville, 9-ii-05 ff.
17   ENGLISH CHURCHMAN, 16-iii-05.
18   THE RECORD, 16-vi-05.   19 THE WITNESS, 17-ii-05.
20   THE RECORD, 6-i-05.
21   METHODIST RECORDER, 26-i-05;   CHRISTIAN HERALD,
27-iv-05.   22 CHURCH TIMES, 10-v-05.
23   THE RECORD, 27-i.   24 ENGLISH CHURCHMAN, 24-iii-05.
25   THE RECORD, 10-ii-05.   26 THE RECORD, 10-ii-05.
27   ENGLISH CHURCHMAN, 2 & 23-ii-05.
28   THE RECORD, 17-ii-05; 17-iii-05.
29   THE RECORD, 10-iii-05.   30 THE RECORD, 17-iii-05.
31   ENGLISH CHURCHMAN, 16-iii-05.
32   METHODIST TIMES, 23-iii-05.
33   ENGLISH CHURCHMAN, 16-iii-05.
34   THE WITNESS, 3-iii-05.   35 THE RECORD, 24-ii-05.
36   ENGLISH CHURCHMAN, 4-v-05.
37   STATESMAN'S YEAR BOOKS, 1905 & 1910.
38   BAPTIST TIMES, 13-x-05, supplement.
39   Issues of 24 & 31-iii-05; 7 & 14-iv-05, BAPTIST TIMES.
40   see issues of BRITISH WEEKLY, and other journals.
41   see issues of WAR CRY, throughout 1905.
42   METHODIST TIMES, 4-v-05.   43 THE WITNESS, 5-v-05
44   METHODIST TIMES, 18-v-05.
45   see issues of METHODIST TIMES, 1905; cf. METHODIST
RECORDER, 1905, and other Methodist connexional journals.
46   WESLEYAN METHODIST MAGAZINE, 1905, p. 513.
47   editorial, WESLEYAN METHODIST MAGAZINE, 1905, p. 129.
48   WESLEYAN METHODIST MAGAZINE, p. 65.
49   Analysis, Annual Reports of the Registrar General, Somerset
House, London, for the years 1904-1907.
50   WESLEYAN METHODIST MAGAZINE, 1905, p. 195.

NOTES on Chapter VII
Awakening in Scandinavia

1   EVANGELICAL CHRISTENDOM, 1909, pp. 78, 26, etc.
2   EVANGELISKA FOSTERLANDS STIFTELSEN, p. 238.
3   S. L. Barratt, T. B. BARRATT; M. Lunde, ALBERT LUNDE.
4   N. Bloch-Hoell, THE PENTECOSTAL MOVEMENT, p. 66.
5   see J. V. Heiberg, UNIONENS OPLOSNING, passim.
6   LUTHERAN HERALD, 1-iii-06.
7   LONDON QUARTERLY REVIEW, October 1905.
8   LUTHERAN HERALD, 22-iii-06.
9   MISSIONARY REVIEW OF THE WORLD, 1907, p. 306.
10 LUTHERAN HERALD, 8-iii-06.
11 THE LUTHERAN, 13-vii-05.
12 LUTHERAN HERALD, 8-iii-06 & 4-iv-07.
13 LUTHERAN STANDARD, 29-vi-05.
14 ENCYCLOPEDIA, LUTHERAN CHURCH, vol. ii, p. 1350.
15 MISSIONARY REVIEW OF THE WORLD, 1906, p. 310.
16 DE UNGAS TIDNING, Stockholm, 1905, p. 134.
17 T. B. Barratt, SJALVBIOGRAFI, pp. 100-101.
18 MISSIONARY REVIEW, 1906, p. 310;   THE CHRISTIAN,
    14-xii-05.   19 LUTHERAN HERALD, 14-vi-06.
20 MISSIONARY REVIEW OF THE WORLD, 1906, p. 458.
21 E. Molland, CHURCH LIFE IN NORWAY, pp. 91-92.
22 LUTHERAN HERALD, 5-iii-06, 1-xi-06.
23 E. Molland, CHURCH LIFE IN NORWAY, pp. 97, 98.
24 LUTHERAN HERALD, 14-vi-06.
25 MISSIONARY REVIEW OF THE WORLD, 1907, p. 527.
26 LUTHERAN HERALD, 12-iv-06, 27-xi-06.
27 DEN INDRE MISSIONENS HISTORIE, p. 363.
28 see DEN INDRE MISSIONENS HISTORIE, pp. 375, 377.
29 INDRE MISSIONS TIDENDE, 1903, p. 327.
30 DE UNGES BLAD, Copenhagen, 1905, p. 111.
31 INDRE MISSIONS TIDENDE, 1906, p. 331.
32 THE CHRISTIAN, 16-xi-05.
33 INDRE MISSIONS TIDENDE, 1907, p. 301, cf. DEN INDRE
    MISSIONENS HISTORIE, pp. 469ff.
34 EVANGELICAL CHRISTENDOM, 1907, p. 7.
35 INDRE MISSIONS TIDENDE, 1909, pp. 3-4.
36 DEN DANSKE PRASTEFORENING, 1906-1907.
37 DEN KIRKHISTORISKE INSTITUTION records, Copenhagen.
38 THE CHRISTIAN, 19-i-05.
39 RECORD OF CHRISTIAN WORK, 1906, p. 309.
40 SVENSKA MORGONBLADET, Stockholm, 22-v-05.
41 RECORD OF CHRISTIAN WORK, 1906, p. 309.
42 THE CHRISTIAN, 25-i-06.
43 EVANGELICAL CHRISTENDOM, 1907, pp. 42 & 74.
44 MISSIONARY REVIEW OF THE WORLD, 1908, p. 111.
45 AMERICAN BAPTIST FOREIGN MISSION, 1913, p. 133.
46 BOARD of FOREIGN MISSIONS, Methodist Episcopal Church,
    1913, p. 393.   47 LUTHERAN HERALD, 1-8-05.
48 P. Brofeldt, TOIVON TAHTI, 1912, pp. 14ff.
49 E. Bernspang, Interviews with elderly folk in Finland, 1967.
50 Ari Haavio, SUOMEN USKONNOLLISET LIIKKEET, 1965.
51 P. Brofeldt, TOIVON TAHTI, 1912, pp. 85-88.

The lengthy treatise written by Professor Paulus Scharpff upon GESCHICHTE DER EVANGELISATION, features a few paragraphs on the 1905 Awakening in Germany, and there is mention of a 'revival given Germany on the eve of the First World War' in Prof. Kupisch's DIE KIRCHE IN IHRER GESCHICHTE. More attention is paid to the disruption of the German Gemeinschaften by Pentecostalism.

1 Scharpff, GESCHICHTE DER EVANGELISATION, pp. 220ff.
2 A. Roth, 50 JAHRE GNADAUER KONFERENZ, passim.
3 O. Hasselman, PASTOR J. DAMMANN, p. 135.
4 J. Vetter, EIN LEBENSBILD.   5 P. Scharpff, p. 279.
6 P. Fleisch, DIE MODERNE GEMEINSCHAFTESBEWEGUNG.
7 F. W. von Viebahn, GEORG VON VIEBAHN, 1918.
8 EVANGELICAL ALLIANCE QUARTERLY, 1905, p. 125.
9 P. Scharpff, pp. 267 & 277.
10 Pagel, DER JUGENBUND FUR E. C.   11 Scharpff, p. 267.
12 Modersohn, ER FUHRET MICH AUF RECHTER STRASSE.
13 CHRISTIAN HERALD, London, 16-iii-05, 11 & 16-xi-05.
14 THE CHRISTIAN, 19-x-05.
15 P. Scharpff, pp. 280-281.
16 A. Ringwald, MENSCHEN VOR GOTT, passim; cf. Kupisch, DER DEUTSCHER C. V. J. M., pp. 56ff.
17 G. Füllkrug, HANDBUCH DER VOLKSMISSION, p. 10.
18 RETTUNGSJUBEL: see P. Scharpff, p. 295.
19 EVANGELICAL CHRISTENDOM, January 1906, p. 3.
20 K. Kupisch, DIE KIRCHE IN IHRER GESCHICHTE, p. 86.
21 CHRISTIAN HERALD, 10-viii-05.
22 Information, Karel Kaleta, born 1893, & Rev. J. Michal, Praha.
23 CHRISTIAN HERALD, 16-xi-05.
24 CHRISTIAN HERALD, 24-viii-05.
25 THE CHRISTIAN, 10-viii-05 & 2-xi-05.
26 MISSIONARY REVIEW OF THE WORLD, 1905, p. 309.
27 EVANGELICAL ALLIANCE QUARTERLY, 1905, p. 141.
28 see R. S. Latimer, UNDER THREE TSARS, pp. 71ff.
29 BAPTIST WORLD ALLIANCE, London, 1911, p. 439.
30 N. I. Saloff-Astakhoff, CHRISTIANITY IN RUSSIA, p. 134; see EVANGELICAL MAGAZINE OF WALES, Oct.-Nov. 1968.
31 N. I. Saloff-Astakhoff, CHRISTIANITY IN RUSSIA, pp. 140ff; see Donald Gee, THE PENTECOSTAL MOVEMENT, p.159.
32 CHRISTIAN HERALD, 30-iii-05.
33 EVANGELISCH ZONDAGSBLAD, 1-x-05.
34 P. Kasteel, ABRAHAM KUYPER, passim.
35 THE CHRISTIAN, 21-ix-05.
36 EVANGELICAL ALLIANCE QUARTERLY, 1905, p. 61.
37 FOREIGN FIELD, Wesleyan Methodist Missionary Society,
38 WESTERN MAIL, reports, iii: 17.   (1905, p. 467.
39 THE CHRISTIAN, 16-ii-05.
40 JOURNAL DE L'EVANGELISATION, cited above 26-x-05.
41 THE CHRISTIAN, 30-xi-05.
42 RECORD OF CHRISTIAN WORK, 1908, p. 172.
43 WESLEYAN METHODIST MISSIONARY SOCIETY, 1906.
44 Houghton, FRENCH & BELGIAN PROTESTANTISM, pp. 81ff.

NOTES on Chapter IX
North American Expectations

Sources for the American chapters are found in religious journals
and in occasional biographies. There is no published work available.

1   N. Carpenter, THE IMMIGRANTS AND THEIR CHILDREN.
2   G. Shaughnessy, HAS THE IMMIGRANT KEPT THE FAITH?
3   J. C. Ramsay, JOHN WILBUR CHAPMAN, p. 74.
4   L.C.Weigle, DICTIONARY OF AMERICAN BIOGRAPHY, 1934.
5   L. M. Jones, THE LIFE AND SAYINGS OF SAM P. JONES.
6   F. C. Ottman, J. WILBUR CHAPMAN, passim.
7   THE GREAT AWAKENING IN COLUMBUS, OHIO—B. Fay
    Mills, pp. 61ff.   8   Walt Holcomb, SAM JONES, passim.
9   WESTERN CHRISTIAN ADVOCATE, 14-ii-1900.
10 Editorial, WESTERN CHRISTIAN ADVOCATE, 4-vii-1900.
11 PRESBYTERIAN JOURNAL, Philadelphia, cited in WESTERN
    CHRISTIAN ADVOCATE, Indiana, 19-ix-1900.
12 F. C. Ottman, J. WILBUR CHAPMAN, pp. 120ff.
13 THE CHRISTIAN, London, 26-iv-06.
14 THE CHURCHMAN, 1905, pp. 11, 218, 256 & 409.
15 THE EXAMINER, 2-ii-05.
16 WESTERN RECORDER, Louisville, 4-v-05.
17 LUTHERAN OBSERVER, 3 & 10-ii-05.
18 THE LUTHERAN, 16-ii-05. 19   METHODIST REVIEW, 1905.
20 CHRISTIAN OBSERVER, Louisville, 15-ii-05.
21 CHRISTIAN HERALD, 1-ii-05.
22 CHRISTIAN ENDEAVOR WORLD, 5-i-05—6-iv-05.
23 CHRISTIAN HERALD, 22-iii-05, 19-iv-05.
24 J. H. McDonald, editor, THE REVIVAL, New York, 1905.
25 BAPTIST ARGUS, Louisville, 2-iii-05.

NOTES on Chapter X
The 1905 American Awakening

1   D. J. Williams, WELSH CALVINISTIC METHODISM, p. 43.
2   THE EXAMINER, 26-i-05 & 16-ii-05.
3   Report of 19-i-05 in THE EXAMINER.
4   PENTECOSTAL HERALD, Louisville, 8-iii-05.
5   see BAPTIST COMMONWEALTH, Philadelphia.
6   BAPTIST ARGUS, 9-iii.   7   CHRISTIAN ADVOCATE, 6-iv.
8   Editorial, CHRISTIAN ADVOCATE, 9-iii-05.
9   CHRISTIAN ENDEAVOR WORLD, 30-iii-05.
10 THE CHRISTIAN, London, 9-iii-05.
11 CHRISTIAN ADVOCATE, 4-i-06.   12   EVENING POST, of
    Schenectady, quoted in CHRISTIAN ADVOCATE, 26-i-05.
13 SCHENECTADY GAZETTE, quoted in above issue.
14 THE EXAMINER, New York, 23-ii-05.
15 CHRISTIAN ADVOCATE, 9-ii-05.
16 MICHIGAN CHRISTIAN ADVOCATE, 11-ii-05.
17 THE WATCHMAN, 9-iii-05. 18   THE WATCHMAN, 4-v-05.
19 THE EXAMINER, 19-i-05.
20 Report of 16-iii-05, THE EXAMINER.
21 THE WATCHMAN, 30-iii-05.
22 Report of 12-x-05, THE WATCHMAN.

23 THE WATCHMAN, 9-iii.   24 THE CHRISTIAN, 7 & 14-ix.
25 CHRISTIAN HERALD, London, 12-i-05.
26 BAPTIST ARGUS, 16-iii-05.
27 THE ADVANCE, 9-iii-05.   28 THE CHRISTIAN, 13-iv-05.
29 WESTERN CHRISTIAN ADVOCATE, 8-iii-05.
30 PENTECOSTAL HERALD, 1-iii-05.
31 CHRISTIAN OBSERVER, 15 & 22-iii-05.
32 CHRISTIAN HERALD, 22-ii-05.
33 Southern Baptist Convention ANNUAL, 1906, p. 46.
34 RELIGIOUS HERALD, Richmond, 2, 23 & 30-iii-05.
35 CHRISTIAN HERALD, 24-v-05.
36 FOREIGN MISSIONS JOURNAL, February 1905.
37 BAPTIST COURIER, 9-ii.   38 BAPTIST ARGUS, 6-iv-05.
39 CHRISTIAN OBSERVER, Louisville, 1-iii-05.
40 BAPTIST ARGUS, 25-v-05.   41 BAPTIST COURIER, 1-iii.
42 BAPTIST ARGUS, 13-iv-05 & 18-v-05.
43 Southern Baptist Convention ANNUAL, 1905, p. 36.
44 OUR HOME FIELD, Southern Baptist Convention, July 1906.
45 THE EXAMINER, 23-ii-05 & 11-v-05.
46 CHRISTIAN HERALD, London, 29-vi-05.
47 MICHIGAN CHRISTIAN HERALD, 26-i-05—23-ii-05; 1-vi-05.
48 MICHIGAN CHRISTIAN ADVOCATE, 4-ii-05.
49 Report of 29-iv-05, MICHIGAN CHRISTIAN ADVOCATE.
50 MICHIGAN CHRISTIAN ADVOCATE, 18-ii-05 & 18-iii-05.
51 Report of 1-iv-05, MICHIGAN CHRISTIAN ADVOCATE.
52 MICHIGAN CHRISTIAN ADVOCATE, 1 & 8-iv-05.
53 Reports of 15-iv-05 & 6-vi-05, in the same journal.
54 MICHIGAN BAPTIST CONVENTION, 1905 & 1906.
55 MICHIGAN CHRISTIAN ADVOCATE, 23-ii-05 & 23-iii-05.
56 BAPTIST OBSERVER, Indianapolis, February 1905 issues.
57 PENTECOSTAL HERALD, 15-iii-05.
58 BAPTIST ARGUS, 16-iii-05.
59 CHRISTIAN ENDEAVOR WORLD, 23-iii-05.
60 CHRISTIAN HERALD, 5-iv-05.
61 SERVICE, Baptist Young People's Union, Chicago, 1905, p. 43.
62 EVENING POST, Iowa, q. in CHRISTIAN ADVOCATE, 2-ii-05.
63 THE ADVANCE, 23-ii 05 & 2-iii-05.
64 CENTRAL BAPTIST, St. Louis, 13 & 27-iv-05.
65 CHRISTIAN ENDEAVOR WORLD, 30-iii-05.
66 THE STANDARD, Chicago, 11-ii-05.
67 CHRISTIAN ADVOCATE, 2-iii-05.
68 BAPTIST ARGUS, Louisville, 23-iii-05.
69 CHRISTIAN HERALD, 19-iv-05.
70 CHRISTIAN ADVOCATE, 2-ii-05; CHRISTIAN HERALD,
    15-ii-05; WITNESS, Belfast, 3-ii-05; EXAMINER, 6-iv-05.
71 THE WATCHMAN, 23-iii-05.
72 CHRISTIAN ADVOCATE, 29-vi-05.
73 CHRISTIAN ENDEAVOR WORLD, 27-iv-05 & 15-vi-05.
74 Report of 15-vi-05, CHRISTIAN ENDEAVOR WORLD.
75 THE WATCHMAN, 20-iv; cf. SERVICE, BYPU, 1905, p. 257.
76 CHRISTIAN HERALD, London, 30-iii-05.
77 WESTERN CHRISTIAN ADVOCATE, 31-i-06.
78 O. J. Smith, THE PEOPLES CHURCH, pp. 15ff.
79 BAPTIST ARGUS, 23-iii-05.
80 RECORD OF CHRISTIAN WORK, 1906, p. 257.

NOTES on Chapter XI
Results in North America

There appears to be no published work, scholarly or otherwise, on the results of the 1905 Awakening in the United States and Canada.

1   MICHIGAN CHRISTIAN ADVOCATE, 9-xii-05.
2   BAPTIST HOME MISSION MONTHLY, 1905, p. 92; & passim.
3   THE STANDARD, Chicago, 6-i-06.
4   MICHIGAN CHRISTIAN ADVOCATE, 21-i-05 & 16-xii-05.
5   METHODIST REVIEW, New York, 1905, p. 999.
6   METHODIST REVIEW, 1905, p. 998.
7   CHRISTIAN ADVOCATE, 22-ii-06.
8   cf. 4 & 25-i-06, CHRISTIAN ADVOCATE.
9   PENTECOSTAL HERALD, 15-ii-05.
10   MICHIGAN CHRISTIAN HERALD, 26-i-05.
11   see W. J. Dawson, THE EVANGELISTIC NOTE, 1905; & THE AUTOBIOGRAPHY OF A MIND, 1925.
12   J. DeForest Murch, CHRISTIANS ONLY, pp. 207ff.
13   LUTHERAN OBSERVER, 10-iii-05.
14   THE LUTHERAN, 30-iii-05; 13 & 27-iv-05; 1 & 15-vi-05; 4 & 11-i-06.
15   LUTHERAN WITNESS, 4-v-05 & 15-vi-05.
16   CHRISTIAN OBSERVER, 8-ii-05.
17   Report of 7-vi-05, CHRISTIAN OBSERVER.
18   Southern Baptist Convention ANNUAL, 1905, p. 37.
19   MICHIGAN CHRISTIAN HERALD, 2-ii-05; cf. Lefferts A. Loetscher, 'Presbyterian Revivals since 1875,' PENNSYL-VANIA MAGAZINE OF HISTORY & BIOGRAPHY, Jan. 1944.
20   CHRISTIAN OBSERVER, 8-iii-05 & 24-v-05.
21   METHODIST REVIEW, 1905, p. 999.
22   CHRISTIAN ADVOCATE, 25-i-06.
23   CHRISTIAN ADVOCATE, 17-i-07.
24   PENTECOSTAL HERALD, Louisville, 19-iv-05.
25   INTERCOLLEGIAN, January & April, 1905; ASSOCIATION MEN, Chicago, February & March, 1905.
26   G. Stewart, LIFE OF HENRY B. WRIGHT, p. 45.
27   INTERCOLLEGIAN, May 1905 & February 1906.
28   JOURNAL & MESSENGER, Cincinnati, 2-ii-05.
29   INTERCOLLEGIAN, April 1906.
30   PACIFIC BAPTIST, 1-iii-05; cf. TELEPHONE-REGISTER, McMinnville, Oregon, issues of February & March 1905.
31   INTERCOLLEGIAN, June 1906.
32   INTERCOLLEGIAN, March 1906.
33   YEARBOOKS, Y.M.C.A. of North America, 1902-03, 1905-06, & 1907-08 statistics of student work.
34   MISSIONARY REVIEW OF THE WORLD, 1906, p. 370.
35   W. T. Ellis, MEN AND MISSIONS, pp. 71-80.
36   Information received from Dr. E. Stanley Jones, in 1969 at Asbury College, Wilmore, Kentucky.
37   C. P. Shedd, THE CHURCH FOLLOWS ITS STUDENTS, p. 9 & pp. 16ff.
38   CHRISTIAN ENDEAVOR WORLD, 4-iv-05 & 13-vii-05.
39   J. E. Stout, THE DAILY VACATION CHURCH SCHOOL, p. 11.
40   THE CHRISTIAN, London, 12-iv-05.

1   ALLIANCE WEEKLY, 1906, p. 222.
2   On Seth Joshua, see ALLIANCE WEEKLY, 1906, p. 177.
3   MISSIONARY REVIEW OF THE WORLD, 1906, p. 4.
4   ALLIANCE WEEKLY, 1906, pp. 305, 316 & 363.
5   E. F. Bayliss, THE GIPSY SMITH MISSIONS IN AMERICA.
6   RECORD OF CHRISTIAN WORK, 1906, p. 23.
7   CHRISTIAN ADVOCATE, 8-ii-06.   8   Report of 15-ii-06,
     CHRISTIAN ADVOCATE.   9   CHRISTIAN ADVOCATE,
     1-ii-06.   10   THE CHRISTIAN, London, 29-iii-06.
11   Following Chapman's campaigns in Denver, Los Angeles,
     Portland and Seattle, local evangelism flourished.
12   THE CHRISTIAN, 29-iii-06.
13   FOREIGN MISSIONS JOURNAL, Richmond, May 1905.
14   THE WATCHMAN, 9-iii-05.
15   Southern Baptist Convention ANNUAL, 1906, p. 40.
16   JOURNAL & MESSENGER, 9-ii-05 & 16-iii-05.
17   Southern Baptist Convention ANNUAL, 1907, pp. 10ff.
18   cf. Southern Baptist Convention ANNUAL, 1905-08 statistics.
19   WESTERN CHRISTIAN ADVOCATE, 17-i-06.
20   F. G. Beardsley, A HISTORY OF AMERICAN REVIVALS,
     p. 320; cf. G. T. B. Davis, TORREY AND ALEXANDER.
21   WESTERN CHRISTIAN ADVOCATE, 21-ii-06 & 9-v-06.
22   J. C. Ramsay, JOHN WILBUR CHAPMAN, pp. 38, 74 & 78.
23   F. C. Ottman, J. WILBUR CHAPMAN, p. 117; cf. Lefferts
     A. Loetscher, PRESBYTERIANISM AND REVIVALS, pp. 81ff.
24   A. Z. Conrad, BOSTON'S AWAKENING, 1909, passim.
25   F. C. Ottman, J. WILBUR CHAPMAN, p. 207.
26   C. E. Schaeffer, A BRIEF HISTORY OF THE DEPARTMENT
     OF EVANGELISM of the Federal Council of Churches, pp. 5ff.
27   W. T. Ellis, BILLY SUNDAY: the Man & His Message; see
     W. G. McLoughlin, BILLY SUNDAY WAS HIS REAL NAME.
28   Dr. McLoughlin took his quotations from Frankenberg's THE
     SPECTACULAR CAREER OF REV. BILLY SUNDAY, p. 213,
     on which the writer passes no judgment. He did hear Rodeheaver
     (Sunday's song-leader) once admit: 'Let's say that he had a
     strong acquisitive instinct.'
29   Stelze, 'The Evangelist in Present Day America,' CURRENT
     HISTORY, November 1931.
30   ZION'S HERALD, 19-i-16 & 28-ii-17.
31   J. Edwin Orr, ALWAYS ABOUNDING, pp. 84ff.
32   METHODIST REVIEW, 1906, p. 279.   33   Ibid., 1906, p. 276.
34   CHRISTIAN ADVOCATE, 2-ii-05, quoting NEW YORK SUN.
35   CHRISTIAN ADVOCATE, 8, 22 & 29-vi-05.
36   MICHIGAN CHRISTIAN ADVOCATE, 9-xii-05.
37   (Inter-Convention) BAPTIST CONGRESS, 1905, p. 3.
38   CHRISTIAN ADVOCATE, 4-i-06.
39   CHRISTIAN OBSERVER, 24-v-05.
40   WESTERN CHRISTIAN ADVOCATE, 31-i-06.
41   THE ADVANCE, 24-vi-15.
42   Mrs. Howard Taylor, BORDEN OF YALE, passim; cf. G.
     Stewart's LIFE OF HENRY B. WRIGHT, pp. 46-47.
43   K. S. Latourette, BEYOND THE RANGES, passim.

1 WMC Executive Committee, 4th meeting, 12-iii-08, Minute 43, p. 28, cf. W. R. Hogg, ECUMENICAL FOUNDATIONS.
2 Silas McBee, 'Catholic Episcopalian' editor (THE CHURCHMAN), seemed to be spokesman for the 'exclude Latin America' lobby, cf. Hogg, ECUMENICAL FOUNDATIONS, pp. 119, 131-133.
3 S. C. Neill, A HISTORY OF CHRISTIAN MISSIONS, p. 389.
4 H. T. Beach, editor: PROTESTANT MISSIONS IN SOUTH AMERICA, article by T. B. Wood.
5 Lauro Bretones, REDEMOINHOS DO SUL, p. 15.
6 MISSIONARY REVIEW, 1901, p. 454; 1902, p. 145.
7 Horton, OUTLINE OF LATIN AMERICAN HISTORY, p. 232.
8 MISSIONARY REVIEW OF THE WORLD, 1907, p. 811.
9 Southern Baptist Convention ANNUAL, 1900, p. 76.
10 MISSIONARY REVIEW OF THE WORLD, 1906, p. 199.
11 W. E. Browning, THE RIVER PLATE REPUBLICS, p. 72.
12 S.B.C. ANNUALS; MISSIONARY REVIEW, 1906, p. 805; & RECORD OF CHRISTIAN WORK, 1906, p. 983.
13 S. Ginsburg, A MISSIONARY ADVENTURE, p. 137.
14 S.B.C. ANNUALS; cf. S. Ginsburg, pp. 216ff.
15 M. Neves, MEIO SECULO, p. 29, cf. Ferreira's HISTORIA.
16 MISSIONARY REVIEW OF THE WORLD, 1907, p. 811.
17 W. R. Read, CHURCH GROWTH IN BRAZIL, pp. 112ff
18 E. Conde, ASSEMBLEIAS DE DEUS NO BRASIL, pp. 11ff
19 W. R. Read, CHURCH GROWTH IN BRAZIL, pp. 22ff
20 D. Berg, ENVIADO POR DEUS, p. 29.
21 Read, CHURCH GROWTH IN BRAZIL, pp. 120-121, 25-26.
22 McLean, LA IGLESIA PRESBITERIANA EN CHILE, pp. 58ff
23 Kessler, PROTESTANT MISSIONS AND CHURCHES IN PERU AND CHILE, pp. 243-244.   24 J. B. A. Kessler, pp. 101ff.
25 W. C. Hoover, AVIVAMIENTO PENTECOSTAL, p. 10.
26 ALLIANCE WEEKLY, 1907, p. 2.
27 J. T. Nichol, PENTECOSTALISM, p. 52.
28 W. C. Hoover, AVIVAMIENTO PENTECOSTAL, p. 17.
29 J. B. A. Kessler, p. 110.   30 W. C. Hoover, pp. 35ff.
31 Donald Gee, THE PENTECOSTAL MOVEMENT, p. 57.
32 MISSIONARY REVIEW OF THE WORLD, 1909, p. 544.
33 cf. (1960) K. S. Latourette, CHRISTIANITY IN A REVOLUTIONARY AGE, volume v, p. 213.
34 Read, Monterroso & Johnson, LATIN AMERICAN CHURCH GROWTH, p. 99.   35 THE CHRISTIAN, 3-viii-05.
36 Letter of J. L. Hart, 1909, Southern Baptist Mission Archives.
37 unpublished paper, Dr. Donald R. Dilworth, Ecuador.
38 CHRISTIAN HERALD, London, 27-iv-05.
39 MISSIONARY REVIEW OF THE WORLD, 1905, p. 229.
40 cf. MISSIONARY REVIEW OF THE WORLD, 1907, p. 683.
41 MISSIONARY REVIEW OF THE WORLD, 1905, p. 467.
42 see MISSIONARY REVIEW, 1906, p. 643, THE CHRISTIAN, 16-iii-05, 30-xi-05, & ALLIANCE WEEKLY, 1906, p. 364.
43 WESLEYAN METHODIST MISSIONARY SOCIETY, 1906, p. 143; 1907 Report, p. 138; cf. THE CHRISTIAN, 12-iv-06.
44 ATLAS OF PROTESTANT MISSIONS, 1903 & WORLD ATLAS OF CHRISTIAN MISSIONS, 1911.

Torrey and Chapman, Lyall and Geil, have left accounts of their evangelistic campaigns in New Zealand and Australia. Lacking other published work, most of this chapter has been culled from journals.

1   MISSIONARY REVIEW OF THE WORLD, 1903, pp. 20ff.
2   H. C. Alexander, CHARLES M. ALEXANDER, p. 48.
3   MISSIONARY REVIEW OF THE WORLD, 1903, pp. 20ff.
4   J. Lyall, RECENT GREAT REVIVAL IN AUSTRALIA AND N.Z., pp. 1-3; cf. W. E. Geil, OCEAN AND ISLE, Sydney, 1902.
5   I. R. Stewart, A SPLENDID OPTIMIST, pp. 47ff.
6   J. Lyall, pp. 9-18—father of the missionary author Leslie T. Lyall)   7   G. T. B. Davis, TORREY & ALEXANDER, p. 57.
8   THE OUTLOOK, Dunedin, 2-viii-02.
9   Report, Australasian Wesleyan Methodist Church in N.Z., 1902, Dunedin.   10   Report, Christchurch, 1903.
11   THE OUTLOOK, 13-xi-02.
12   cf. G. T. B. Davis, & THE OUTLOOK, 20-ix-02.
13   THE OUTLOOK, 27-ix-02.
14   J. Lyall, RECENT GREAT REVIVAL, pp. 27-37.
15   THE OUTLOOK, 11-18-x-02.
16   MISSIONARY REVIEW OF THE WORLD, 1903, p. 220.
17   THE OUTLOOK, 21-i-05.   18   THE CHRISTIAN, 23-xi-05.
19   THE OUTLOOK, 30-ix-05 & 7-x-05.
20   AUSTRALIAN CHRISTIAN WORLD, 10-ii-05.   21   10-iii-05.
22   AUSTRALIAN CHRISTIAN WORLD, 12-v-05.   23   25-viii-05.
24   F. C. Ottman, J. WILBUR CHAPMAN, pp. 146ff.
25   MISSIONARY HERALD, Boston, 1906, pp. 345-346.
26   MISSIONARY REVIEW, 1906, p. 83, & 1907, p. 566.
27   Edinburgh MISSIONARY CONFERENCE, 1910, vol. i, p. 41.
28   BAPTIST MISSIONARY MAGAZINE, 1902, p. 687.
29   U. S. Senate Document 331, 1902;   cf. C. Osias & Avelina Lorenzana, EVANGELICAL CHRISTIANITY IN PHILIPPINES; & Homer C. Stuntz, THE PHILIPPINES & THE FAR EAST.
30   J. B. Rodgers, FORTY YEARS IN THE PHILIPPINES, 1940.
31   MISSIONARY REVIEW OF THE WORLD, 1905, p. 399.
32   W. N. Roberts, THE FILIPINO CHURCH, pp. 69ff.
33   MISSIONARY REVIEW OF THE WORLD, 1906, p. 644.
34   MISSIONARY REVIEW, 1907, p. 530; J. Flierl, 30 JAHRE MISSIONSARBEIT IN WUSTEN UND WILDNISSEN.
35   INTERNATIONAL REVIEW OF MISSIONS, 1912, p. 586.
36   MISSIONARY REVIEW OF THE WORLD, 1908, p. 167.
37   see T. M. Kruger, SEDJARAH GEREDJA DI INDONESIA; MISSIONARY REVIEW, 1916, p. 324; 1920, p. 398; 1922, p. 505; 1924, p. 439.   (There are sources also in Dutch and German.)
38   Rauws, Kraemer, Van Hasselt & Slotemaker de Bruine, eds. THE NETHERLANDS INDIES, pp. 50, 122.
39   Indonesian Bible Society figures, 1966. T. M. Kruger's work (1959) contains an informative chapter on the Church in Nias.
40   J. Richter, EVANGELISCHE MISSION IN NIEDERLANDISCH INDIEN & Kruger, SEDJARAH GEREDJA DI INDONESIA.
41   see ATLAS OF PROTESTANT MISSIONS, 1903, & WORLD ATLAS OF CHRISTIAN MISSIONS, 1911.

42 G.Mondain, MISSION PROTESTANTE A MADAGASCAR, p. 344.
43 A.Thunem, NY FIFOHAZANA ETO MADIGASKARA.
44 MISSIONARY REVIEW OF THE WORLD, 1904, p. 616.
45 G.Mondain, MISSION PROTESTANTE A MADAGASCAR, p. 346.
46 Chapus & Bothun, AU SOUFFLE DE L'ESPRIT, p. 7.
47 MISSIONARY REVIEW OF THE WORLD, 1906, p. 566.
48 Report of 1905, MISSIONARY REVIEW, p. 878.
49 MISSIONARY REVIEW OF THE WORLD, 1906, pp. 134ff.
50 Report of 1905, MISSIONARY REVIEW, p. 449.
51 MISSIONARY REVIEW, 1907, p. 151 & 1908, p. 6.

NOTES on Chapter XV
South African Resurgence

Apart from the writer's own researches on the subject, there is
no published work treating the decade of revival in Southern Africa.
There is coverage of Gipsy Smith's 1904 evangelistic campaigns in
MISSION OF PEACE, and material in Dutch and Afrikaans on the
prisoner-of-war awakenings among the Boers overseas, particularly
Dr. W. M. Retief's HERLEWINGS IN ONS GESKIEDENIS. Most of
the material in this chapter is derived from periodicals and archives.

1   DE KERKBODE, Capetown, 1901, pp. 315, 510; also a letter
    from Ds. W. Robertson, 2-vii-01 (p. 398).
2   MS Diary of Rev. William Meara, deceased friend of the writer,
    in Cory Library at Rhodes University, lists 173 Boer women
    and children buried in a month at the civilian camp, Barberton.
3   CHRISTIAN STUDENT, Capetown, April 1902 (Louis Hofmeyr),
    cf. MISSIONARY REVIEW OF THE WORLD, 1903, pp. 616ff.
4   DE KERKBODE, 1901, indexed references.
5   Indexed references, DE KERKBODE, cf. CHRISTIAN STU-
    DENT, September 1901 and March 1902.
6   DE KERKBODE, 1901, indexed references.
7   Indexed references, DE KERKBODE, 1901 & 1902.
8   MISSIONARY REVIEW OF THE WORLD, 1903, pp. 317, &
    616ff; cf. G. B. A. Gerdener, RECENT DEVELOPMENTS IN
    THE SOUTH AFRICAN MISSION FIELDS, p. 15.
9   DE KONINGSBODE, July 1903, 'De Opwekking.'
10 CHRISTIAN EXPRESS, Lovedale, June 1902, p. 81.
11 MISSIONARY REVIEW OF THE WORLD, 1904, p. 271.
12 Gipsy Smith, A MISSION OF PEACE, 1904, passim.
13 DE KERKBODE, 1905, pp. 35, 46ff; see also METHODIST
    CHURCHMAN, 11-i-05 & 8-iii-05; and CHRISTIAN EXPRESS,
    July 1905.
14 CAPE ARGUS, Capetown, 18-iv-04.
15 DE KERKBODE, 1904, p. 71.
16 KIMBERLEY FREE PRESS, 14-v-04.
17 METHODIST CHURCHMAN, 8-vi-04.
18 Report of 22-vi-04, METHODIST CHURCHMAN.
19 THE STAR, Johannesburg, 11 & 13-vi-04.
20 DE KERKBODE, report of 30-vi-04, p. 315.
21 NATAL MERCURY, Durban, 25 & 26-vii-04.
22 Gipsy Smith, A MISSION OF PEACE, pp. 100ff; cf. August
    issues of NATAL WITNESS for both sides the controversy.
23 METHODIST CHURCHMAN, 7-ix-04.

24 Address of South African Conference, 1905, to the British Wesleyan Methodist Conference.
25 METHODIST CHURCHMAN, 4-vii-05 & 8-viii-05.
26 DE KERKBODE, 3-viii-05.
27 see DE CHRISTELIJKE STREVER, September 1905.
28 DE KERKBODE, 24-viii-05.
29 see DE KERKBODE, 1905, pp. 400 & 493.
30 DE CHRISTELIJKE STREVER, September 1905, p. 12.
31 Report of September 1905, DE CHRISTELIJKE STREVER.
32 cf. Dr. H. C. Hopkins, in his centenary history of the Dutch Reformed congregation at Heidelberg, Cape Province.
33 METHODIST CHURCHMAN, 29-viii-05.
34 Report of 19-ix-05, METHODIST CHURCHMAN.
35 METHODIST CHURCHMAN, 17-x-05.
36 cf. THE CHRISTIAN, London, 10-viii-05.
37 METHODIST CHURCHMAN, 7-xi-05.
38 Report of 12-xii-05, METHODIST CHURCHMAN.
39 METHODIST CHURCHMAN, 31-x-05 & 7-xi-05.
40 Reports of 21 & 28-xi-05, METHODIST CHURCHMAN.
41 METHODIST CHURCHMAN, 19-xii-05.
42 personal knowledge of 'Oupa' Douglas.
43 Minutes of Grahamstown District Methodist Synod, at Graaff-Reinet, 7-13 February 1906, in Cory Library.
44 South African Methodist Conference, Capetown, 1901-10.
45 Methodist Synod Meetings, Rhodesia District, 1900-02.
46 Minutes of 1903-1904, Rhodesia District, Archives, Salisbury.
47 WESLEYAN METHODIST MISSIONARY SOCIETY, 1906, p. 108.

NOTES on Chapter XVI
The African Awakenings

This chapter on African Awakenings in the first two decades of the twentieth century has been compiled from notes in missionary periodicals, supplemented by information in missionary biography. There is no published work on the movement.

1   MISSIONARY REVIEW OF THE WORLD, 1903, pp. 616ff.
2   see G. B. A. Gerdener, RECENT DEVELOPMENTS IN THE SOUTH AFRICAN MISSION FIELD, p. 15.
3   M. W. Retief, HERLEWINGS IN ONS GESKIEDENIS, p. 100.
4   MISSIONARY REVIEW OF THE WORLD, 1903, p. 317.
5   MISSIONARY REVIEW OF THE WORLD, 1903, p. 79.
6   J. du Plessis in INTERNATIONAL REVIEW OF MISSIONS, October 1912, pp. 37ff.
7   MISSIONARY REVIEW OF THE WORLD, 1906, pp. 645ff.
8   G. & N. Pamla, AMABALANA NGO BOMI BUKA.
9   Minutes, South African Methodist Conference, 1913, p. 5.
10 W. Searle, booklet on REVIVAL AT LUTUBENI.
11 SOUTH AFRICAN PIONEER, January 1914.
12 August-September 1916, SOUTH AFRICAN PIONEER.
13 N. P. Grubb, REES HOWELLS, INTERCESSOR, passim.
14 SOUTH AFRICAN PIONEER, October 1916.
15 Conference Report, SOUTH AFRICAN PIONEER, Dec. 1917.
16 SOUTH AFRICAN PIONEER, July 1918.
17 Letters of Evelyn Richardson, 25-v-18, 6 & 13-vi-18.

18   Letter of Evelyn Richardson, 25-v-18, Archives of S. A. G. M.
19   Letter of Evelyn Richardson, 13-vi-18, Archives of S. A. G. M.
20   SOUTH AFRICAN PIONEER, January & March 1919.
21   see booklets by Bessie Porter Head, 1916 & 1918; cf. SOUTH
      AFRICAN PIONEER, August 1919ff.
22   MISSIONARY REVIEW OF THE WORLD, 1910, p. 883.
23   MISSIONARY REVIEW OF THE WORLD, 1910, p. 465; &
      1911, p. 81; Donald Fraser, WINNING A PRIMITIVE PEOPLE,
      pp. 279-288.
24   Donald Fraser, WINNING A PRIMITIVE PEOPLE, pp. 279ff.
25   Dan Crawford, THINKING BLACK, pp. 354ff.
26   see C. P. Groves, THE PLANTING OF CHRISTIANITY IN
      AFRICA, vol. iii, p. 234.
27   S. C. Neill, A HISTORY OF CHRISTIAN MISSIONS, p. 380.
28   S. C. Neill, A HISTORY OF CHRISTIAN MISSIONS, p. 381.
29   MISSIONARY REVIEW OF THE WORLD, 1901, pp. 556ff.
30   MISSIONARY REVIEW OF THE WORLD, 1902, p. 715.
31   MISSIONARY REVIEW OF THE WORLD, 1906, p. 308.
32   cf. W. H. Sheppard, PRESBYTERIANS IN THE CONGO.
33   MISSIONARY REVIEW OF THE WORLD, 1907, p. 952.
34   MISSIONARY REVIEW OF THE WORLD, 1906, p. 325.
35   ALLIANCE WEEKLY, 8-vi-07, p. 211.
36   Report of 1908, ALLIANCE WEEKLY, p. 177.
37   BAPTIST MISSIONARY MAGAZINE, 1910, pp. 398ff.
38   MISSIONARY REVIEW OF THE WORLD, 1913, p. 953.
39   N. P. Grubb, C. T. STUDD, CRICKETER AND PIONEER.
40   J. T. Tucker, ANGOLA, p. 67 & p. 70.
41   MISSIONARY REVIEW OF THE WORLD, 1911, p. 954.
42   ASSEMBLY HERALD, January 1907, p. 119.
43   Report of 1908 in ASSEMBLY HERALD, 1909, p. 5.
44   ASSEMBLY HERALD, 1909, p. 105.
45   Report of 1910, ASSEMBLY HERALD, p. 121.
46   G. von Götzen, DEUTSCH-OSTAFRIKA IM AUFSTAND.
47   PROCEEDINGS of the Church Missionary Society, 1905-1906,
      p. 57.
48   H. R. A. Philp, A NEW DAY IN KENYA, p. 20.
49   CHURCH MISSIONARY INTELLIGENCER, 1906, p. 50.
50   PROCEEDINGS of the Church Missionary Society, 1905-1906,
      p. 89; 1906-1907, p. 95; cf. MISSIONARY REVIEW OF THE
      WORLD, 1907, p. 405.
51   CHURCH MISSIONARY INTELLIGENCER, 1906, p. 371.
52   CHURCH MISSIONARY INTELLIGENCER, 1906, p. 615.
53   MISSIONARY REVIEW OF THE WORLD, 1908, p. 463.
54   see J. H. Maxwell, NIGERIA—and Christian Progress.
55   J. H. Hunter, A FLAME OF FIRE, the biography of Rowland
      Bingham.
56   W. J. Platt, AN AFRICAN PROPHET, a biography of William
      Wade Harris.
57   MISSIONARY REVIEW OF THE WORLD, 1909, p. 871.
58   MISSIONARY REVIEW, 1917, p. 542, & 1918, p. 236.
59   MISSIONARY REVIEW OF THE WORLD, 1903, pp. 795ff.
60   MISSIONARY REVIEW OF THE WORLD, 1906, p. 458.
61   MISSIONARY REVIEW, 1906, p. 308 & p. 405.
62   q. David Barrett, in CHURCH GROWTH BULLETIN.
63   Edinburgh MISSIONARY CONFERENCE, 1910, vol. i, p. 40.

Helen S. Dyer, friend of Pandita Ramabai of Mukti, compiled an account of REVIVAL IN INDIA, based on the experience of Mukti teams and on correspondence in India; but it gives a limited and unsystematic record of events in the 1905 Awakening throughout India.

1   H. S. Dyer, REVIVAL IN INDIA, p. 28.

2   H. S. Dyer, REVIVAL IN INDIA, p. 29.

3   J. M. Thoburn, ISABELLA THOBURN, p. 106.

4   ECUMENICAL MISSIONARY CONFERENCE, New York, 1900, vol. ii, p. 116.   5   H. S. Dyer, REVIVAL IN INDIA, p. 29.

6   J. N. Hyde, LIFE AND LETTERS OF PRAYING HYDE.

7   F. McGaw, PRAYING HYDE, p. 13.

8   Student Volunteer Movement, STUDENTS & THE MODERN MISSIONARY CRUSADE, 1906, p. 367.

9   BAPTIST MISSIONARY REVIEW, February 1907, p. 55.

10   Nicol MacNicol, PANDITA RAMABAI, p. 117.

11   In May 1903, Torrey reported: 'There is much prayer for a great revival in India, and there is a very widespread expectation that God is going to do such things as He has never done before in this great and needy Empire.' JAPAN EVANGELIST.

12   J. Meirion Lloyd, ON EVERY HIGH HILL, p. 52.

13   Mrs. John Roberts, THE REVIVAL IN THE KHASSIA HILLS.

14   H. S. Dyer, REVIVAL IN INDIA, pp. 31ff.

15   Mrs. John Roberts, THE REVIVAL IN THE KHASSIA HILLS.

16   AMERICAN BAPTIST MISSIONARY UNION, 1907 Report.

17   In 1905, 5100 Khasis were received into membership, and in 1906, 2771, bringing the total to 28,000 out of a population of 250,000. RECORD OF CHRISTIAN WORK, 1907, p. 508.

18   AMERICAN BAPTIST MISSIONARY UNION, 1906 Report.

19   ABMU 1906 Report, p. 88.   20   ABMU 1906 Report, p. 92.

21   BAPTIST MISSIONARY REVIEW, January 1907.

22   ABMU 1905 Report, p. 165.   23   ABMU 1906 Report, p. 100.

24   ABMU 1906 Report, p. 101.   25   ABMU 1905 Report, pp. 157f. MS Reports of O. L. Swanson, Golaghat, 1906: 'meetings can hardly be described . . . impressive'; A. J. Tuttle, Gauhati: 'More encouraging this year than any time previous.' Archives.

26   ABMU 1905 Report, p. 161.   27   ABMU 1905 Report, p. 69.

28   ABMU 1905 Report, p. 77.

29   V. H. Sword, BAPTISTS IN ASSAM, p. 110.

30   J. Meirion Lloyd, ON EVERY HIGH HILL, p. 52.

31   J. Meirion Lloyd, p. 53.   32   J. Meirion Lloyd, p. 54.

33   J. Meirion Lloyd, p. 55.   34   J. Meirion Lloyd, p. 64.

35   J. Meirion Lloyd, p. 55.

36   M. M. Thomas & Taylor, TRIBAL AWAKENING, p. 29.

37   Thomas & Taylor, TRIBAL AWAKENING, pp. 23 & 24.

38   Thomas & Taylor, TRIBAL AWAKENING, p. 61.

39   Thomas & Taylor, TRIBAL AWAKENING, pp. 226 & 228.

40   cf. MISSIONARY REVIEW OF THE WORLD, 1907, p. 563; and BAPTIST MISSIONARY REVIEW, February 1907.

41   H. S. Dyer, REVIVAL IN INDIA, pp. 119ff.

42   H. S. Dyer, REVIVAL IN INDIA, pp. 122-123. see also Orr, EVANGELICAL AWAKENINGS IN INDIA, 1968.

Apart from Helen S. Dyer's narrative, REVIVAL IN INDIA, and K. K. Kuruvilla's REVIVAL IN KERALA (Malayalam), material for this chapter was found in missionary periodicals and biography.

1   BAPTIST MISSIONARY REVIEW, February 1907, p. 58.
2   CANADIAN BAPTIST TELUGU MISSIONS, 1905 Report.
3   Report of 1905, CANADIAN BAPTIST TELUGU MISSIONS.
4   J. A. Craig, FORTY YEARS AMONG THE TELUGUS, p. 150.
5   Letter quoted in J. A. Craig, p. 152.
6   CANADIAN BAPTIST TELUGU MISSIONS, Report of 1906; cf. J. A. Craig, p. 158.
7   D. Downie, FROM MILL TO MISSIONFIELD, pp. 50ff. (The reports of 23-iv-06 & 18-iii-07 are in ABMU Archives).
8   J. A. Baker, CONTENDING THE GRADE, pp. 103ff.
9   Letter of J. A. Baker, 18-iv-06, Archives of the ABMU.
10 J. A. Baker, CONTENDING THE GRADE, pp. 105-106.
11 Field Report, Ongole 1906, and letter of J. A. Baker, 18-iv-06, citing 245 candidates baptized that month, Archives ABMU.
12 CANADIAN BAPTIST TELUGU MISSIONS, 1906 Report, p. 3.
13 1906 Report, CANADIAN BAPTIST TELUGU MISSIONS, p. 66.
14 CANADIAN BAPTIST TELUGU MISSIONS, 1904-1914 Reports.
15 BAPTIST MISSIONARY REVIEW, February 1907, p. 74.
16 C. H. Swavely, 100 YEARS IN THE ANDHRA COUNTRY, p. 19. Drach and Kuder, TELUGU MISSION OF THE LUTHERAN CHURCH, p. 355.   17 M. L. Dolbeer, Jr. A HISTORY OF LUTHERANISM IN THE ANDHRADESA.
18 see chapter v. Though references are taken from this work by Dolbeer, he makes no mention of the Awakening of 1905-06.
19 M. L. Dolbeer, p. 292.   20 M. L. Dolbeer, p. 261.
21 M. L. Dolbeer, p. 266.   22 M. L. Dolbeer, p. 288.
23 M. L. Dolbeer, p. 265.
24 PROCEEDINGS of the Church Missionary Society, 1907-08, pp. 164-165; cf. Graham, AZARIAH OF DORNAKAL, p. 42.
25 Carol Graham, AZARIAH OF DORNAKAL, pp. 31ff.
26 PROCEEDINGS of the Church Missionary Society, 1905-06, p. 222.   27 H. S. Dyer, REVIVAL IN INDIA, p. 147.
28 Church Missionary Society PROCEEDINGS, 1905-06, pp. 162ff.
29 H. S. Dyer, REVIVAL IN INDIA, pp. 113-114.
30 Revival among Christian Brethren in India caused some dismay in Britain, their missionary editor commenting: 'We do not understand 'prophesying' and 'visions' of which we read, and prefer to say little about them.' ECHOES OF SERVICE, October 1906.
31 H. S. Dyer, REVIVAL IN INDIA, pp. 113-114.
32 London Missionary Society, 111th Report, 1906.
33 H. S. Dyer, REVIVAL IN INDIA, p. 64.   4   p. 150.
35 F. Houghton, AMY CARMICHAEL OF DOHNAVUR, p. 146.
36 MISSIONARY REVIEW OF THE WORLD, 1906, p. 542.
37 Letter of R. A. Stott, Tumkur, 15-xii-05, in the Archives of the Methodist Missionary Society, Marylebone, London.
38 1904-07 Reports, Wesleyan Methodist Missionary Society.
39 1906 Report, Wesleyan Methodist Missionary Society.
40 see A. W. Carmichael, WALKER OF TINNEVELLY, passim.

41 J. Richter, INDISCHE MISSIONGESCHICHTE, passim.
42 Hollister, THE METHODIST CHURCH IN SOUTHERN ASIA, p. 292.　　　43 H. S. Dyer, REVIVAL IN INDIA, p. 115.
44 see JOURNAL, South India (Methodist) Conference.
45 Church Missionary Society PROCEEDINGS, 1905-06, p. 246.
46 MISSIONARY REVIEW OF THE WORLD, 1906, p. 162.
47 K. K. Kuruvilla, REVIVAL IN KERALA, pp. 48ff.
48 K. K. Kuruvilla, REVIVAL IN KERALA, pp. 54ff.
49 MISSIONARY REVIEW OF THE WORLD, 1906, p. 162.
50 PROCEEDINGS of the Church Missionary Society; Letter of F. N. Askwith, Kottayam, 10-i-08, Archives of the C. M. S.
51 A. W. Carmichael, WALKER OF TINNEVELLY, p. 391.
52 K. K. Kuruvilla, REVIVAL IN KERALA, pp. 61 (V. P. Mammen).
53 A. J. Thottungal, unpublished thesis on the History and Growth of the Mar Thoma Church, School of World Mission, Pasadena.

NOTES on Chapter XIX
Revival, Western India

Much of the following is taken from Helen S. Dyer's account of the part played in 1905-06 by Pandita Ramabai's Mukti Bands—on which the verdict of time is cited in Dr. Nicol McNicol's biography.

1 Nicol MacNicol, PANDITA RAMABAI, p. 64.
2 Nicol MacNicol, PANDITA RAMABAI, p. 61.
3 H. S. Dyer, REVIVAL IN INDIA, p. 41.
4 There were 24,000,000 widows in India, every fifth female— see MISSIONARY REVIEW OF THE WORLD, 1904, p. 274.
5 Nicol MacNicol, PANDITA RAMABAI, p. 117.
6 J. C. Winslow, NARAYAN VAMAN TILAK, p. 35.
7 Nicol MacNicol, PANDITA RAMABAI, p. 117; MISSIONARY REVIEW OF THE WORLD, 1906, p. 552.
8 H. S. Dyer, REVIVAL IN INDIA, p. 44.
9 H. S. Dyer, PANDITA RAMABAI, p. 11.
10 H. S. Dyer, REVIVAL IN INDIA, p. 55.
11 Nicol MacNicol, PANDITA RAMABAI, p. 118.
12 Nicol MacNicol, PANDITA RAMABAI, p. 117.
13 H. S. Dyer, REVIVAL IN INDIA, p. 47.
14 G. H. Lang, AN ORDERED LIFE, p. 134.
15 BOMBAY GUARDIAN: cf. H. S. Dyer, p. 48.
16 H. S. Dyer, REVIVAL IN INDIA, p. 49.　　　17　p. 53.
18 H. S. Dyer, REVIVAL IN INDIA, p. 61.　　　19　p. 62.
20 H. S. Dyer, REVIVAL IN INDIA, p. 63.　　　21　p. 67.
22 H. S. Dyer, REVIVAL IN INDIA, p. 68.
23 MISSIONARY REVIEW OF THE WORLD, 1906, p. 162.
24 H. S. Dyer, REVIVAL IN INDIA, p. 72.
25 Missionary Board, General Assembly, Presbyterian Church in the U.S.A., 1905; Letter of A. L. Wiley, Ratnagiri, p. 206.
26 MISSIONARY REVIEW OF THE WORLD, 1906, p. 169.
27 H. S. Dyer, REVIVAL IN INDIA, pp. 89ff.　　　28　p. 93.
29 MISSIONARY REVIEW OF THE WORLD, 1906, p. 542.
30 H. S. Dyer, REVIVAL IN INDIA, pp. 103ff.
31 ALLIANCE WEEKLY, 16-v-08.
32 Donald Gee, THE PENTECOSTAL MOVEMENT, p. 29, stated that the first glossolalia occurred at Aurangabad in 1906.

NOTES on Chapter XX
North India Awakenings

No published work describes the Awakening of 1905 in the North of India, confirmed in the Archives of the Presbyterian Church in the U.S.A. John Hyde, better known as Praying Hyde, is the subject of several biographies, but few seem to know that he was one figure in a much wider movement. Other details are taken from H. S. Dyer and from missionary reports and periodicals.

1   Student Volunteer Movement, STUDENTS & THE MODERN MISSIONARY CRUSADE, pp. 380ff.
2   H. S. Dyer, REVIVAL IN INDIA, pp. 97ff.
3   Basil Miller, PRAYING HYDE, p. 47.
4   Archives of the General Assembly of the Presbyterian Church in the United States of America, Philadelphia, microfilmed letters and reports, series 266ff.
5   H. S. Dyer, REVIVAL IN INDIA, pp. 97ff.
6   B. Miller, PRAYING HYDE, pp. 63ff.
7   H. S. Dyer, REVIVAL IN INDIA, p. 101.
8   H. S. Dyer, REVIVAL IN INDIA, p. 99.
9   H. S. Dyer, REVIVAL IN INDIA, p. 101.
10 B. Miller, PRAYING HYDE, p. 96; cf. J. N. Hyde, LIFE AND LETTERS OF PRAYING HYDE.
11 A. J. Appasamy, SUNDAR SINGH: a Biography.
12 H. S. Dyer, REVIVAL IN INDIA, p. 98.
13 PROCEEDINGS, Church Missionary Society, 1906-07, p. 188.
14 PROCEEDINGS, Church Missionary Society, 1907-08, p. 147.
15 H. S. Dyer, REVIVAL IN INDIA, p. 101.
16 H. S. Dyer, REVIVAL IN INDIA, p. 102.
17 H. S. Dyer, REVIVAL IN INDIA, p. 59.
18 H. S. Dyer, REVIVAL IN INDIA, p. 60.
19 PROCEEDINGS, Church Missionary Society, 1905-06, p. 171; cf. H. S. Dyer, p. 62.
20 H. S. Dyer, REVIVAL IN INDIA, p. 62.
21 H. S. Dyer, REVIVAL IN INDIA, p. 124.
22 H. S. Dyer, REVIVAL IN INDIA, p. 125.
23 H. S. Dyer, REVIVAL IN INDIA, p. 126.
24 MISSIONARY REVIEW OF THE WORLD, 1907, p. 564.
25 PROCEEDINGS, Church Missionary Society, 1905-06, p. 164.
26 A. W. Carmichael, WALKER OF TINNEVELLY, p. 369.
27 A. W. Carmichael, WALKER OF TINNEVELLY, p. 356.
28 ASSEMBLY HERALD, Philadelphia, April 1907.
29 INTERNATIONAL REVIEW OF MISSIONS, 1913, p. 442.
30 INTERNATIONAL REVIEW OF MISSIONS, 1912, p. 28.
31 YEAR BOOK OF MISSIONS IN INDIA, 1912, credited Roman Catholics with 25% growth (379,251) during the revival decade, Syrians (including Mar Thoma) 27%, and Protestants 42.5% (or 488,982). As the Syrians included the badly-divided Jacobites, most of the growth must be credited to the Mar Thoma Church, which supported the Revival.
32 ALLIANCE WEEKLY, 1907, p. 234.
33 CANADIAN BAPTIST TELUGU MISSIONS, Report of 1905.
34 A. W. Carmichael, WALKER OF TINNEVELLY, p. 389.
35 BAPTIST MISSIONARY REVIEW, September 1907, p. 392.

Andrew Gih, best-known survivor of the China-wide Awakening of 1927-39, told the writer (who served with him in that movement) that he was unaware of any spiritual revival in China during the first decade of the century, other than a post-Boxer increase in attendance due to change of community feeling. Other than the writings of Jonathan Goforth of Manchuria, there is no work that deals with the China-wide Awakenings of 1900-1910. Sources for this chapter were found in periodicals of the time, published in Shanghai and overseas.

1   A. H. Smith, CHINA IN CONVULSION, passim.
2   ENCYCLOPEDIA BRITANNICA, 1960, China, history.
3   A. E. Glover, A THOUSAND MILES OF MIRACLE IN CHINA, & Marshall Broomhall, editor, MARTYRED MISSIONARIES OF THE CHINA INLAND MISSION.
4   P. A. Varg, MISSIONARIES, CHINESE & DIPLOMATS, p. 86.
5   D. MacGillivray, A CENTURY OF PROTESTANT MISSIONS IN CHINA, pp. 277-278.
6   MISSIONARY REVIEW OF THE WORLD, 1900, p. 652.
7   D. MacGillivray, A CENTURY OF PROTESTANT MISSIONS IN CHINA, p. 211.
8   CHINESE RECORDER, Shanghai, 1905, p. 221.
9   ASSEMBLY HERALD, February 1903.
10 MISSIONARY REVIEW OF THE WORLD, 1909, p. 483.
11 D. MacGillivray, PROTESTANT MISSIONS IN CHINA, p. 58; cf. MISSIONARY REVIEW OF THE WORLD, 1909, p. 483.
12 MISSIONARY REVIEW OF THE WORLD, 1905, p. 936.
13 CHINA'S MILLIONS, 1906, p. 141.
14 CHINA'S MILLIONS, 1907, p. 14.
15 MISSIONARY REVIEW OF THE WORLD, 1907, p. 485.
16 MISSIONARY REVIEW OF THE WORLD, 1906, p. 802.
17 CHINA'S MILLIONS, 1906, p. 141.
18 MISSIONARY REVIEW OF THE WORLD, 1906, p. 643.
19 CHINA'S MILLIONS, 1906, p. 141.
20 MISSIONARY HERALD, 1906, p. 357.
21 MISSIONARY HERALD, 1905, pp. 80-81.
22 CHINA'S MILLIONS, 1906, p. 143.
23 MISSIONARY REVIEW, 1907, p. 642 & 1908, p. 451.
24 ALLIANCE WEEKLY, 1906, pp. 234 & 318; CHINA'S MILLIONS !1906, p. 154.
25 S. R. Clarke, AMONG THE TRIBES IN SOUTHWEST CHINA, pp. 140ff.   26 CHINA'S MILLIONS, 1907, pp. 10ff.
27 MISSIONARY REVIEW OF THE WORLD, 1907, pp. 207ff.
28 R. E. Kendall, THE EYES OF THE EARTH (Diary of Samuel Pollard), p. 73.
29 R. Toliver, unpublished research on the Awakenings of 1905 in Tribes of Southwest China, School of World Mission, Pasadena.
30 R. Goforth, GOFORTH OF CHINA, passim.
31 Jonathan Goforth, 'BY MY SPIRIT,' pp. 33ff.
32 Jonathan Goforth, 'BY MY SPIRIT,' pp. 74ff.
33 J. Webster, REVIVAL IN MANCHURIA, passim; cf. Austin Fulton, THROUGH EARTHQUAKE, WIND AND FIRE, Church and Mission in Manchuria, 1867-1950, pp. 47ff.

34 K. S. Latourette, A HISTORY OF THE EXPANSION OF CHRISTIANITY, volume vi, p. 344.
35 CHINESE RECORDER, 1908, p. 333.
36 MISSIONARY REVIEW OF THE WORLD, 1913, pp. 529ff.
37 Edinburgh MISSIONARY CONFERENCE, 1910, vol. i, pp. 36ff.
38 MISSIONARY REVIEW OF THE WORLD, 1908, pp. 16ff.
39 CHINA'S MILLIONS, 1909, pp. 74, 147 & passim.
40 CHINA'S MILLIONS, 1909, passim.
41 CHINA'S MILLIONS, 1910, p. 22.
42 CHINA'S MILLIONS, 1909, p. 9.
43 MISSIONARY REVIEW OF THE WORLD, 1909, pp. 884ff, & BAPTIST MISSIONARY MAGAZINE, 1909, p. 355.
44 MISSIONARY HERALD, 1910, p. 51.
45 MISSIONARY HERALD, 1910, p. 51.
46 CHINA'S MILLIONS, 1909, p. 123.
47 ALLIANCE WEEKLY, 1909, p. 173.
48 RECORD OF CHRISTIAN WORK, 1907, p. 371.
49 CHINA'S MILLIONS, February 1911.
50 CHINA'S MILLIONS, May 1911.
51 Edinburgh MISSIONARY CONFERENCE, 1910, vol. i, p. 37.
52 L. T. Lyall, A BIOGRAPHY OF JOHN SUNG, passim.
53 K. S. Latourette, A HISTORY OF THE EXPANSION OF CHRISTIANITY, volume vi, pp. 441ff.

NOTES on Chapter XXII
The Korean Pentecost

Unlike other countries of the world, Korea possesses a wealth of literature on the Awakening of the 1900s, and every volume of Korean church history deals with the subject. But there is a tendency to begin with the 1907 outbreak, the most extraordinary manifestation, and neglect the movements from 1903 till the end of 1906. The writer has talked with survivors of the Revival, studied their books, read reports made at the time, and cited periodicals Korean and overseas. A most up-to-date treatment has been given by Mrs. Hazel Watson in an unpublished M.A. thesis, 'Revival and Church Growth in Korea.'

1   A. W. Wasson, CHURCH GROWTH IN KOREA, p. 29.
2   Report, Methodist Episcopal Church, South, 1904, pp. 23-24.
3   Hazel T. Watson, 'Revival and Church Growth in Korea,' 1884-1910, pp. 145-146.
4   O. C. Grauer, FREDRIK FRANSON, pp. 160ff; cf. Woodward, AFLAME FOR GOD, p. 155.
5   A. W. Wasson, CHURCH GROWTH IN KOREA, p. 31.
6   A. W. Wasson, CHURCH GROWTH IN KOREA, p. 32.
7   O. C. Grauer, FREDRIK FRANSON, p. 161.
8   W. N. Blair, GOLD IN KOREA, chapter xv.
9   MISSIONARY REVIEW, 1905, pp. 474-475, 555ff, 955.
10 Annual Meeting, Korea Mission of the Presbyterian Church in U.S.A., Seoul 1906. Johnston addressed meetings in Pyongyang and Taegu also, telling of the Awakenings in Wales and India.
11 THE KOREA MISSION FIELD (II: 12: 228), & MISSIONARY REVIEW OF THE WORLD, 1906, p. 395.
12 G. T. Brown, MISSION TO KOREA, p. 59.
13 MISSIONARY REVIEW OF THE WORLD, 1906, p. 556.

14 cf. R. E. Shearer, WILDFIRE: CHURCH GROWTH IN KOREA; & MISSIONARY REVIEW OF THE WORLD, 1907, p. 15.

15 MISSIONARY REVIEW OF THE WORLD, 1907, p. 15.

16 MISSIONARY REVIEW OF THE WORLD, 1907, p. 323.

17 G. H. Jones & W. A. Noble, THE KOREAN REVIVAL.

18 MISSIONARY REVIEW OF THE WORLD, 1907, p. 323.

19 Microfilm Report, George McCune, Pyongyang, 15-i-05, in the Archives of the Presbyterian Church in the U.S.A.

20 MISSIONARY REVIEW OF THE WORLD, 1907, p. 168.

21 W. N. Blair, GOLD IN KOREA, chapter xvi.

22 Details were still vivid in the mind of a 90-year-old survivor, William Newton Blair, interviewed by the writer.

23 G. McCune, Pyongyang, 15-i-07. (Mrs. Watson supposed that praying simultaneously and audibly is an oriental custom, but the writer has heard this phenomenon among European, African and American peoples, in times of spiritual revival.

24 L. G. Paik, THE HISTORY OF PROTESTANT MISSIONS IN KOREA, p. 357.

25 William L. Swallen, Pyongyang, 18-i-07, in the microfilm reports of the Presbyterian Church in the U.S.A., Philadelphia.

26 W. N. Blair, GOLD IN KOREA, p. 64.

27 L. G. Paik, THE HISTORY OF PROTESTANT MISSIONS IN KOREA, p. 357.

28 L. G. Paik, p. 359.

29 1908 Report, Board of Missions, Methodist Episcopal Church.

30 A. H. Wasson, CHURCH GROWTH IN KOREA, p. 420.

31 The missionary journal, KOREAN MISSION FIELD, featured thirty-two different reports from observers in the field.

32 W. N. Blair, GOLD IN KOREA, p. 64.

33 There was a surprising unanimity of agreement.

34 Student Volunteer Movement, STUDENTS & THE MODERN MISSIONARY CRUSADE, 1910, p. 307; A. W. Wasson, p. 419; & INTERNATIONAL REVIEW OF MISSIONS, July, 1912.

35 STUDENTS AND THE MISSIONARY CRUSADE, 1910, p. 307.

36 JOURNAL of the Methodist Episcopal Church, South, 1908.

37 L. G. Paik, PROTESTANT MISSIONS IN KOREA, p. 364.

38 G. T. Ladd, IN KOREA WITH MARQUIS ITO, 1908.

39 see WHO WAS WHO, 1947, volume ii, p. 599.

40 G. T. Ladd, IN KOREA WITH MARQUIS ITO, p. 408.

41 ANNALS OF THE AMERICAN ACADEMY, June 1909, p. 197.

42 A. W. Wasson, CHURCH GROWTH IN KOREA, p. 53.

43 W. N. Blair, GOLD IN KOREA, pp. 67ff.

44 A. W. Wasson, CHURCH GROWTH IN KOREA, p. 54.

45 F. C. Ottman, J. WILBUR CHAPMAN, p. 197.

46 J. E. Adams, Annual Report, Board of Foreign Mission of the Presbyterian Church in the U.S.A., (Taegu, 1910-1911).

47 Clark, THE KOREAN CHURCH & NEVIUS METHODS, p. 155.

48 cf. figures 3 & 16 in the well-documented book upon church growth in Korea, by Roy E. Shearer.

49 Dr. Han Kyung-Chik, Young Nak Church, Seoul.

50 Edinburgh MISSIONARY CONFERENCE, 1910, vol. i, p. 77.

51 cf. Shearer, WILDFIRE: CHURCH GROWTH IN KOREA.

52 W. N. Blair, PENTECOST IN KOREA, passim.

53 C. A. Clark, THE KOREAN CHURCH AND THE NEVIUS METHODS, pp. 73-74.

Evangelical Christians have often asked the question, 'Why is it that the Korean Church has often experienced spiritual revival while Japanese Christianity has lacked it?' Without herein analysing the reasons for the recurring of Evangelical Awakenings in Korea, one must point out that extraordinary revival broke out in Japan in 1884 when missionaries were first penetrating Korea. Few foreigners and few Japanese Christians seem aware of the extent and success of the evangelistic movement of 1901, and the measure of revival that followed it. For lack of either scholarly or popular works on the subject, the researchist was compelled to assemble material from religious periodicals, such as the interdenominational JAPAN EVANGELIST and denominational journals, with occasional use of published biographies and church histories.

1   Otis Cary, A HISTORY OF CHRISTIANITY IN JAPAN, vol. ii, pp. 164ff.
2   Student Volunteer Movement, Toronto, 1902, pp. 390ff.
3   see PAUL KANAMORI'S LIFE STORY, & MISSIONARY REVIEW OF THE WORLD, 1900, p. 689.
4   MISSIONARY HERALD, Boston, June 1900.
5   MISSIONARY HERALD, October 1901.
6   J. H. DeForest, SUNRISE IN THE SUNRISE KINGDOM, p. 194.
7   JAPAN EVANGELIST, July 1901, p. 227.
8   see JAPAN EVANGELIST, 1901 onwards.
9   JAPAN EVANGELIST, June 1901, p. 195.
10   JAPAN EVANGELIST, July 1901, p. 226.
11   Student Volunteer Movement, Toronto, 1902, pp. 390ff.
12   JAPAN EVANGELIST, April 1902, pp. 109ff.
13   J. H. DeForest, SUNRISE IN THE SUNRISE KINGDOM, p. 194.
14   BAPTIST MISSIONARY MAGAZINE, 1907, p. 406.
15   MISSIONARY HERALD, 1907, pp. 80ff.
16   see C. W. Iglehart, A CENTURY OF PROTESTANT CHRISTIANITY IN JAPAN, p. 119.
17   A. Ebisawa, NIPPON KIRISTOKYO HYAKUNENSHI, p. 168.
18   A. Ebisawa, NIPPON KIRISTOKYO HYAKUNENSHI, p. 169.
19   C. W. Iglehart, PROTESTANT CHRISTIANITY, p. 128.
20   MISSIONARY REVIEW OF THE WORLD, 1907, p. 325.
21   Basil Matthews, JOHN R. MOTT, World Citizen, p. 183.
22   MISSIONARY REVIEW OF THE WORLD, 1908, p. 3.
23   ALLIANCE WEEKLY, New York, 1906-1907, p. 235.
24   ASSEMBLY HERALD, Philadelphia, 1908, pp. 405ff.
25   MISSIONARY REVIEW OF THE WORLD, 1910, p. 598.
26   JAPAN EVANGELIST, November 1901, pp. 338ff.
27   Edinburgh MISSIONARY CONFERENCE, 1910, vol. i, p. 36.
28   cf. MISSIONARY REVIEW OF THE WORLD, 1903, p. 521; 1909, p. 74.
29   see T. Yanagita, A SHORT HISTORY OF CHRISTIANITY IN JAPAN, p. 63.
30   Taikyo Dendo's extraordinary success dismayed the Buddhists, who responded by trying to form a Buddhist Evangelistic Association, cf. JAPAN EVANGELIST, February 1902, pp. 46ff.
31   see K. Aoyoshi, DR. MASAHISA UEMURA, passim.

There is a growing literature dealing with the beginnings of the Pentecostal Movement of the twentieth century. A scholarly work in Norwegian, PINSEBEVEGELSEN, by Dr. Nils Bloch-Hoell, has been translated as THE PENTECOSTAL MOVEMENT, which is the title of a smaller, less technical book by Donald Gee, one of the movement's most informed leaders. There is also (in German) Walter J. Hollenweger's ENTHUSIASTISCHES CHRISTENTUM, combining scholarship and information, being presented in English. To the knowledge of the writer, no study deals adequately (if at all) with the relationship between the Pentecostal movement and the worldwide Evangelical Revival which preceded it—not surprisingly, for there has been to date no publication, scholarly or popular, that presents the full story of that Awakening. Many writings on the Pentecostal movement refer to the Welsh Revival, and recognize the important place of the meetings in Azusa Street, Los Angeles, in spreading Pentecostalism. None trace the movement through the general awakening that swept every state in the U.S.A. in 1905-06—including California—to provide a needed explanation of the outburst. This chapter was compiled from the religious press of the decade, from works cited and from Pentecostal biographies in the languages read by the writer. It is written from outside the movement, with insights gained through fraternal association in ministry of the Word.

1   N. Bloch-Hoell, THE PENTECOSTAL MOVEMENT, ch. iv.
2   M. Neiiendam, FRIKIRKER OG SEKTER, pp. 96-97.
3   E. Linderholm, PINGSTRORELSEN, pp. 231ff.
4   S. H. Frodsham, WITH SIGNS FOLLOWING, p. 187.
5   Frodsham, p. 31; cf. Hollenweger for a recent account.
6   Frank Bartleman, WHAT REALLY HAPPENED AT AZUSA STREET.   7   THE CHRISTIAN, 17-v-06.
8   EVANGELII HAROLD, Stockholm, 1916, p. 173.
9   Donald Gee, THE PENTECOSTAL MOVEMENT, pp. 11ff.
10 J. L. Sherrill, THEY SPEAK WITH OTHER TONGUES, p. 40.
11 F. Bartleman, p. 28.   12 LOS ANGELES TIMES, 18-iv-06.
13 J. T. Nicol, PENTECOSTALISM, p. 36.
14 ALLIANCE WEEKLY, 26 January & 9, 16 February 1907.
15 S. Barratt Lange, T. B. BARRATT, passim.
16 T. B. Barratt, autobiography, p. 102.
17 T. B. Barratt, autobiography, p. 103.
18 ALLIANCE WEEKLY, 1908, p. 245.
19 ALLIANCE WEEKLY, 1908, p. 246.
20 'Kom hit, hver torstig sjæl.' ('Come near, O thirsty soul.')
21 T. B. Barratt, autobiography, pp. 165ff.
22 T. B. Barratt, autobiography, p. 101.
23 T. B. Barratt, autobiography, pp. 185ff.
24 T. B. Barratt, autobiography, p. 192.
25 POLITIKEN, Copenhagen, 8, 9, & 10 November 1908.
26 S. H. Frodsham, WITH SIGNS FOLLOWING, pp. 77ff.
27 L. Pethrus, HUR JAG FICK ANDENS DOP, pp. 14ff.
28 ALLIANCE WEEKLY, 1908, p. 246.
29 Donald Gee, THE PENTECOSTAL MOVEMENT, pp. 175ff.
30 E. Bernspang, interviews in Finland, 1967.

31 TOIVON TAHTI, Helsinki, series of articles, 1932-1934.
32 Donald Gee, pp. 15 & 20ff.   33   Donald Gee, pp. 34ff.
34 Donald Gee, pp. 31ff.   35   Donald Gee, pp. 33ff, 97ff.
36 While unconnected with the Pentecostal movement, the writer had contact with such leaders as George Jeffreys and Donald Gee (Britain), Lewi Pethrus (Scandinavia), David du Plessis (South Africa), Howard Carter (New Zealand) and Oral Roberts (USA).
37 Scharpff, GESCHICHTE DER EVANGELISATION, pp. 265ff.
38 Fleisch, PFINGSTBEWEGUNG IN DEUTSCHLAND, pp. 277ff
39 ZEITSCHRIFT FUR RELIGIONSPSYCHOLOGIE, Halle, 1908, cites various newspapers in its discussion of phenomena.
40 P. Fleisch, MODERNE GEMEINSCHAFTSBEWEGUNG, p. 408.
41 T. B. Barratt, autobiography, p. 231.
42 Krust, 50 JAHRE DEUTSCHE PFINGSTBEWEGUNG, Mulheim Richtung.   43   see BYPOSTEN, Oslo, 1909-1913, passim.
44 Donald Gee, pp. 27, 68ff, & 159ff.   45   pp. 27-29.
46 Donald Gee, pp. 43-44.   47   p. 85.
48 CHIAO HUI SAN SHIH CHOU NIEN CHI NIEN KAN, 1956, Taichung, Taiwan.   49   Donald Gee, pp. 46-49.
50 THE APOSTOLIC FAITH, Los Angeles, September 1906.
51 United States Census, Religious Bodies, 1936.
52 YEARBOOK OF THE AMERICAN CHURCHES, 1906.
53 A. J. Tomlinson, ANSWERING THE CALL, pp. 14ff.
54 The writer observed this most acutely between 1930 and 1940.
55 see M. Neiiendam, FRIKIRKER OG SEKTER, p. 115.
56 Bloch-Hoell, PENTECOSTAL MOVEMENT, topic indexed. It is strange that the notion that speaking in tongues is xenolalic (foreign language) rather than glossolalic (unknown) is claimed oftener in Charismatic than Pentecostal circles, where pastors know that their missionaries master languages for evangelism.

NOTES on Chapter XXV
Rent Heavens—Ravaged Earth

1 Preface to Gabriel Vahanian's THE DEATH OF GOD, 1961.
2 J. Edwin Orr, THE SECOND EVANGELICAL AWAKENING IN BRITAIN, pp. 35ff, 207 & 269ff. Numbers added in Welsh churches in the Revival of 1904 matched those of 1859.
3 In many countries, the fastest-growing denomination.
4 Editor of the BRITISH WEEKLY, London.
5 W. R. Nicoll, PRINCES OF THE CHURCH, p. 108.
6 Sigmund Freud, THE FUTURE OF AN ILLUSION, 1928.
7 1st July 1916. The Ulster Division was decimated in battle.
8 F. C. Ottman, J. WILBUR CHAPMAN, p. 272.
9 Distinction is made between evangelism based on organization and publicity and evangelism sustained by revival of the churches.
10 An observation based on thirty years' experience in evangelism on all six continents.   11   Keir Hardie died in 1915.
12 STATESMAN'S YEARBOOK, 1905 & 1911 data.
13 STATESMAN'S YEARBOOK, 1905 & 1909 figures.
14 Minutes, South African Methodist Conferences, 1901-10.
15 INTERNATIONAL REVIEW OF MISSIONS, 1912, p. 28, cf. YEAR BOOK OF MISSIONS IN INDIA, 1912.
16 92nd ANNUAL REPORT, American Baptist Missionary Union, pp. 99 & 119; cf. 93rd Annual Report, Boston.

17 R. E. Shearer, WILDFIRE: CHURCH GROWTH IN KOREA.
18 CHINA MISSION YEAR BOOK, 1915.
19 ATLAS OF PROTESTANT MISSIONS, 1903, AND WORLD ATLAS OF CHRISTIAN MISSIONS, 1911.
20 Malagasy figures are deducted from the totals.
21 BAPTIST MISSIONARY MAGAZINE, 1907, p. 232.
22 BAPTIST MISSIONARY MAGAZINE, 1907, p. 189.
23 Archives, American Baptist Foreign Mission Society, Letter of David Downie, 23-iv-06.
24 Rev. Duncan Campbell in Edinburgh told the writer that during the 1949 Hebrides Revival a woman fell into a trance for several hours, awoke in great agitation, urging him to go immediately to a village on the other side of Lewis to stop a man from committing suicide. In the only cottage lighted at 2 a.m., Campbell and his friends found a number of men restraining a hysterical man.
25 Coleman's treatise, ABNORMAL PSYCHOLOGY & MODERN LIFE, is the standard work on the subject.
26 William James, VARIETIES OF RELIGIOUS EXPERIENCE.
27 Walter Houston Clark, 'Psychology of Religious Experience,' in PSYCHOLOGY TODAY, February 1968.
28 In the Reavivamento Espiritual Brasileiro (1952), the writer insisted: 'Let the circle of the sin be the circle of confession.' Scandal was thus avoided. Lauro Bretones, REDEMOINHOS DO SUL, & J. Edwin Orr, PLENA SUBMISSAO, pp. 33ff.
29 CHINESE RECORDER, June 1908, p. 335.
30 BAPTIST MISSIONARY REVIEW, January 1907.
31 see Theodor Reik, on THE COMPULSION TO CONFESS.
32 BAPTIST MISSIONARY REVIEW, January 1907.
33 William Sargant, THE BATTLE FOR THE MIND, pp. 99ff: 'The frantic scenes of the Welsh Revival are forgotten in the new and respectable chapels where the 'hwyl' (a Welsh device exciting a congregation by breaking into wild chant) is now rarely heard.' The Welsh Revival packed respectable churches (including Anglican) and the 'hwyl' was noticeably absent.
34 one judged the best sense to be the scriptural (Ephesian) one.
35 Orr, THE SECOND EVANGELICAL AWAKENING, ch. xiii.
36 Orr, THE SECOND EVANGELICAL AWAKENING, ch. x.
37 Latourette, A HISTORY OF THE EXPANSION OF CHRISTIANITY, volume iv, chapter xi.
38 J. Strong, THE NEXT GREAT AWAKENING and A. C. Dixon, EVANGELISM, OLD AND NEW, for pros and cons. The term 'new evangelism' was used by some for visitation in preference to mass evangelism, a matter of method rather than of message.
39 see DEN DANSKE PRASTEFORENING, Maanadsblad for den Danske Folke Kirke, 1906-07.
40 Acts i, 7-8.   41 ii, 1-4.   42 ii, 16-21.   43 ii, 37-38.
44 Robertson, WORD PICTURES IN THE NEW TESTAMENT, vol. iii, p. 36.   45 Acts ii, 41-47.
46 'A concert of voices' (Robertson, p. 54), the obvious explanation of I Samuel vii, 6.
47 Too often the claims of xenolalia are unspecific, lacking names of witnesses or authorities quoted, second-hand references being often given.
48 G. F. Barbour, LIFE OF ALEXANDER WHYTE, pp. 88ff.
49 THE KESWICK HYMN-BOOK, Hymn 149.

BIBLIOGRAPHY

In collecting material for this book, the writer consulted archives on all six continents, not only libraries in Britain and United States and depositories of missionary societies, but collections as far apart as Ramapatnam in India and Stellenbosch in the Cape, seeking notes in the far east in Japan and in Chile in the far south, in Uganda and in the Ukraine. Of about 1250 footnotes, 900 were primary sources.

Periodicals:

THE ADVANCE, Chicago, 1905.
ALLIANCE WEEKLY, New York, 1906-08.
AMERICAN BAPTIST FOREIGN MISSION, New York, 1905.
ASSEMBLY HERALD, Philadelphia, 1903-08.
YR ARGYFWNG, Cardiff, 1954.
AUSTRALIAN CHRISTIAN WORLD, Sydney, 1905.
BAPTIST ARGUS, Louisville, 1905.
BAPTIST COMMONWEALTH, Philadelphia, 1905.
BAPTIST CONGRESS, Cincinnati, 1905.
BAPTIST COURIER, Greeville, S.C., 1905.
BAPTIST HOME MISSION MONTHLY, Philadelphia, 1905-06.
BAPTIST MISSIONARY MAGAZINE, Boston, 1900-07.
BAPTIST MISSIONARY REVIEW, Guntur, India, 1907.
BAPTIST OBSERVER, Indianapolis, 1905.
BAPTIST TIMES, London, 1905.
BRITISH WEEKLY, London, 1905.
BYPOSTEN, Oslo, 1905-13.
CATHOLIC TIMES, London, 1905.
CENTRAL BAPTIST, St. Louis, 1905-06.
CHINA MISSION YEAR BOOK, Shanghai, 1915.
CHINA'S MILLIONS, London, 1901-10.
CHINESE RECORDER, Shanghai, 1903-09.
CHRISTELIJKE STREVER, Capetown, 1904-05.
THE CHRISTIAN, London, 1901-09.
CHRISTIAN ADVOCATE, New York, 1900-06.
CHRISTIAN ENDEAVOR WORLD, Boston, 1905.
CHRISTIAN EXPRESS, Lovedale, South Africa, 1900-05.
CHRISTIAN HERALD, London, 1905-06.
CHRISTIAN HERALD, Philadelphia, 1905-06.
CHRISTIAN OBSERVER, Louisville, 1905.
CHRISTIAN STUDENT, Capetown, 1901-02.
CHURCH MISSIONARY INTELLIGENCER, London, 1905.
CHURCH TIMES, London, 1905.
THE CHURCHMAN, New York, 1905.
Y CYFAILL EGLWSIG, Cardiff, 1902.
Y DRYSORFA, Aberystwyth, 1902.
THE ENGLISH CHURCHMAN, London, 1905.
YR EURGRAWN WESLEYAIDD, Cardiff, 1905.
EVANGELICAL ALLIANCE QUARTERLY, London, 1905.
EVANGELICAL CHRISTENDOM, London, 1905-10.
EVANGELICAL MAGAZINE OF WALES, Cardiff, 1968.
EVANGELII HAROLD, Stockholm, 1916.
EVANGELISCH ZONDAGSBLAD, Leiden, 1905.
THE EXAMINER, New York, 1905.
THE FOREIGN FIELD, W.M.M.S., London, 1905.

FOREIGN MISSIONS JOURNAL, Richmond, Virginia, 1905.
THE FRIEND, London, 1905.
Y GOLEUAD, Aberystwyth, 1900-05.
YR HAUL, Aberystwyth, 1902.
INDRE MISSIONS TIDENDE, Copenhagen, 1903.
INTERNATIONAL REVIEW OF MISSIONS, London, 1911-12
IRISH CHRISTIAN ADVOCATE, Belfast, 1905-06.
IRISH ENDEAVOURER, Belfast, 1905.
THE HOSPITAL, London, 1905.
JAPAN EVANGELIST, Tokyo, 1900-09.
JOURNAL AND MESSENGER, Cincinnati, 1905.
JOURNAL DE L'EVANGELIZATION, Paris, 1905.
JOURNAL, South India Methodist Conference, Madras, 1902.
DE KERKBODE, Capetown, 1901-05.
DE KONINGSBODE, Capetown, 1902-05.
KOREAN MISSION FIELD, Seoul, 1905-09.
THE LANCET, London, 1905.
THE LIFE OF FAITH, London, 1901-10.
LONDON QUARTERLY REVIEW, London, 1905.
THE LUTHERAN, Lebanon, Pennsylvania, 1905.
LUTHERAN HERALD, Decorah, Iowa, 1905-06.
LUTHERAN STANDARD, Columbus, Ohio, 1905.
MAANADSBLAD, Danske Folke Kirke, Copenhagen, 1906-07.
METHODIST CHURCHMAN, Capetown, 1904-05.
METHODIST RECORDER, London, 1905.
METHODIST REVIEW, New York, 1905.
METHODIST TIMES, London, 1905.
MICHIGAN BAPTIST CONVENTION, Lansing, 1905-06.
MICHIGAN CHRISTIAN ADVOCATE, Adrian, 1905.
MINUTES, Irish Methodist Conference, Belfast, 1905.
MISSIONARY HERALD, Boston, 1905-06.   (1905-06.
MISSIONARY RECORD, United Free Church of Scotland,
MISSIONARY REVIEW OF THE WORLD, London, 1900-15.
OUR HOME FIELD, Atlanta, 1905.
THE OUTLOOK, Dunedin, New Zealand, 1901-05.
PENTECOSTAL HERALD, Louisville, 1905.
POLITIKEN, Copenhagen, 1908.   (1905-07.
PROCEEDINGS of the CHURCH MISSIONARY SOCIETY, London,
PSYCHOLOGY TODAY, New York, 1968.
THE RECORD, London, 1905.
RECORD OF CHRISTIAN WORK, Chicago, 1905-08.
RELIGIOUS JOURNAL, Richmond, Virginia, 1905.   (1903-09.
REPORT of the Wesleyan Methodist Church in New Zealand,
REPORT of the Canadian Baptist Telugu Mission, 1906.   (U.S.A.
REPORT, Missionary & Benevolent Board, Presbyterian Church,
REPORT of the Wesleyan Methodist Missionary Society, 1906.
SCOTTISH BAPTIST MAGAZINE, Glasgow, 1905-08.
SERVICE, Baptist Young People's Union, Chicago, 1905-07.
SOUTH AFRICAN PIONEER, Capetown, 1914-19.
SOUTHERN BAPTIST CONVENTION ANNUALS, 1905-1907.
THE STANDARD, Chicago, 1905.
THE STATESMAN'S YEARBOOKS, London, 1905-11.
THE SUNDAY COMPANION, London, 1905.
Y TYST, Aberystwyth, 1904.
DE UNGAS TIDNING, Stockholm, 1905.

DE UNGES BLAD, Copenhagen, 1905.
THE WAR CRY, London, 1905.
THE WATCHMAN, Boston, 1905.
WESTERN CHRISTIAN ADVOCATE, Indianapolis, 1902-05.
WESTERN RECORDER, Louisville, 1905.
THE WITNESS, Belfast, 1904-05.
YEAR BOOK OF MISSIONS IN INDIA, 1912.
ZEITSCHRIFT FUR RELIGIONSPSYCHOLOGIE, Halle, 1908.
ZION'S HERALD, Nashville, 1917.

Theses & Published Books

Alexander, H. C., CHARLES M. ALEXANDER, London, 1920.
Appasamy, A. J., SUNDAR SINGH, a biography, London, 1958.
Appasamy, A. J., WRITE THE VISION! London, 1964.
ATLAS OF PROTESTANT MISSIONS, New York, 1903.
Baker, J. A., CONTENDING THE GRADE, Asheville, N.C., 1947.
BAPTIST WORLD ALLIANCE, London, 1911.   (1923.
Barbour, G. F., THE LIFE OF ALEXANDER WHYTE, London,
Barratt, S. Lange, T. B. BARRATT, Oslo, 1962.
Barratt, T. B., SJÄLVBIOGRAFI (Autobiography), Stockholm, 1942.
Bartleman, F. WHAT REALLY HAPPENED AT AZUSA STREET,
    Los Angeles, 1962.   (1907.
Bayliss, E. F., GIPSY SMITH MISSIONS IN AMERICA, Boston,
Beach, H. T., PROTESTANT MISSIONS IN SOUTH AMERICA,
    Chicago, 1900.   (1912.
Beardsley, F. G., HISTORY OF AMERICAN REVIVALS, New York,
Berg, D., ENVIADO POR DEUS (Portuguese), Sao Paulo, 1959.
Blair, W. N., GOLD IN KOREA, Topeka, 1946.
Bloch-Hoell, N., THE PENTECOSTAL MOVEMENT, Oslo, 1964.
Bodensieck, J. (ed.), AN ENCYCLOPEDIA OF THE LUTHERAN
    CHURCH, Minneapolis, 1965.
Bois, H., LE REVEIL AU PAYS DE GALLES, Toulouse, 1905.
Bretones, L., REDEMOINHOS DO SUL; um Ano de Reavivamento
    no Brasil com o Dr. J. Edwin Orr, Teresopolis, 1953.
Broomhall, M., MARTYRED MISSIONARIES OF THE CHINA
    INAND MISSNO, London, 1901.
Brown, G. T., MISSION TO KOREA, Nashville, 1962.
Browning, W. E. THE RIVER PLATE REPUBLICS, London, 1928.
Carmichael, A. W., WALKER OF TINNEVELLY, London, 1916.
Carpenter, N., THE IMMIGRANTS AND THEIR CHILDREN, 1920.
Cary, Otis, HISTORY OF CHRISTIANITY IN JAPAN, New York,
    1909.   (Antananarivo, Madagascar, 1951.
Chapus, G. S. & Bothun, F., (French) AU SOUFFLE DE L'ESPRIT,
Clark, C. A., THE KOREAN CHURCH AND THE NEVIUS
    METHODS, New York, 1930.   (London, 1911.
Clarke, S. R., AMONG THE TRIBES IN SOUTHWEST CHINA,
Coleman, J. C., ABNORMAL PSYCHOLOGY AND MODERN LIFE,
    Chicago, 1960.   (Rio de Janeiro, 1960.
Conde, E., HISTORIA DOS ASSEMBLEIAS DE DEUS NO BRASIL,
Conrad, A. Z., BOSTON'S AWAKENING, Boston, 1909.   (1912.
Craig, J. A., FORTY YEARS AMONG THE TELUGUS, Toronto,
Crawford, D., THINKING BLACK: 22 years without a break in the
    long grass of Central Africa, London, 1912.
Danske Indremission, DEN INDREMISIONENS HISTORIE, 1912.
Davis, G. T. B., TORREY AND ALEXANDER, New York, 1905.

Davis, G. T. B., WHEN THE FIRE FELL, Philadelphia, 1945.
Dawson, W. J., AUTOBIOGRAPHY OF A MIND, New York, 1925.
Dawson, W. J., THE EVANGELISTIC NOTE, London, 1905. (1904.
DeForest, J. H. SUNRISE IN THE SUNRISE KINGDOM, New York,
Dixon, A. C., EVANGELISM, OLD AND NEW, New York, 1905.
Dolbeer, M. L., Jr., A HISTORY OF LUTHERANISM IN THE
   ANDHRADESA, New York, 1959.
Downie, D., FROM MILL TO MISSIONFIELD, Philadelphia, 1928.
Drach, G. & Kuder, THE TELUGU MISSION OF THE LUTHERAN
   CHURCH, Philadelphia, 1914.
Dyer, H. S., PANDITA RAMABAI, London, undated.
Dyer, H. S., REVIVAL IN INDIA, London, 1907.
Ebisawa, A., NIPPON KIRISTOKYO HYAKUNENSHI, Tokyo, 1959.
ECUMENICAL MISSIONARY CONFERENCE, New York, 1900.
Ellis, W. T., MEN AND MISSIONS, Philadelphia, 1909.
Ellis, W. T., BILLY SUNDAY, New York, 1936.
Evangeliska Fosterlands Stiftelsen (E. F. S.), MED GUD OCH
   HANS VANSKAP, Stockholm, 1956.
Evans, E. K., FY MHERERINDOD YSBRYDOL, Liverpool, 1938.
Ferreira, J. A., A HISTORIA DA IGREJA PRESBITERIANA DO
   BRASIL, São Paulo, 1959.
Fleisch, P., DIE MODERNE GEMEINSCHAFTSBEWEGUNG IN
   DEUTSCHLAND, Leipzig, 1912.
Flierl, J. CHRIST IN NEW GUINEA, Tanunda, Australia, 1932.
Fraser, Donald, WINNING A PRIMITIVE PEOPLE, London, 1922.
Freud, S., THE FUTURE OF AN ILLUSION, New York, 1928.
Frodsham, S. H., WITH SIGNS FOLLOWING, Springfield, 1946.
Füllkrug, G., HANDBUCH DER VOLKSMISSION, Schwerin, 1919.
Garrard, M. N., MRS. PENN-LEWIS, London, undated.
Gee, Donald, THE PENTECOSTAL MOVEMENT, London, 1949.
Geil, W. E., OCEAN AND ISLE, Sydney, 1902.
Gerdener, G. B. A., RECENT DEVELOPMENTS IN THE SOUTH
   AFRICAN MISSION FIELD, London, 1958.
Gibson, Rupert, AN ABUNDANT MINISTRY, Belfast, 1960.
Ginsburg, S. L., A MISSIONARY ADVENTURE, Nashville, 1921.
Glover, A. E., A THOUSAND MILES OF MIRACLE IN CHINA,
   London, 1901.
Goforth, Jonathan, "BY MY SPIRIT," London, undated.
Goforth, R., GOFORTH OF CHINA, London, undated.
Graham, Carol, AZARIAH OF DORNAKAL, London, 1946.
Grauer, O. C., FREDRIK FRANSON, Chicago, 1940.
Groves, C. P., THE PLANTING OF CHRISTIANITY IN AFRICA,
   four volumes, London, 1948-1958.
Grubb, N. P., C. T. STUDD, Cricketer and Pioneer, London, 1933.
Grubb, N. P., REES HOWELLS, INTERCESSOR, London, 1952.
Haavio, A. SUOMEN USKONNOLLISET LIIKKEET, Helsinki, 1965.
Hasselman, O., PASTOR JULIUS DAMMANN, Schwerin, 1930.
Head, B. P., ADVANCE IN GAZALAND: the continued story of
   Revival, (booklet), London, 1918.
Head, B. P., RETROSPECT AND REVIVAL IN GAZALAND,
   (booklet), London, 1916.
Hogg, W. R., ECUMENICAL FOUNDATIONS, New York, 1952.
Holcomb, W., SAM JONES, Nashville, 1947.
Hollister, J. N., CENTENARY OF THE METHODIST CHURCH IN
   SOUTHERN ASIA, Lucknow, 1956.

Hoover, W. C., HISTORIA DEL AVIVAMIENTO PENTECOSTAL EN CHILE, Santiago, 1931.
Hopkins, H. C., EEUFEES GEDENKBOEK VAN DIE NEDERDUITS GEREFORMEERDE GEMEENTE VAN HEIDELBERG, 1949.
Horton, A. G., AN OUTLINE OF LATIN AMERICAN HISTORY, Dubuque, 1966.
Houghton, F., AMY CARMICHAEL OF DOHNAVUR, London, 1954.
Houghton, L. S., A HANDBOOK OF FRENCH AND BELGIAN PROTESTANTISM, New York, 1919.
Hunter, J. H., A FLAME OF FIRE (The Life and Work of R. V. Bingham), Toronto, 1961.
Hyde, J. N., (edited), THE LIFE AND LETTERS OF PRAYING HYDE, undated, Springfield, Illinois.
Iglehart, C. W. A CENTURY OF PROTESTANT CHRISTIANITY IN JAPAN, Tokyo, 1959.
James, W., VARIETIES OF RELIGIOUS EXPERIENCE, New York, 1902. (1906.
Jones, L. M., LIFE AND SAYINGS OF SAM JONES, Atlanta,
Jones, G. H. & Noble, THE KOREAN REVIVAL, New York, 1906.
R. B. Jones, RENT HEAVENS, London, 1909.
Kanamori, P. M. KANAMORI'S LIFE STORY, Philadelphia, 1921.
Kasteel, P., ABRAHAM KUYPER, Kampen, Holland, 1938.
Kemp, W., JOSEPH W. KEMP, London, 1934.
Kendall, R. E., THE EYES OF THE EARTH, Diary of Samuel Pollard, London, 1954.
Kessler, J. B. A., PROTESTANT MISSIONS AND CHURCHES IN PERU AND CHILE, Goes, Holland, 1967. (1959.
Kruger, T. M., SEDJARAH GEREDJA DI INDONESIA, Jakarta,
Krust, C., 50 JAHRE DEUTSCHE PFINGSTBEWEGUNG MUHL-HEIMER RICHTUNG, Altdorf, 1958.
Kupisch, K., DER DEUTSCHE C. V. J. M., Kassel, 1958. (1966.
Kupisch, K., DIE KIRCHE IN IHRE GESCHICHTE, Göttingen,
Kuruvilla, K. K., REVIVAL IN KERALA, (in Malayalam), 1950.
Ladd, G. T., WITH MARQUIS ITO IN KOREA, New York, 1910.
Lang, G. H., AN ORDERED LIFE, London, 1919.
Latimer, R. S., UNDER THREE TSARS: Liberty of Conscience in Russia, 1856-1909, London, 1909.
Latourette, K. S. A HISTORY OF CHRISTIAN MISSIONS IN CHINA, London, 1919.
Latourette, K. S., A HISTORY OF THE EXPANSION OF CHRISTIANITY, volume vi, New York, 1945.
Linderholm, E., PINGSTRORELSEN, Stockholm, 1924.
Lloyd, J. Meirion, ON EVERY HIGH HILL, London, 1950.
Lunde, M., ALBERT LUNDE, Minner fra hans Liv, Oslo, 1939.
Lyall, J., THE RECENT GREAT REVIVAL IN AUSTRALIA AND NEW ZEALAND, Edinburgh, 1905.
Lyall, L. T., A BIOGRAPHY OF JOHN SUNG, London, 1954.
MacDonald, J. H., (editor), REVIVAL, New York, 1905.
MacFarlan, D., THE REVIVALS OF THE EIGHTEENTH CENTURY, Edinburgh, undated.
McGaw, F., PRAYING HYDE, Chicago, 1933.
MacGillivray, D. (ed.), A CENTURY OF PROTESTANT MISSIONS IN CHINA, Shanghai, 1907.
McLean, J. H., HISTORIA DE LA IGLESIA PRESBITERIANA EN CHILE, Santiago, 1954.

McLoughlin, W. G., BILLY SUNDAY WAS HIS REAL NAME, Chicago, 1955.
MacNicol, Nicol, PANDITA RAMABAI, Calcutta, 1926.   (1934.
Matthews, Basil,   JOHN R. MOTT, World Citizen, New York,
Maxwell, J. H., NIGERIA, THE LAND, THE PEOPLE, AND CHRISTIAN PROGRESS, London, undated.
Miller, Basil, PRAYING HYDE, Grand Rapids, 1943.   (1953.
Modersohn, E., ER FUHRET MICH AUF RECHTER STRASSE,
Molland, E., CHURCH LIFE IN NORWAY, Minneapolis, 1957.
Mondain, Gustave, UN SIECLE DE MISSION PROTESTANTE A MADAGASCAR, Paris, 1920.
Morgan, J. V., THE WELSH RELIGIOUS REVIVAL, London, 1909.
Murch, J. De Forest, CHRISTIANS ONLY, Cincinnati, 1962.
Neiiendam, M., FRIKIRKER OG SEKTER, Copenhagen, 1939.
Neill, S. C., A HISTORY OF CHRISTIAN MISSIONS, London, 1964.
Neves, M., MEIO SECULO, São Paulo, 1955.
Nichol, J. T., PENTECOSTALISM, New York, 1966.
Nicoll, W. Robertson, PRINCES OF THE CHURCH, London, 1909.
Orr, J. Edwin, ALWAYS ABOUNDING, London, 1939.
Orr, J. Edwin, THE LIGHT OF THE NATIONS, London, 1965.
Orr, J. Edwin, THE SECOND EVANGELICAL AWAKENING IN BRITAIN, London, 1949.
Ottman, F. C., J. WILBUR CHAPMAN, New York, 1920.
Pagel, A., DER JUGENBUND FUR E. C., Kassel, 1954.
Paik, L. G., HISTORY OF PROTESTANT MISSIONS IN KOREA, Pyongyang, 1929.
Pamla, G. & N., AMABALANA NGO BOMI BUKA (Xhosa biography of the Rev. Charles Pamla), Palmerton, Cape, 1934.
Penn-Lewis, J., THE AWAKENING IN WALES, London, 1905.
Pethrus, L., HUR JAG FICK ANDENS DOP, Stockholm, 1953.
Philip, H. R. A., A NEW DAY IN KENYA, London, 1936.
Phillips, D. M., EVAN ROBERTS, Welsh Revivalist, London, 1923.
Platt, W. J., AN AFRICAN PROPHET, William Harris, London,
Pollock, J. C., BILLY GRAHAM, New York, 1966.   (1934.
Pollock, J. C., THE KESWICK STORY, London, 1964.
Pollock, J. C., MOODY: a Biographical Portrait, London, 1963.
Ramsay, J. C., JOHN WILBUR CHAPMAN, New York, 1962.
Rauws, J., et al., THE NETHERLANDS INDIES, London, 1935.
Read, W. R., Monterroso & Johnson, LATIN AMERICAN CHURCH GROWTH, Grand Rapids, 1969.
Read, W. R., NEW PATTERNS OF CHURCH GROWTH IN BRAZIL, Grand Rapids, 1965.
Rees, T. M., SETH JOSHUA AND FRANK JOSHUA, Cardiff, 1926.
Reik, Th., THE COMPULSION TO CONFESS, New York, 1966.
Retief, M. W., HERLEWINGS IN ONS GESKIENDENIS, Capetown.
Richter, J., EVANGELISCHE MISSION IN NIEDERLANDISCH INDIEN, Gutersloh, 1931.
Richter, J., INDISCHE MISSIONSGESCHICHTE, Gutersloh, 1924.
Ringwald, A., MENCHEN VOR GOTT, Stuttgart, 1958.
Roberts, G. M. & Evans, S., CYFROL GOFFA DIWYGIAD 1904-1905, Carnarvon, 1954.   (1909.
Roberts, Mrs. J., REVIVAL IN THE KHASSIA HILLS, London,
Robertson, A. T., WORD PICTURES IN THE NEW TESTA-MENT, volume iii, New York, 1930.   (1940.
Rodgers, J. B., FORTY YEARS IN THE PHILIPPINES, New York,
Roth, A., 50 JAHRE GNADAUER KONFERENZ, Giessen, 1938.

St. John, Patricia, HAROLD ST. JOHN, London, 1960.   (1941.
Saloff-Astakhoff, N. I., CHRISTIANITY IN RUSSIA, New York,
Schaeffer, C. E., A BRIEF HISTORY OF THE DEPARTMENT OF
    EVANGELISM OF THE FEDERAL COUNCIL OF CHURCHES
    New York, 1951.
Searle, W., REVIVAL AT LUTUBENI, (booklet), London, 1911.
Shaffer & Shobin, PSYCHOLOGY OF ADJUSTMENT, Boston,
    1956, 'Emotion.'   (Rapids, 1966.
Shearer, R. E., WILDFIRE: CHURCH GROWTH IN KOREA, Grand
Shedd, C. P., THE CHURCH FOLLOWS ITS STUDENTS, New
    Haven, 1938.   York, (1964.
Sherrill, J. L., THEY SPEAK WITH OTHER TONGUES, New
Sloan, W. B., THESE SIXTY YEARS (Keswick), London, 1935.
Smith, A. H., CHINA IN CONVULSION, Chicago, 1901.
Smith, Gipsy, A MISSION OF PEACE, London, 1904.
Smith, O. J., THE PEOPLES CHURCH, Toronto, 1951.
Stauffer, H., THE GREAT AWAKENING IN COLUMBUS, OHIO,
    under the Labors of the Rev. B. Fay Mills, Columbus, 1895.
Stewart, I. R., A SPLENDID OPTIMIST, Edinburgh, 1952.
Stout, J. E., DAILY VACATION BIBLE SCHOOL, New York, 1923.
Strong, J., THE NEXT GREAT AWAKENING, New York, 1902.
Student Volunteer Movement, STUDENTS AND THE MODERN
    MISSIONARY CRUSADE, Nashville, 1906.   (1952.
Swavely, C. H., 100 YEARS IN THE ANDHRA COUNTRY, Madras,
Sword, V. H., BAPTISTS IN ASSAM, Chicago, 1935.
Thoburn, J. M., ISABELLA THOBURN, New York, 1903.
Thottungul, A. J., 'History and Growth of the Mar Thoma Church,'
    unpublished thesis, School of World Mission, Pasadena, 1967.
Thunem, A., NYFIFOHAZANA ETO MADIGASKARA, (Malagasy),
    Antananarivo, 1935.
Tomlinson, A. J., ANSWERING THE CALL, Cleveland, Tenn.
Townsend, Workman & Eayrs, NEW HISTORY OF METHODISM,
    London, 1909.   (1933.
Tucker, J. T., ANGOLA, Land of the Blacksmith Prince, London,
Vahanian, G., THE DEATH OF GOD, New York, 1961.   (1953.
Varg, P. A., MISSIONARIES, CHINESE & DIPLOMATS, Princeton,
Vetter, J., EIN LEBENSBILD, Geisweid, 1922.   (1909.
von Götzen, G., DEUTSCH-OSTAFRIKA IM AUFSTAND, Berlin,
von Viebahn, F. W., GEORG VON VIEBAHN, Berlin, 1918.
Wasson, A. W., CHURCH GROWTH IN KOREA, New York, 1934.
Watson, H. T., 'Revival and Church Growth in Korea, 1884-1910,'
    unpublished thesis, School of World Mission, Pasadena, 1968.
Webster, J., THE REVIVAL IN MANCHURIA, London, 1910.
Weigle, L. C., DICTIONARY OF AMERICAN BIOGRAPHY, New
    York, 1934—a concise biography of B. Fay Mills.
Williams, D. J., A HUNDRED YEARS OF WELSH CALVINISTIC
    METHODISM IN AMERICA, Philadelphia, 1937.   (1968.
Williams, Stewart (ed.), THE GLAMORGAN HISTORIAN, Cardiff,
Winslow, J. C., NARAYAN VAMAN TILAK, Calcutta, 1930.
Wood, F. P. & M. S., YOUTH ADVANCING, London, 1961.
Woodward, D. B., AFLAME FOR GOD, (popular style biography
    of Fredrik Franson), Chicago, 1966.
WORLD ATLAS OF CHRISTIAN MISSIONS, 1910.
Yanagita, T., SHORT HISTORY OF CHRISTIANITY IN JAPAN,
    Sendai, 1957.

237

INDEX OF PERSONS

Place names, being contained in chapters
arranged geographically, are unindexed